AF894981

At Home in the West

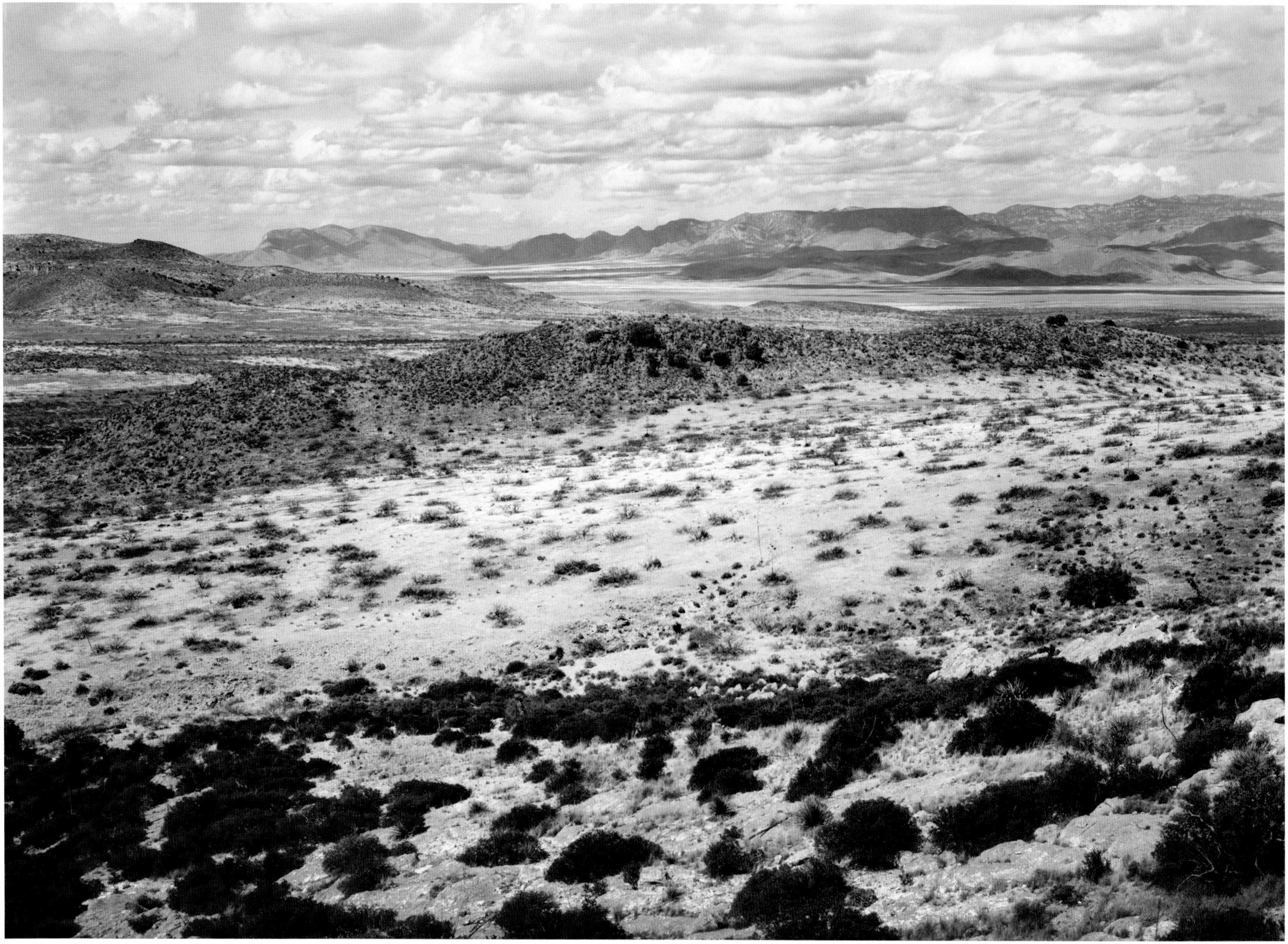

At Home in the West

The Lure of Public Land

by William S. Sutton

with concluding essays by Toby Jurovics
and Susan B. Moldenhauer

George F. Thompson Publishing
in association with
the American Land Publishing Project

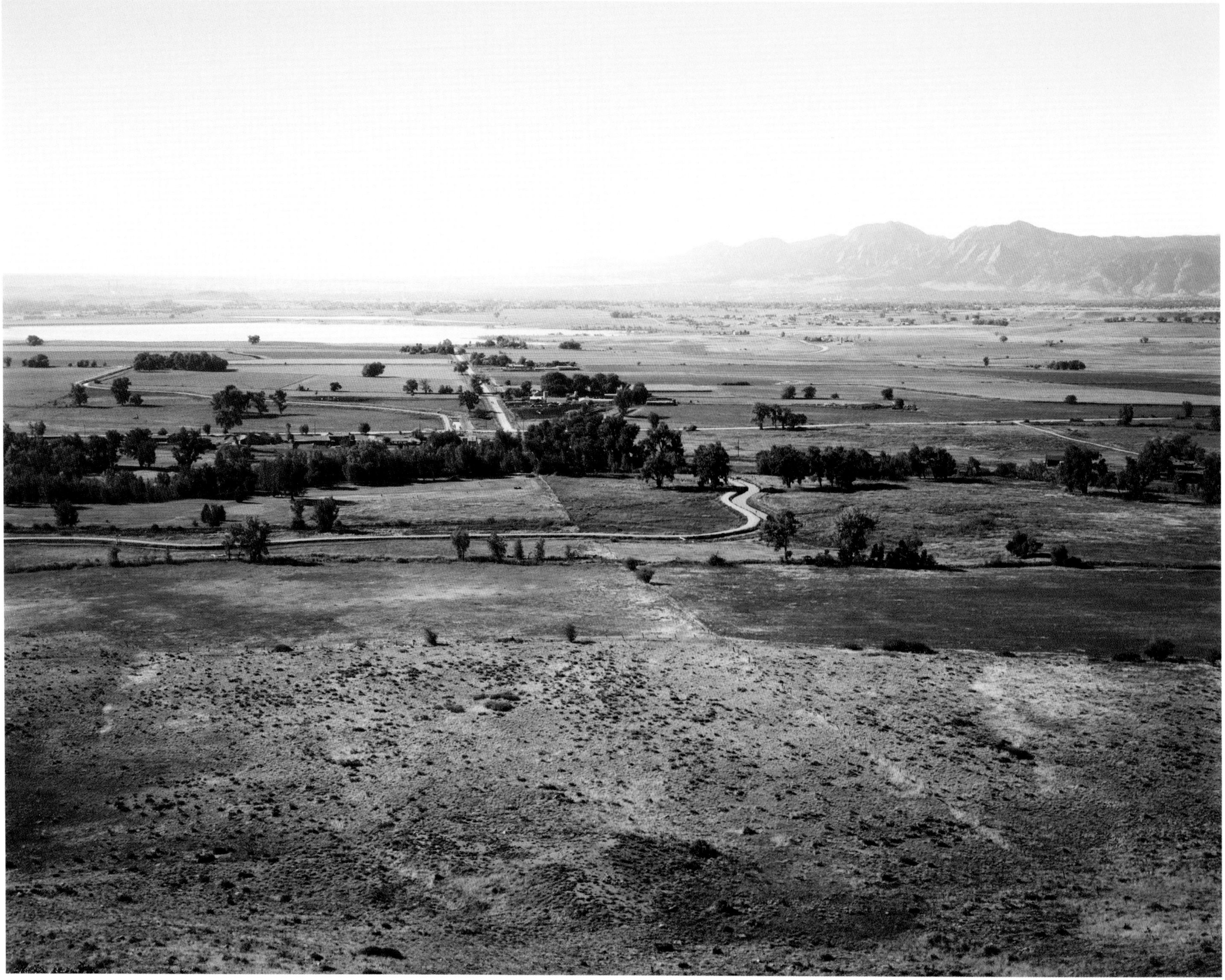

For Lynn, Justin, and Jaime

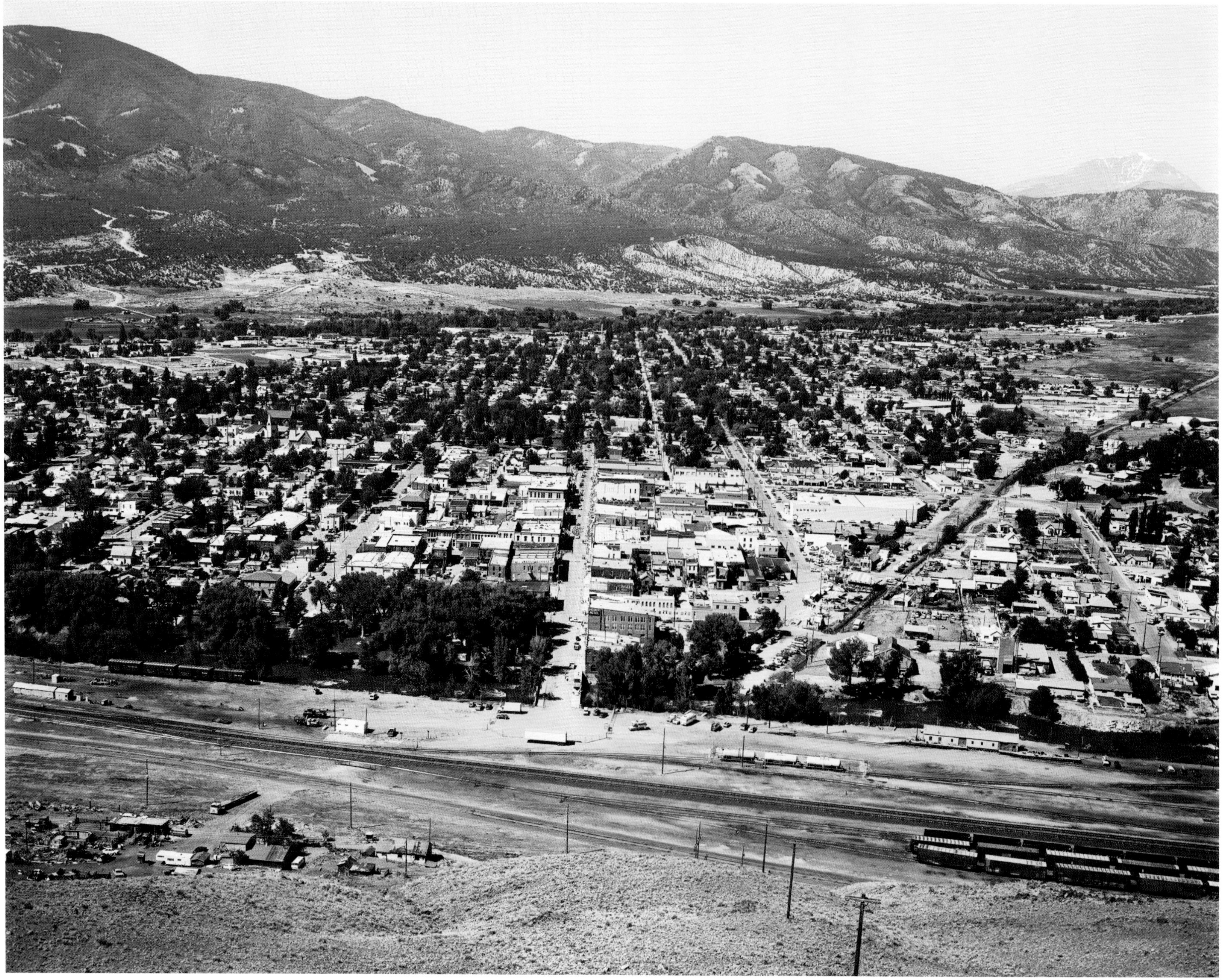

Contents

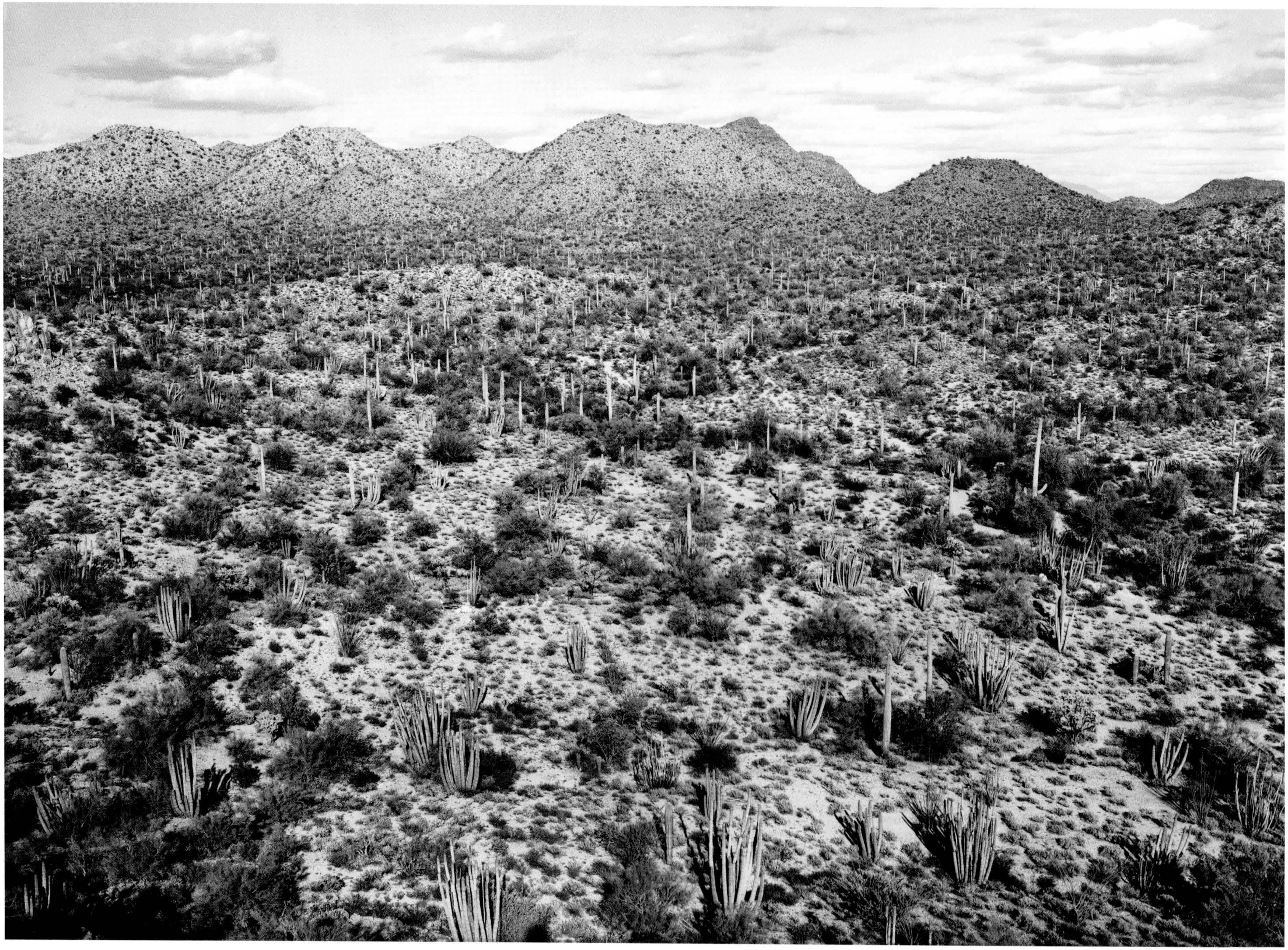

Finding My Place

"Oh, I feel so good, I wanna' ramble."[1]
—John Lee Hooker

When I was six years old, my father moved our family from New York State to Scottsdale, Arizona. That was my first experience of the West. It was 1962.

Dad was an ambitious businessman with an M.B.A. from Harvard who took a new job every few years, moving us from place to place, this time to Arizona. He worked in the tallest building in Phoenix: the Guaranty Bank downtown, at twenty stories tall, with vertical sky-blue-and-white stripes and a bold, black GB emblazoned on the building's top corner.

Dad went ahead of the rest of the family to find our new home in Arizona and to get things settled. He stayed with my Mom's Uncle Pete, who was the gun editor for *Sports Afield* magazine. While showing Dad around the desert in his Toyota Land Cruiser, Uncle Pete stopped the truck, picked up a rattlesnake by the tail, whirled it around over his head, and then smashed the snake on the ground. By the time we got to Phoenix, my Dad had bought an old, light-blue convertible, and he wore white jeans and a straw cowboy hat. There is a photograph from this time of Dad with a large six-shooter strapped around his leg.

Phoenix, like Tucson, was different back then, Although the population had already surged to around 400,000, it still felt like a big town rather than a big city; now, it is a burgeon-

1. John Lee Hooker (1917–2001) added "Oh, I feel so good" to the classic song, "I Wanna' Ramble," by Junior Parker (1932–1971), on Hooker's album, *Get Back Home*, released in 1969 on Disques Black and Blue.

(Left) Organ Pipe Cactus National Monument (elevation 1,670–4,808 feet), Arizona, 1994.

ing metropolis with a population of more than 1,500,000 and growing. As a boy, the desert and its rattlesnakes, roadrunners, scorpions, and cacti fascinated me. Almost every place had an American Indian or Hispanic name: we shopped at Papago Plaza and lived on Coronado Road. There were huge, red sandstone formations on the edge of town with cavernous openings. Camelback Mountain, to the north, was framed in our living room's picture window. I resonated with the dry heat and big open sky.

We children played in a tangerine orchard next to our neighborhood. During the hot summer, neighbors would irrigate their lawns by flooding them with ten inches of water, and we had a grand time splashing around. As a little boy, all of Arizona was magic. I remember my parents saying, "If we drive out of town ten miles, we will be out in the middle of nowhere."

After only three years in Arizona, Dad announced that we were moving once again: this time to Chicago. I did not want to go but had no choice in the matter. I attended junior high and high school in the western suburbs. It seemed to me there was always at least one roaring jetliner in the sky coming in or out of O'Hare International Airport and the constant noise of traffic from nearby Interstate 294. As high school graduation approached, my parents asked me, "Where do you want to go to college?" They were hopeful they could interest me in an Ivy League school or its equivalent, but the only school I applied to was Arizona State University. So, in 1973 at age seventeen, I packed up my Ford van and drove the 2,000 miles to Tempe to attend ASU. The liberation I felt of being on my own and attending the university was linked with the landscape of the West. And, during my first year at college, I explored a lot of Arizona and northern New Mexico and even made a few trips to California.

But then I dropped out, to travel around the country with a friend. We backpacked out of my Grandpa's cabin in New York's Catskill Mountains and along the Appalachian Trail. Eventually, we ended up in Arizona again and I attended ASU for one more semester before transferring to the University of Colorado in Boulder. There, I discovered the high expanse and rugged wildness of the Rocky Mountains.

(Right) Near home along North Boulder Creek, Roosevelt National Forest (elevation 5,800–13,392 feet), Colorado, 1991.

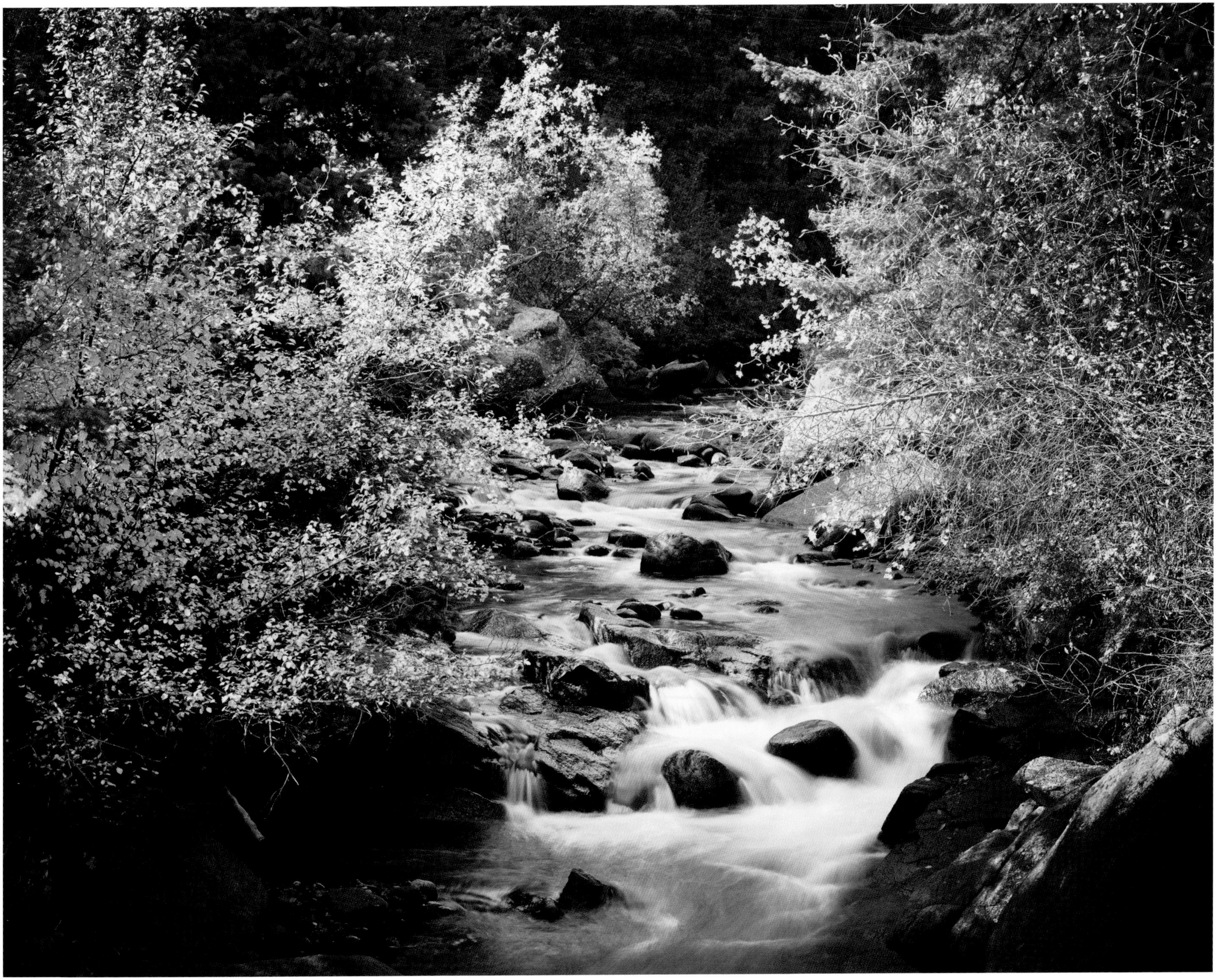

It was during those early college years when I discovered of a life-long passion for exploring the West and using photography to investigate notions about living in a place, especially in the West where humanity and nature are so intertwined in the landscape. In 1984, I started this project when I began to visit thousand-year-old Indian rock art sites and cliff dwellings in northern New Mexico and southern Utah. The rock art provided a destination and access point to the landscape, and the images from an ancient time and culture stimulated my imagination. How did these ancestral people craft a living from this environment, this place? What did their inscriptions say about their society and their outlook on life? Permeating these musings were my own questions and concerns about the sustainability of contemporary society and a youthful yearning for a meaningful life.

The pictures that came from these places often describe layers of inhabitation. Looking at the landscape, I could see where past societies had grown their food and where they had moved up and down protective canyon walls. I imagined family groups, rituals, and an alternative social and environmental reality among the ancestral Pueblo people. Their marks, imbedded within the land, described societal activity; they were integrated simultaneously into a much older biology, climate, and geology along with the more recent erosion of wind and rain and often a layer of contemporary human activity, as seen in fences, footprints, paths, and signs in the dusty soil.

I recall reading somewhere that all places on Earth have been inhabited by human beings at some point in time. There is a long history of human occupation and a broad range of dependency on the landscape for resource acquisition, from hunter-gatherers to contemporary industrial practices and technologies for agriculture and mining. Human life is also dependent on larger cycles and movements of the planet, such as the hydrologic cycle, weather patterns, and the balance of oxygen and carbon dioxide in the atmosphere. Biologically, we cannot exist without the air that we breathe, or the water that flows through us, or the soils that sustain us, or the thousands of nurturing and consuming organisms that live around us and within us.

(Right) Luke in Horseshoe Canyon, Canyonlands National Park (elevation 3,700–7,200 feet), Utah, 1984.

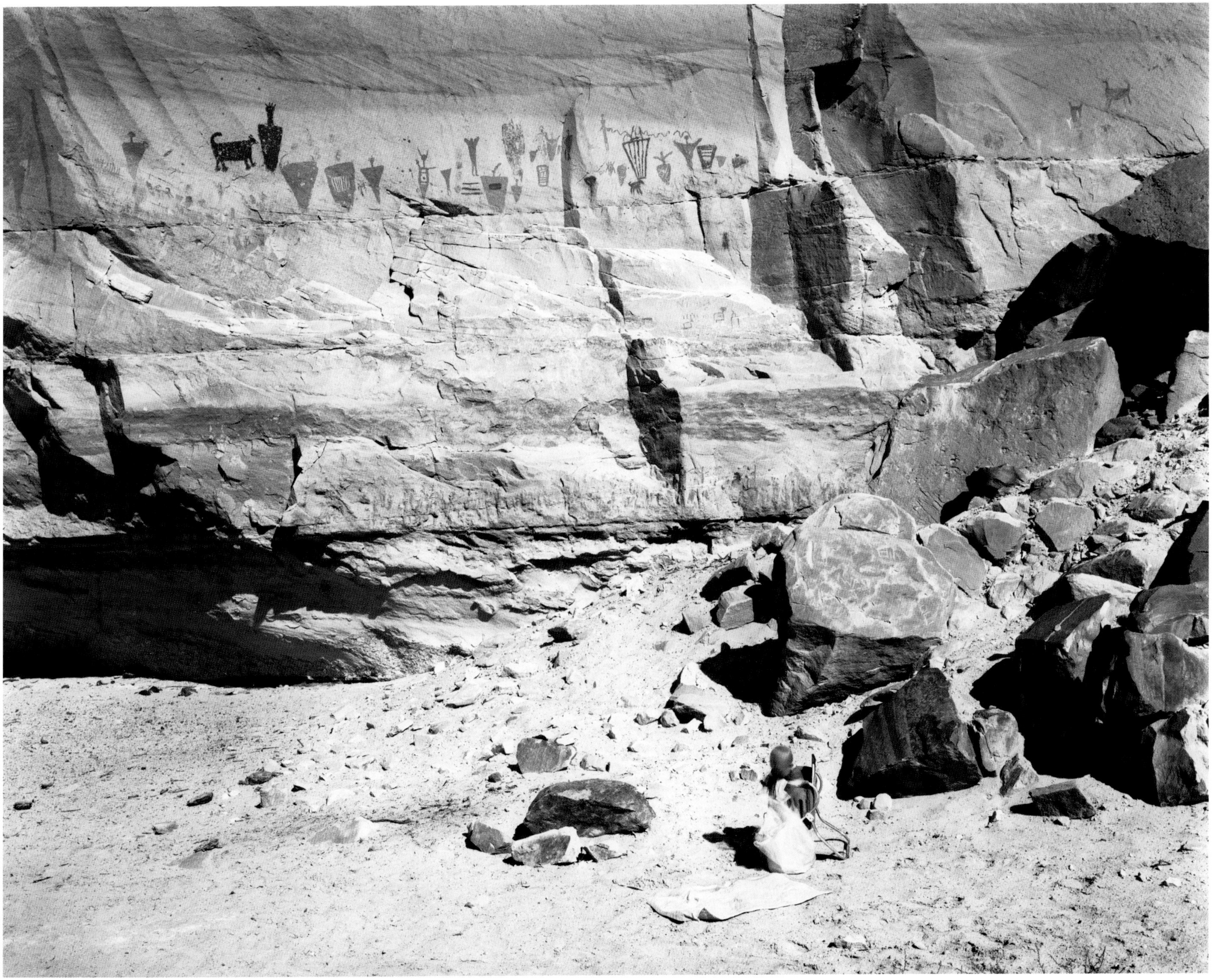

J. B. Jackson (1909–1996), the founder of landscape studies, advanced the idea that the landscape is a record of the people who have inhabited and created it and that we have an obligation to learn how to read it—in all its myriad of forms. The writer Wendell Berry (b. 1934) further described a relationship of identity between humanity and the land: "It is impossible to care for each other more or differently than we care for the earth."[2] These views form the basis for my landscape photography: I seek to create images that express layers of human aspirations in the context of biology and the deep time of geology.

The original idea for the photographs in this book was to document the public lands of the American West in a large swath of land generally west of the 100th meridian: a region that includes, on the easternmost edge, the Sandhills of western Nebraska and Badlands of southwestern South Dakota and all the way west to the Pacific Coast. I imagined an ambitious project: to photograph a full spectrum of the public land that belongs to all Americans, illustrating the famous lyrics by Woody Guthrie (1912–1967), "This land is your land, this land is my land . . . "[3] To what use can we employ this land for the greatest good?

Our public lands are used for a wide range of activities: the enjoyment of nature; the extraction of resources, in particular logging and mining; food production, in particular grazing, fishing, and hunting; recreation, including hiking, backpacking, and mountain biking; the preservation of habitat and biologic reserves where the diversity of nature is provided a place to flourish; and the acknowledgment and celebration of human history and culture as historic monuments on the landscape. All of these activities are important, but, within various interests and value systems, they also involve benefits, costs, and compromises. How do we, as a continental community with varying geographics, balance our necessary resource extraction with conservation goals to ensure that the land is maintained for future generations? I aspired to form an encompassing vision of the contemporary Western landscape, one that would not only reveal the deep beauty of the West—as if one were to discover the region for the first time—but also express the integration of humanity in the natural landscape.

2. Wendell Berry, *The Unsettling of America: The Body and the Earth* (San Francisco, CA: Sierra Club Books, 1977), 123.

3. Guthrie wrote his famous song, "This Land Is Your Land," in New York City in February 1940 while on shore leave from the Merchant Marines. He recorded it in NYC in April 1944, published the lyrics in 1945, and released the song in 1951 on the Folkways label.

(Right) The Keyhole (elevation 14,245 feet), Longs Peak Trail, Rocky Mountain National Park, Colorado, 2001.

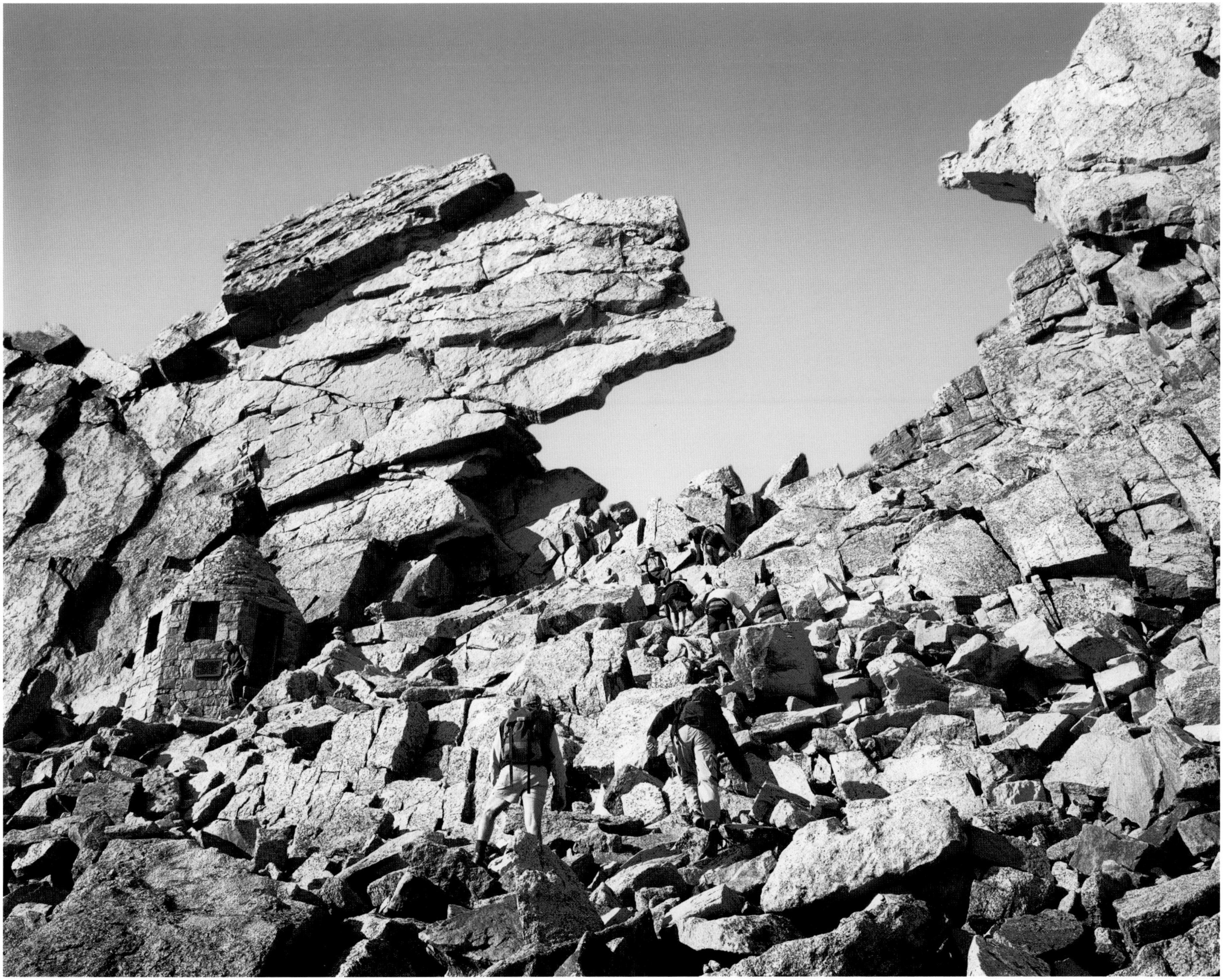

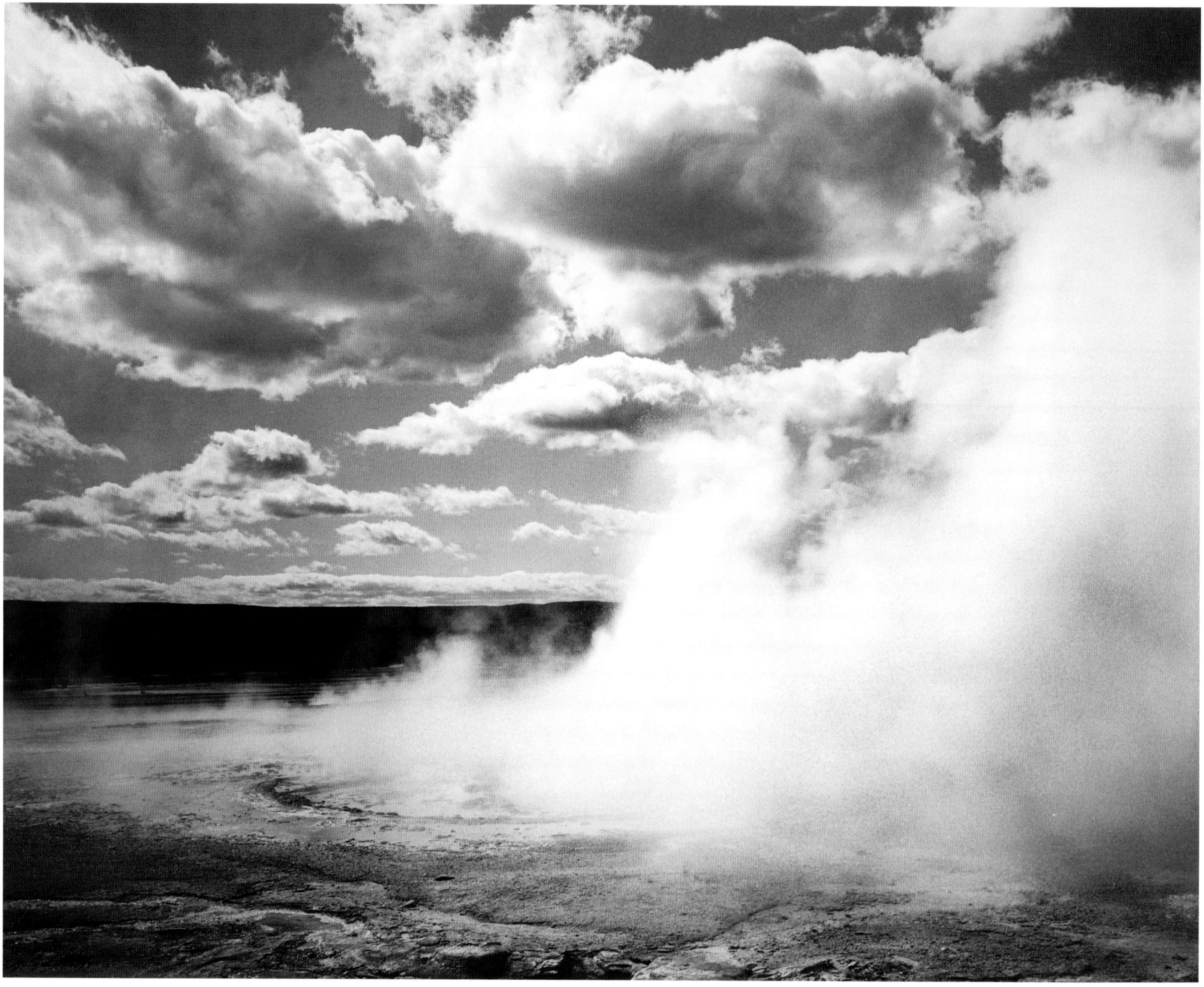

I live in the West because of its topography and its abundance of federal public lands. The eleven states officially comprising the West contain eighty-five percent of all the public lands in the lower forty-eight states.[4] Almost one-half of the total area of these eleven states is held in the public domain. Nowhere else in the lower forty-eight states is there so much accessible land as in the American West. From the drama of red-rock canyons and high-altitude mountaintops to the subtle quiet of grassland meadows and arid deserts, our public lands contain beauties that any of us can freely access and engage. This abundance of public land is what ultimately defines the American West.

Federal public lands are comprised of national forests and grasslands, national monuments and historic sites, national parks and scenic and wild rivers, national wildlife refuges and recreation areas, Bureau of Land Management (BLM) holdings and Indian lands. In many ways, they represent the real wealth of the United States. Pivotal acts by Congress helped to usher in these great gifts to the world, among them the creation of the U.S. Forest Service in 1905, the establishment of the National Park Service in 1916, and the passage of the Antiquities Act of 1906, Wilderness Act of 1964, and National Historic Preservation Act of 1966.

The U.S. Forest Service (USFS) and BLM roughly split management of ninety-three percent of the public lands in the eleven Western states. Congress established the Forest Service in 1905 to provide quality water and timber resources. USFS lands are defined as "land of many uses"; hence, there are often conflicts of interest between grazing, logging, mining, recreation, and wildlife habitat. BLM land is literally the land that was left over after homesteading and claim-staking had run their course. It is mostly range land used for grazing, for oil, gas, and mineral extraction, and increasingly for recreation.

National parks are set aside specifically for the preservation of their natural and scenic values. In 1872, Congress established Yellowstone National Park in northwestern Wyoming as the first national park in the United States and the world because of its exceptional geologic features and natural beauty, but the National Park Service was not created until 1916.

4. All percentages were calculated from statistics gathered from: *Annual Report of Lands Under Control of the U.S. Fish and Wildlife Service 2010* (Washington, DC: U.S. Department of the Interior, 2011); *Land Areas of the National Forest Systems* (Washington, DC: U.S. Department of Agriculture Forest Service, 2011); *NPS Stats Reports* (Washington, DC: National Park Service Public Use Statistics Office, Land Resource Division, 2010); and *Public Land Statistics* (Washington, DC: U.S. Department of the Interior, Bureau of Land Management, 2009).

(Left) Geyser, Yellowstone National Park (elevation 5,282–11,358 feet), Wyoming, 1998.

A national park is established through an act of Congress, and a national monument is established by presidential proclamation from land that is already federally owned. National parks and national monuments are both under the National Park Service's management. Today, national parks and national monuments comprise five and one-half percent of the total area of the public lands in the eleven Western states. Theodore Roosevelt (1858–1919) was the first president to use the Antiquities Act of 1906 to create a series of national monuments, including Chaco Canyon in New Mexico, Devils Tower in Wyoming, and the Grand Canyon in Arizona, which later became a national park in 1919.

In 1964, Congress passed the Wilderness Act to preserve areas "of undeveloped federal land retaining its primeval character and influence . . ." Wilderness areas are also defined to protect wildlife and habitat: "A wilderness . . . is hereby recognized as an area where the earth and its community of life are untrammeled by man . . ."[5] The 2008 Congressional Research Service report on wilderness states: "In total, more than 17% of all federal land, and nearly 5% of all land in the United States, has been designated as wilderness. Alaska, because of its size and relatively pristine condition, dominates wilderness statistics—more than 54% of designated wilderness is in Alaska. In total, nearly 16% of all land (federal, state, private, and other) in Alaska has been designated as wilderness. In contrast, 3% of all land in the United States outside Alaska has been designated as wilderness."[6]

There are many reasons to preserve wilderness and maintain biodiversity. One is that we find wildlife and natural landscapes beautiful, inspiring, and wondrous. Another is the realization that we are part of, and dependent upon, the natural world; therefore, we have an interest in preserving the environmental systems that support us. Additionally and provocatively, deep ecologists maintain a moral position that wildlife has an intrinsic right to exist separate from human uses or perceptions.

5. 1964 Federal Wilderness Act.

6. These statistics are the most recent available. See Ross W. Gorte, *Wilderness: Overview and Statistics* (Washington, DC: Congressional Research Service, Report for Congress, Library of Congress, 2008; available online at http://digitalcommons.unl.crsdocs/22 (accessed August 22, 2012).

(Right) Campground, Chaco Culture National Historical Park (elevation 6,000–6,800 feet), New Mexico, 1986.

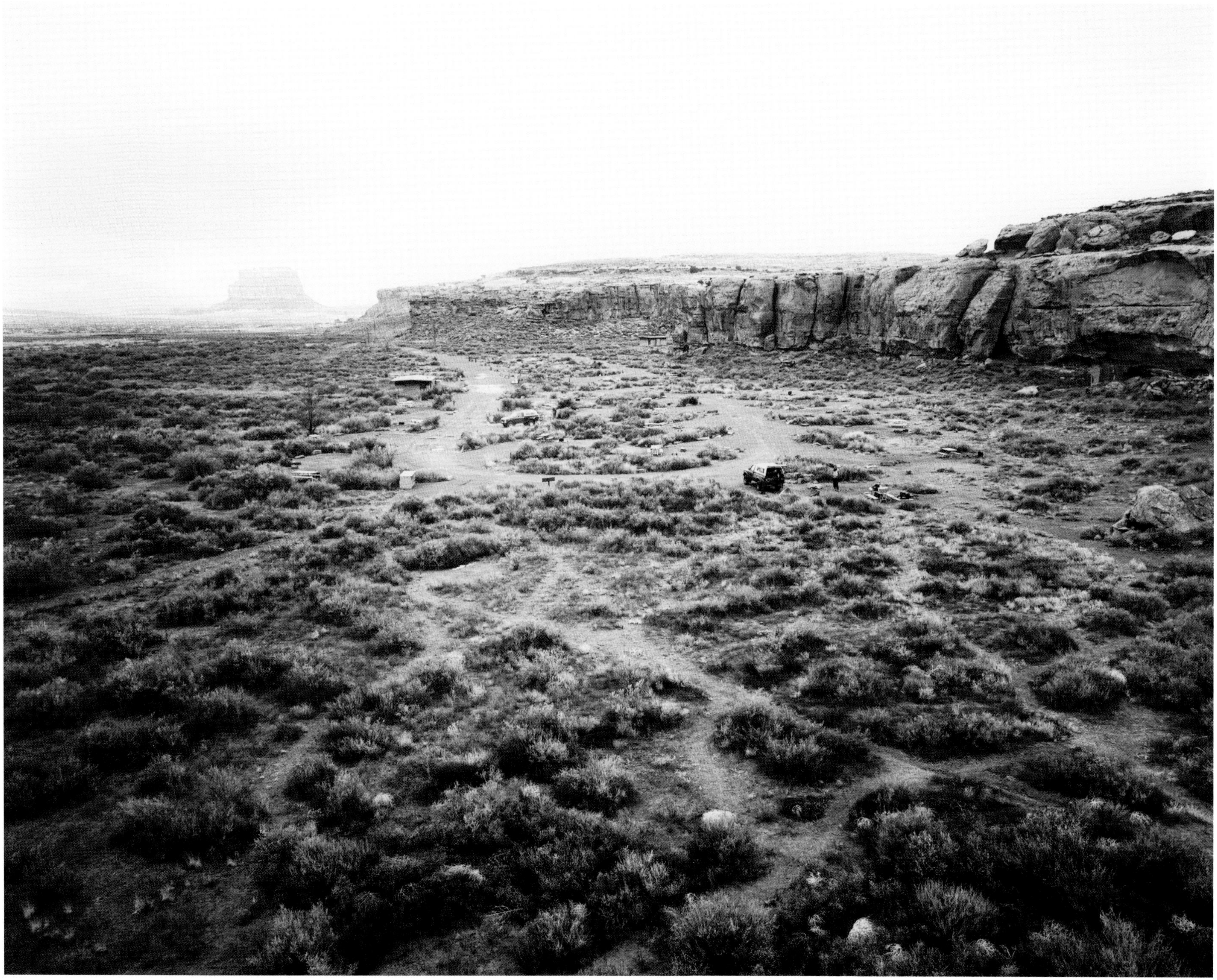

I ACCESSED THE LANDSCAPE primarily from dirt roads and on foot by way of a four-wheel-drive pickup truck. I had a camper shell over the truck bed and a futon inside where I could sleep. I stowed food, a stove, backpacking gear, and, at times, more than twenty gallons of water. My original truck had an additional gas tank, allowing me to drive more than 400 miles. I could camp almost anywhere. In my little pickup, I was temporarily self-sufficient.

I did not use a systematic or scientific approach to exploring the West's public lands, but neither was I an aimless wanderer. I was interested in some places, but, for the most part, I had little more than a general plan: to have the freedom to go or stay depending upon what I found. Sometimes I would travel with a friend, or we would meet up for awhile and then go our separate ways. We would journey to special places where the land might reveal some magic: to the deserts, grasslands, and mountains for the freedom of big spaces, the forms of animated vegetation, and the inspiration of illuminating light. Other times I thought of myself as assessing the condition of the public lands. I would come across overgrazed rangeland, valleys full of cow pies, and trampled riparian habitats. In the mountains, I found enormous wastelands from mining and logged-out forests denuded of trees, with stumps and broken branches splayed about.

The public lands are legacies of the ever-changing frontier, and within them can be found wild lands, and within those wild lands is a psychological and spiritual horizon. The poet Gary Snyder, in an essay in *The Practice of the Wild*, offered a definition of "wild" as the state or place where one is totally connected and aware of one's environment.[7] Wild animals need to be aware of their surroundings to survive, to know the location of prey and predators and of water and nesting ground. When something moves through a forest, the vegetation makes a sound, insects crawl, birds fly, and through these movements the inhabitants of the forest communicate in an intricate web. To be wild is to be *in place*, aware, entirely conscience of one's surroundings, and intimately connected to the environment.

7. Gary Snyder, *The Practice of the Wild: The Etiquette of Freedom* (New York: North Point Press, 1990), 3–26.

(Right) Shell Canyon, Bighorn National Forest (elevation 5,500–13,175 feet), Wyoming, 2012.

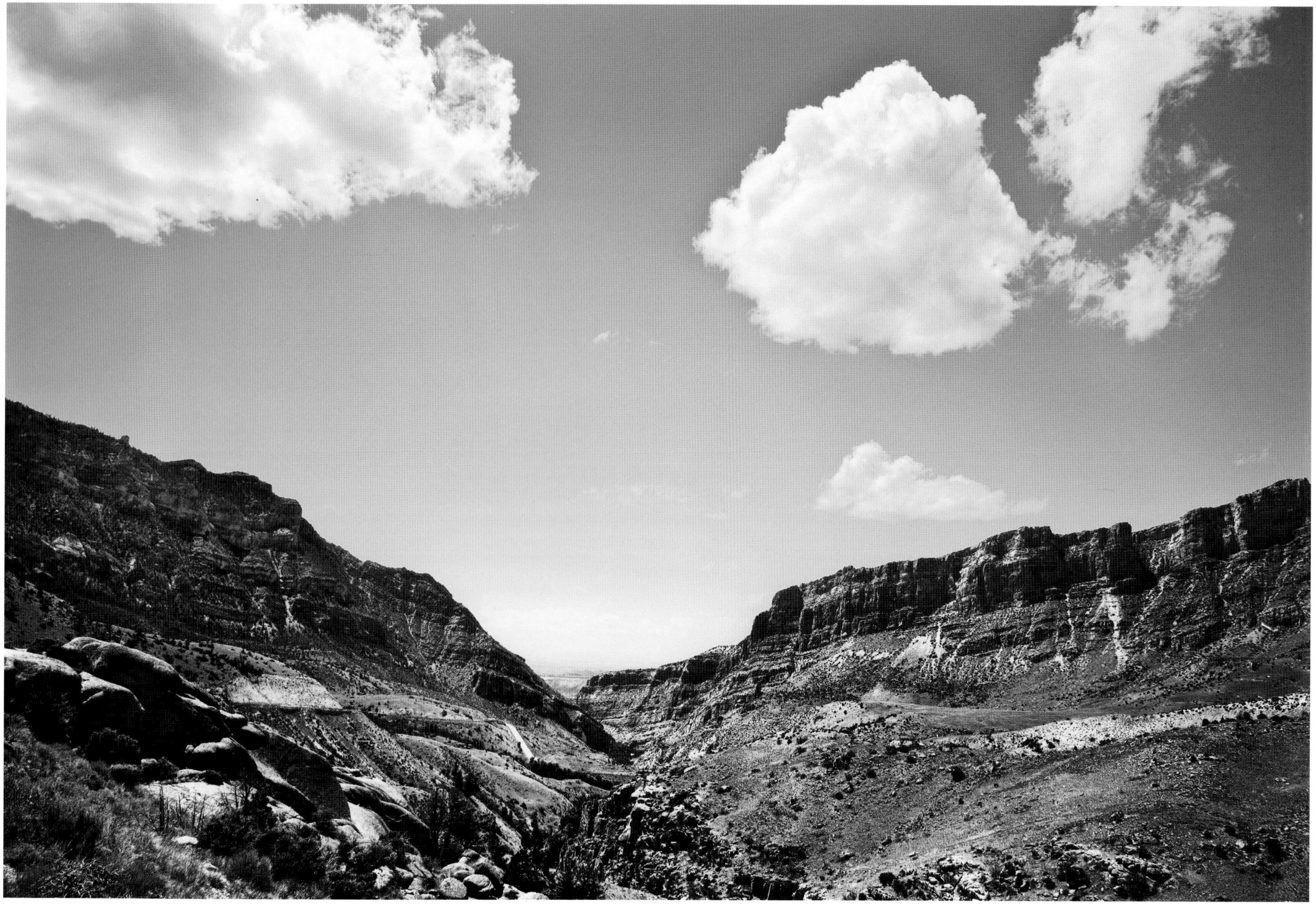

As time passed, my pictures of public lands became something other than the documentation I had originally imagined. My path as a photographer is to interact with the world through walking and looking and making pictures. I am an idealist. I am committed to working towards a better world. I believe in the power of pictures to change the way we think and act. I was different after I saw my first Jackson Pollock painting, after I first saw an exhibition of Edward Weston's photographs, and each time I poured over Robert Frank's influential book, *The Americans* (1958). Art addresses us and challenges us in psychologically and intellectually complex ways. Art nourishes and informs; it broadens our world and makes it bigger and deeper. Ultimately, making pictures and engaging art is a way of knowing the world.

The American West has long been a cultural icon, an archetypical form, which includes notions of conquest and freedom, heroic struggle and exploitation, grandeur and the sublime. Much has been written about the myths and realities of the West and about the clash of human aspirations and the limits of the land. Still, the West remains a place of hope, dreams, and aspirations, a place where the interactions of nature and culture are laid bare in spare, dry, and dramatic landscapes.

In *The Natural West,* environmental historian Dan Flores suggests that we recognize something within us when we experience the vastness of the Great Plains, with the West's mountain ranges appearing in the distance and with a big sky overhead, something that was written forever into our being at the dawn of human consciousness on an African savanna.[8] Perhaps, then, there is also something inside us that we can re-remember about living in a place and caring about the consequences of our actions for the health of future generations, something about the connections within us, and between us, and the places we create and inhabit.

We all come from somewhere, and we all have a territorial range. We move in distinct circles: from home to work and back home again, among family and friends, from the places where we do business to the places that hold mystery for us. One of my circles takes place in the mountains west of Boulder, Colorado, where I live. My walks lead me in a large circle around

8. Daniel Flores, *The Natural West: Islands in the Desert* (Norman: University of Oklahoma Press, 2001), 110–11.

my house, hiking along ridges and hilltops in a clockwise direction. I look west to the snowy ridges of the West's Continental Divide and then gaze back upon the house I have been building for the past three decades. I look at the way it fits into the meadow and our children's toys scattered about and see the clothesline and piles of firewood. My footprints wear a path into the spaces I repeatedly walk upon. Since I follow the topography, I am often walking along game trails made by deer. Sometimes, to move faster or just for the fun of it, I run up and down the hills.

When I was much younger, I wanted to be a Westerner, a mountain man. I wanted to be of this place we call the American West. I believed that, if I spent enough time out there, its landscapes would form me and I could earn a mantle of belonging. I could find my place. Now, a half century after first moving to Arizona, I have instead been formed by the grandeur and foolishness of my dreams and desires, together with the challenges and failures of living. After returning to the West from Chicago, I wanted to escape from the noise and pollution of the big city and to live in an authentic manner, responsive to the cycles and patterns of the land. The process of living has made it evident how dependent and absolutely woven into society and flow of the economy that I am—that we all are. We are like the grass that the wind moves, reaching for the sky, rooted and entwined together in this special home we call Earth.

At Home in the West

View from Mount Sneffels (elevation 14,157 feet), Uncompahgre National Forest, Colorado, 1999.

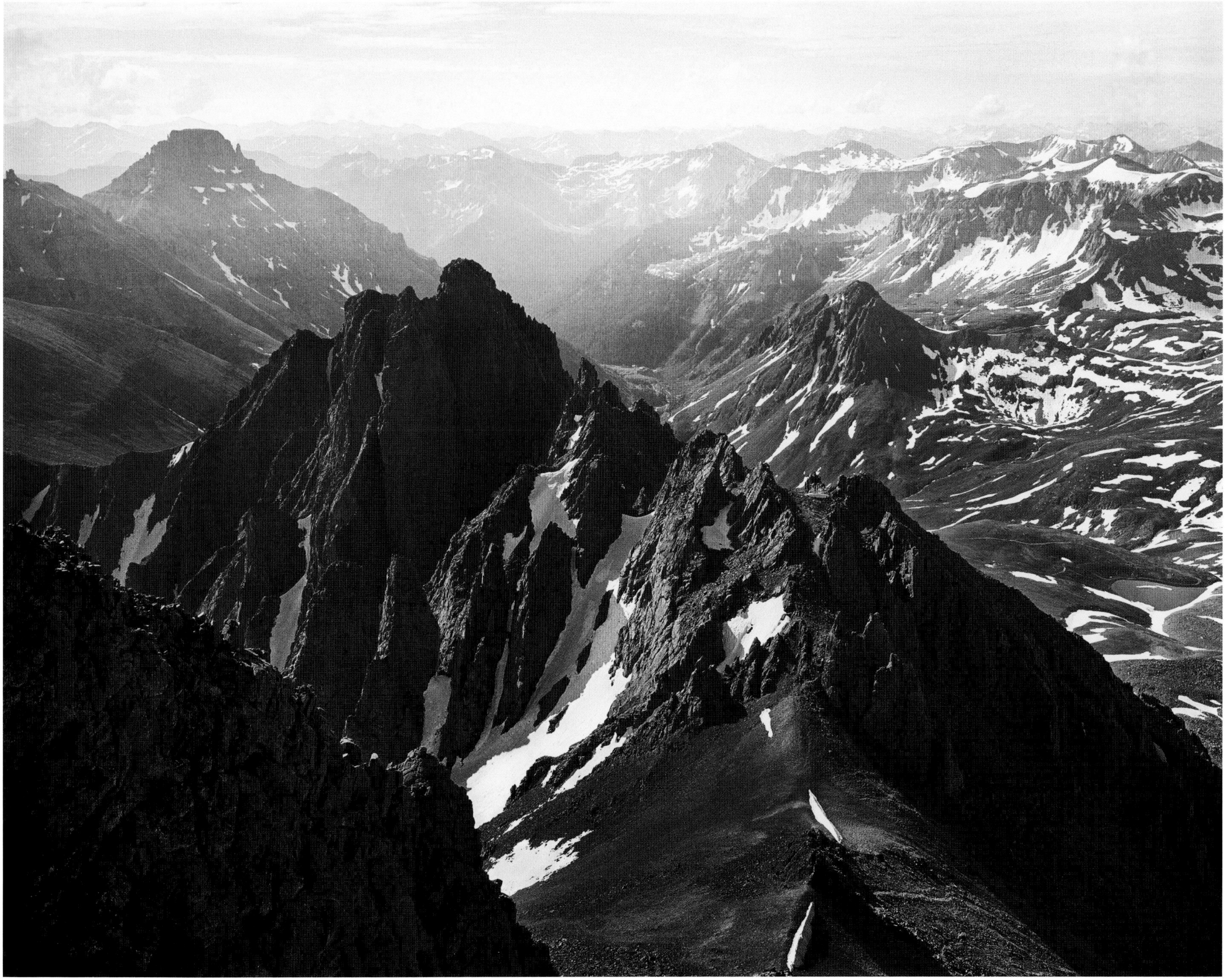

The Sandhills, Samuel R. McKelvie National Forest (elevation 2,932–3,180 feet), Nebraska, 1989.

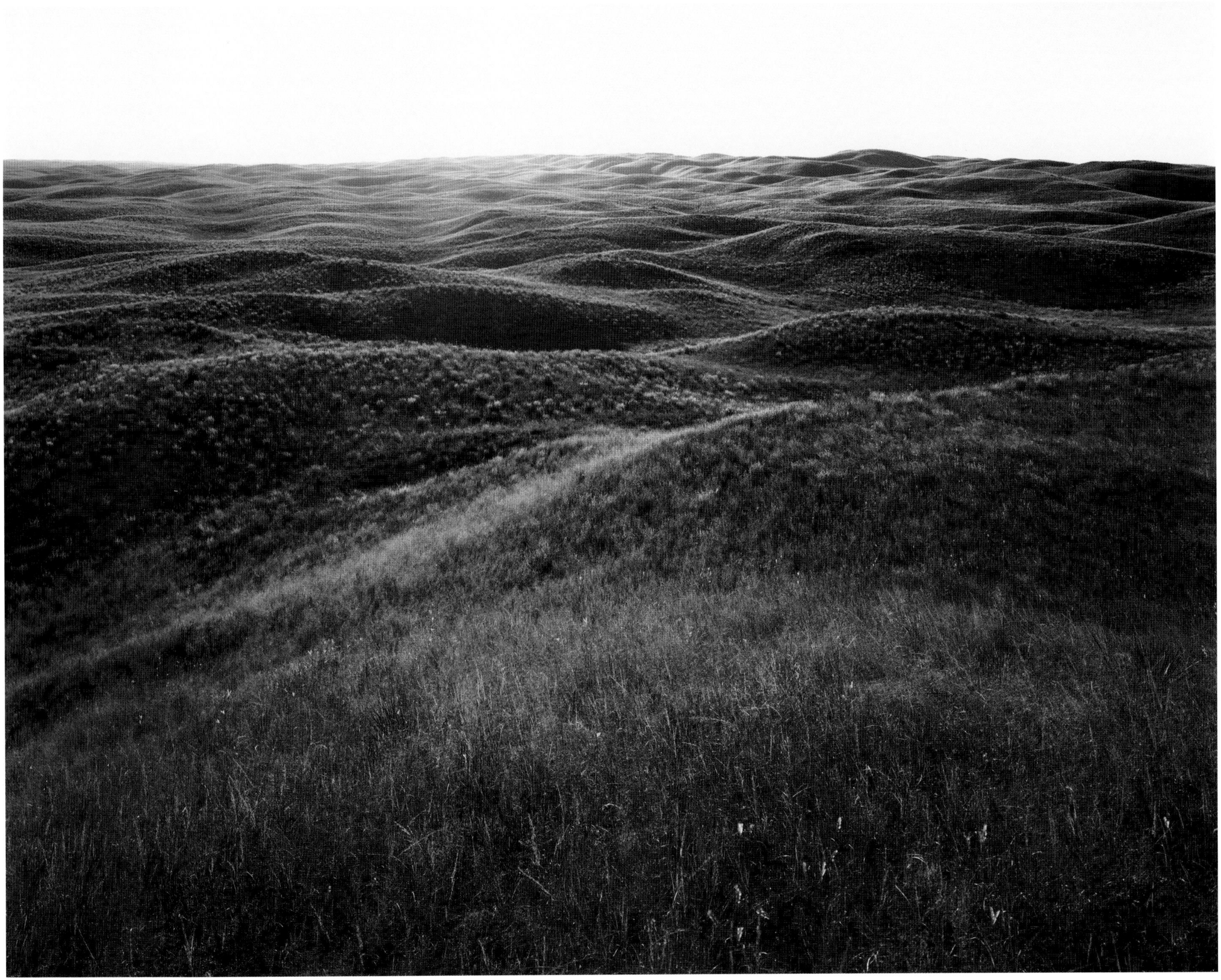

Bison in Lamar Valley (average elevation 6,500 feet), Yellowstone National Park, Wyoming, 1995.

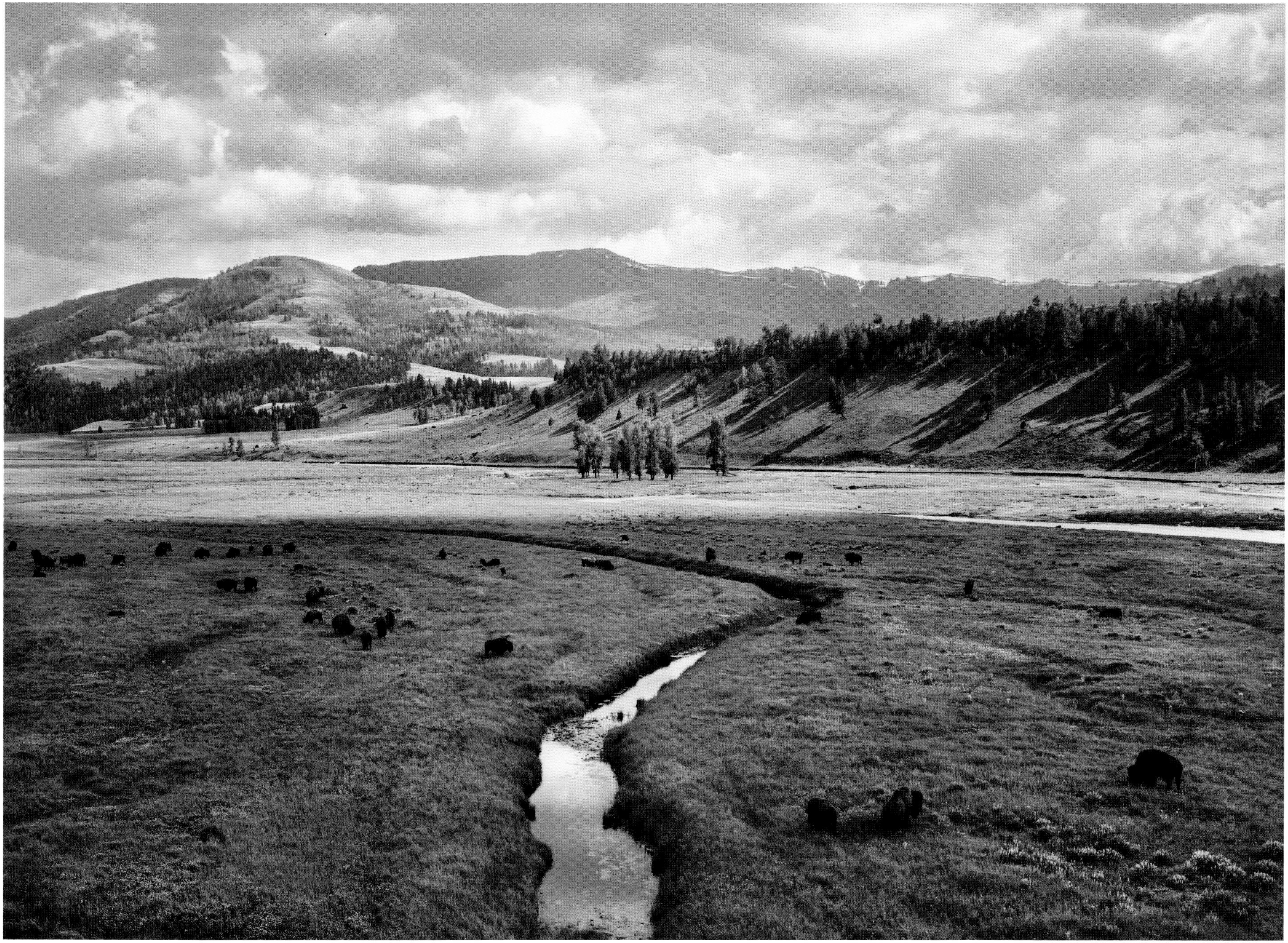

Bison in Badlands National Park (elevation 2,443–3,340 feet), South Dakota, 1985.

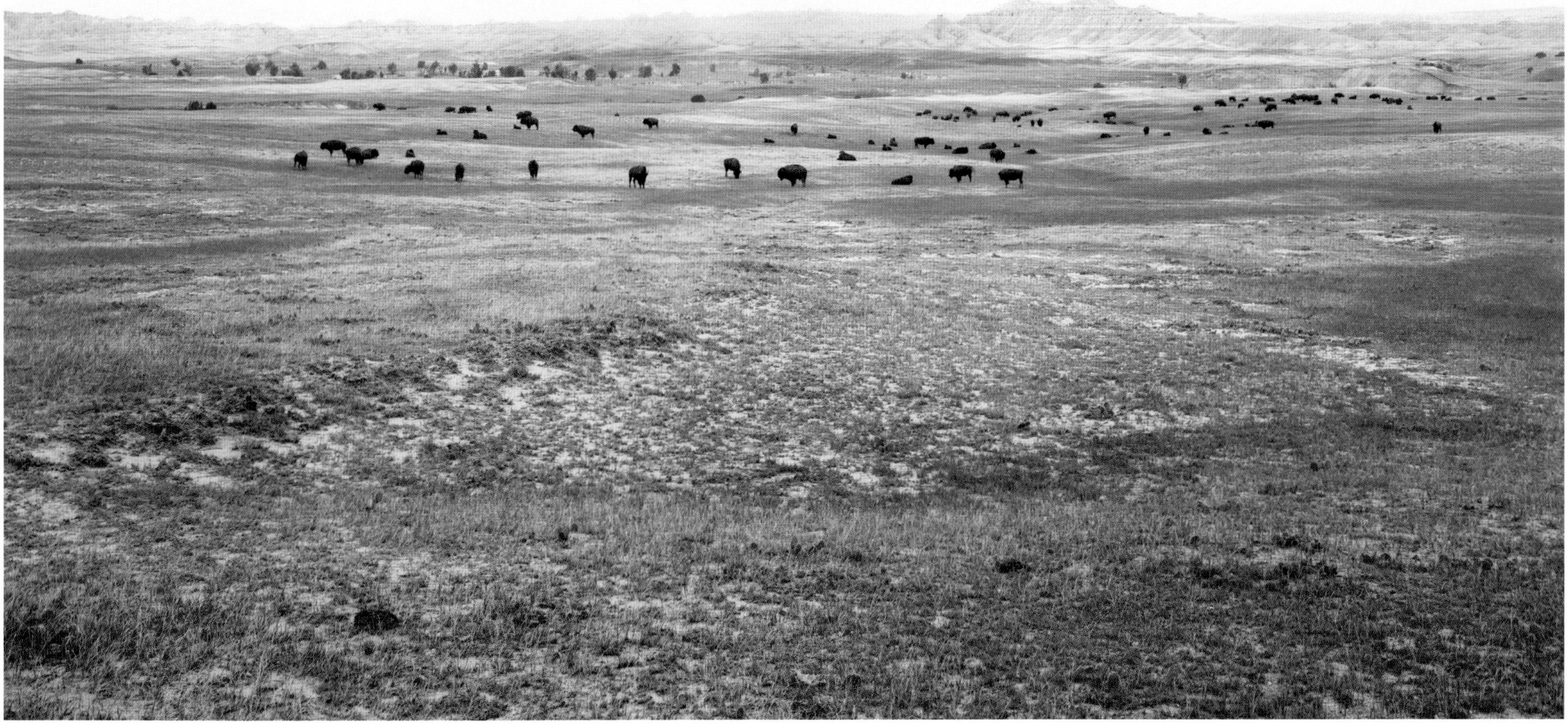

View from Sheep Mountain Table (elevation 3,282 feet), Badlands National Park, South Dakota, 1997.

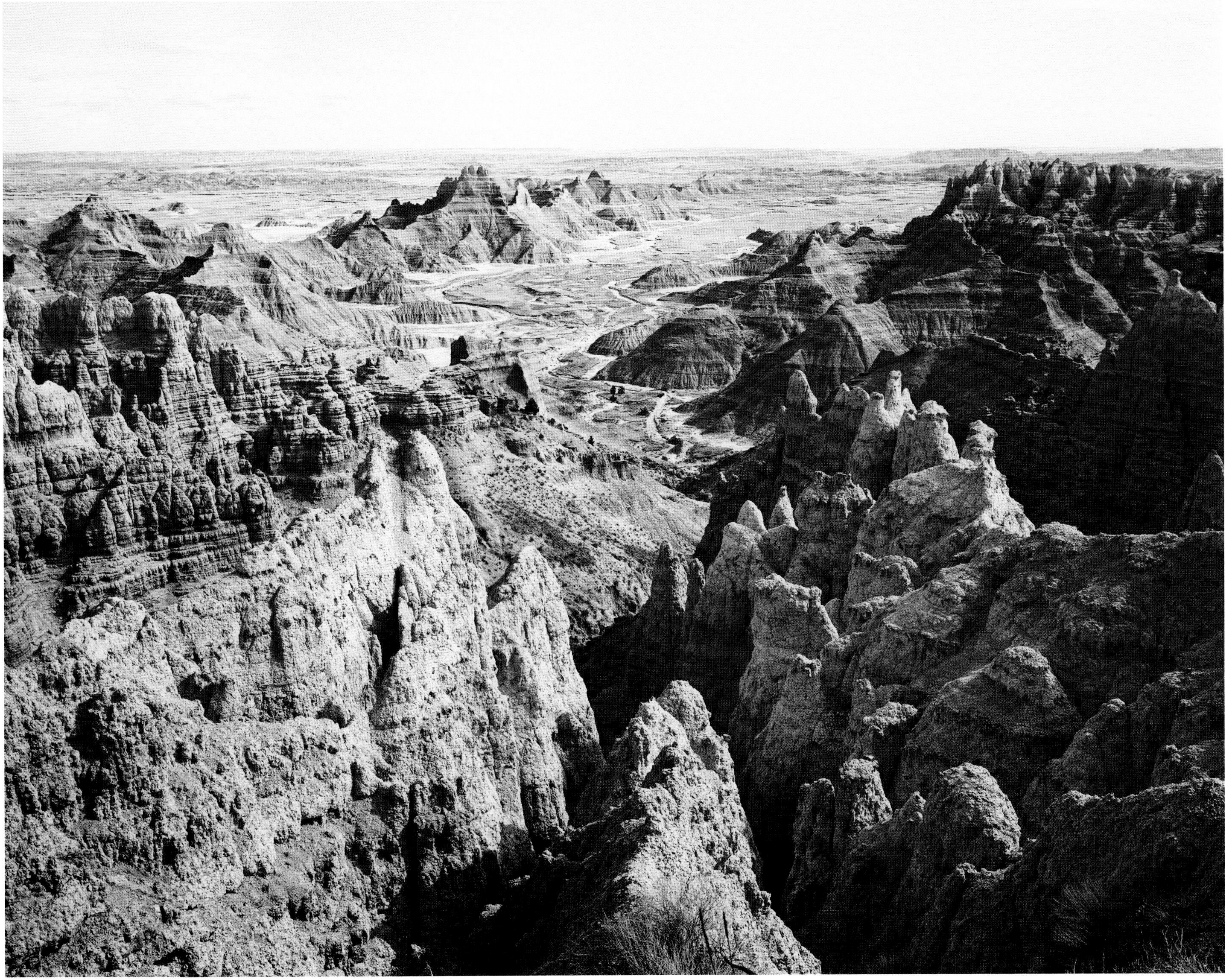

Colorado River, Canyonlands National Park (elevation 3,700–7,200 feet), Utah, 1989.

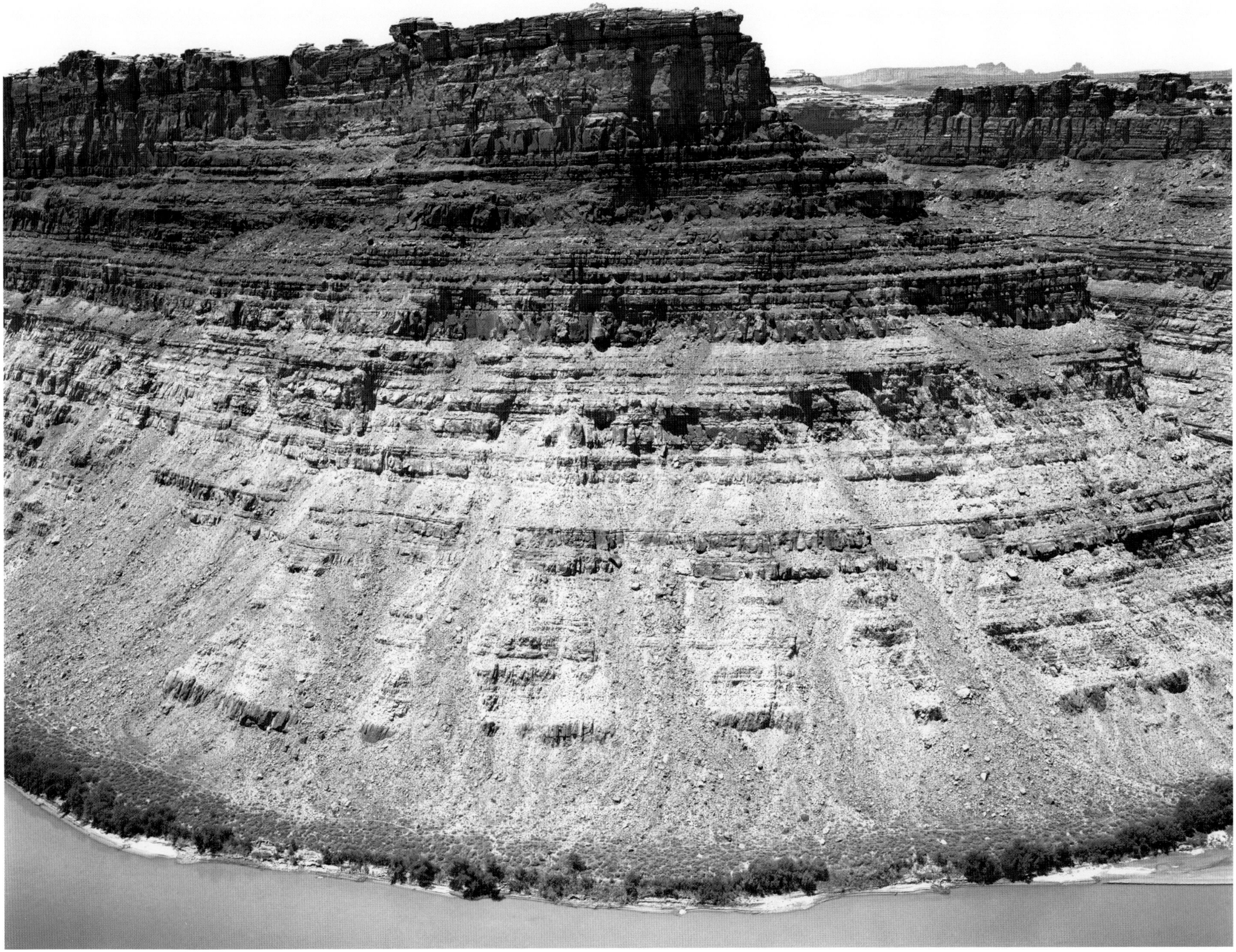

Strawberry Crater (elevation 5,500–6,526 feet), Coconino National Forest, Arizona, 1989.

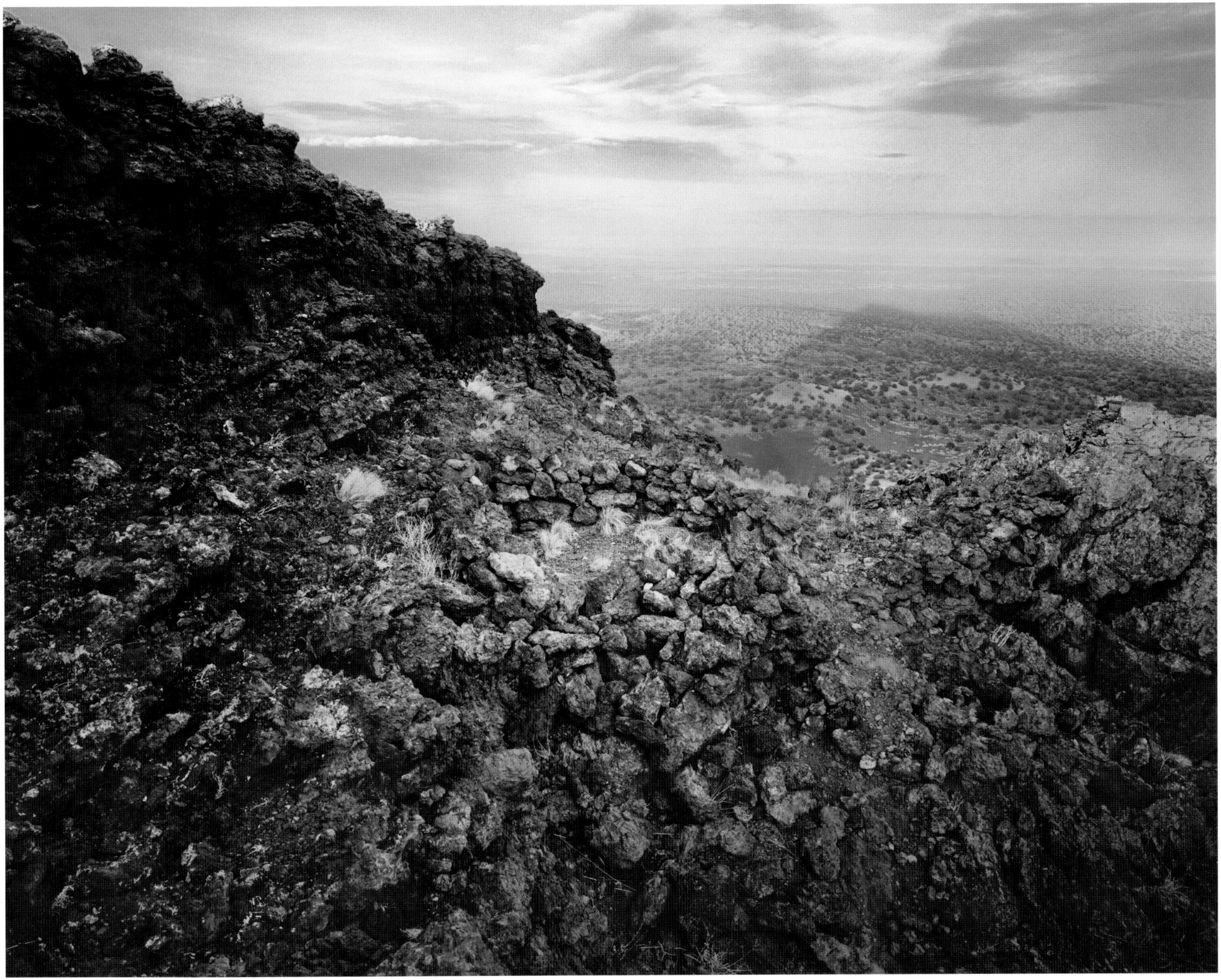

Desert View Point (elevation 7,450 feet), Grand Canyon National Park, Arizona, 1980.

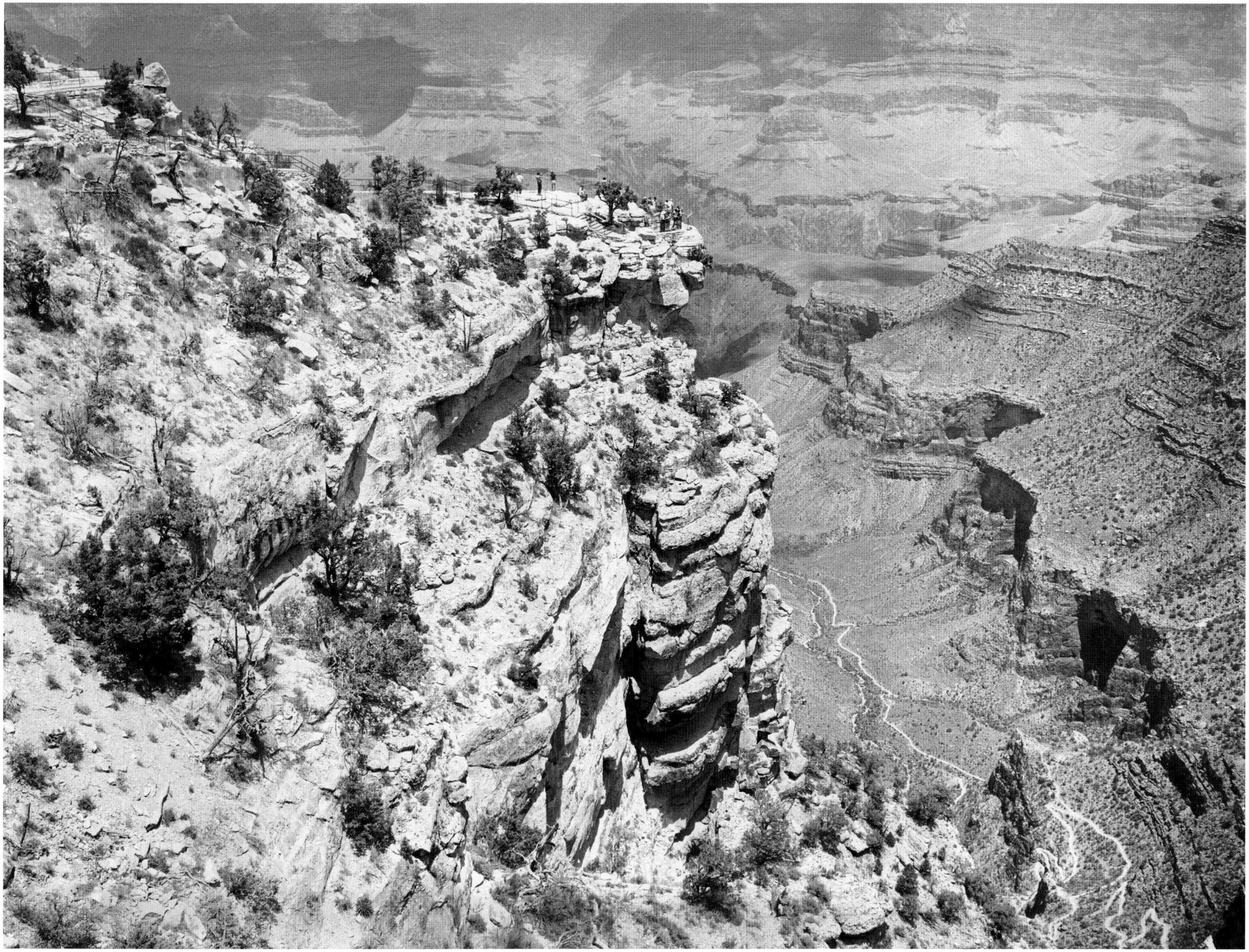

San Rafael Swell (elevation 4,000–7,000 feet) at Interstate 70, Utah, 1989.

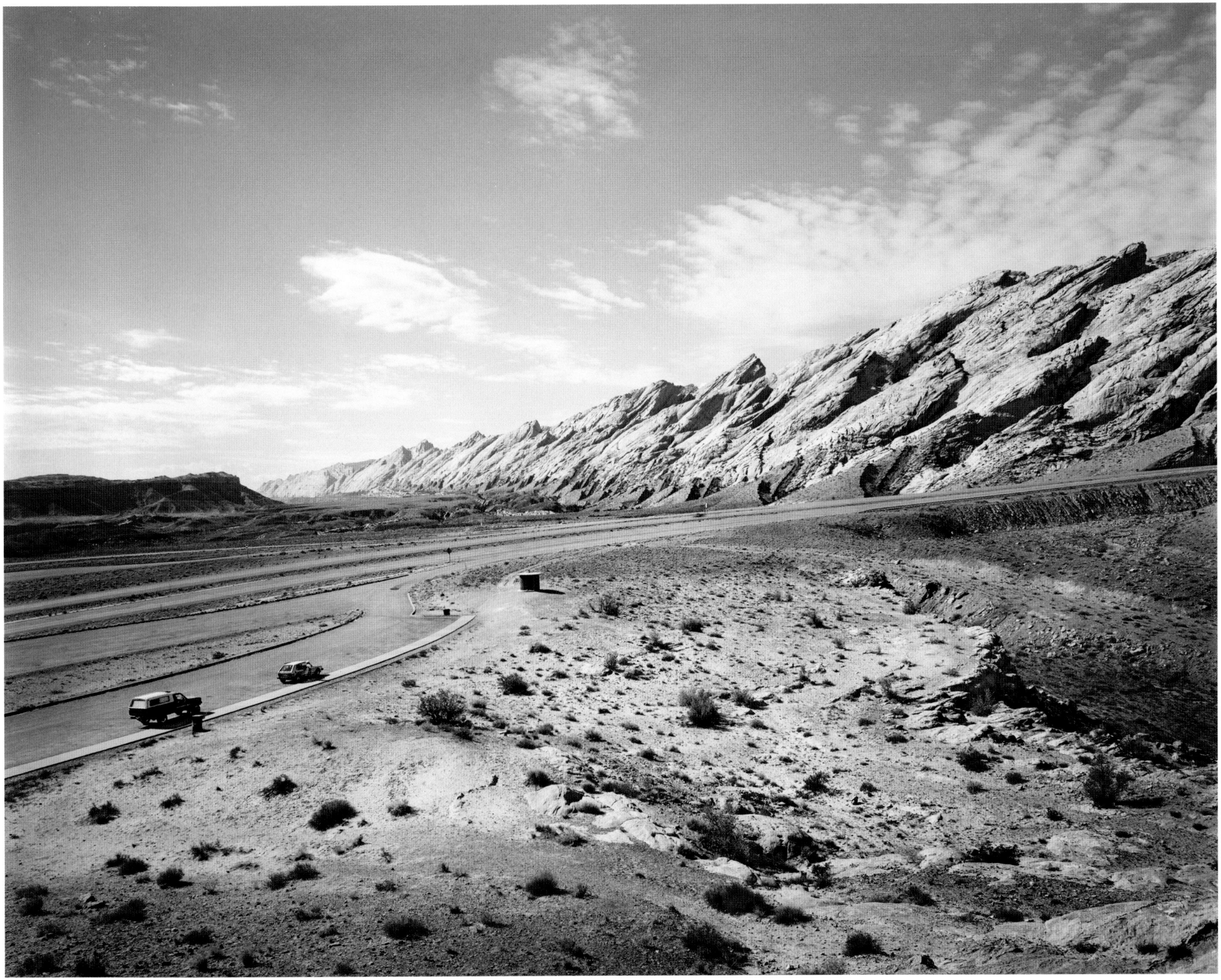

Comb Ridge (elevation 5,374 feet at its center), Utah, 1989.

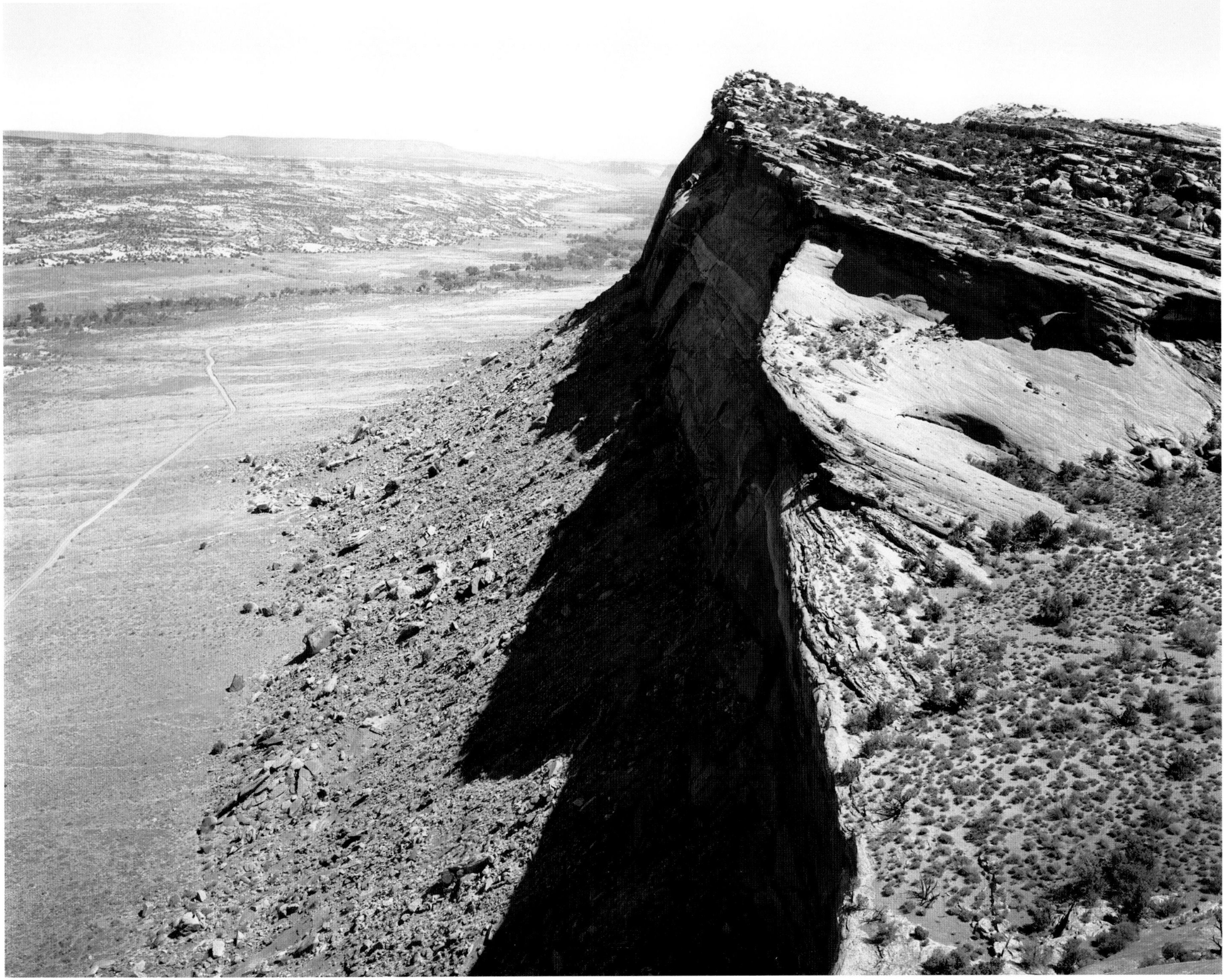

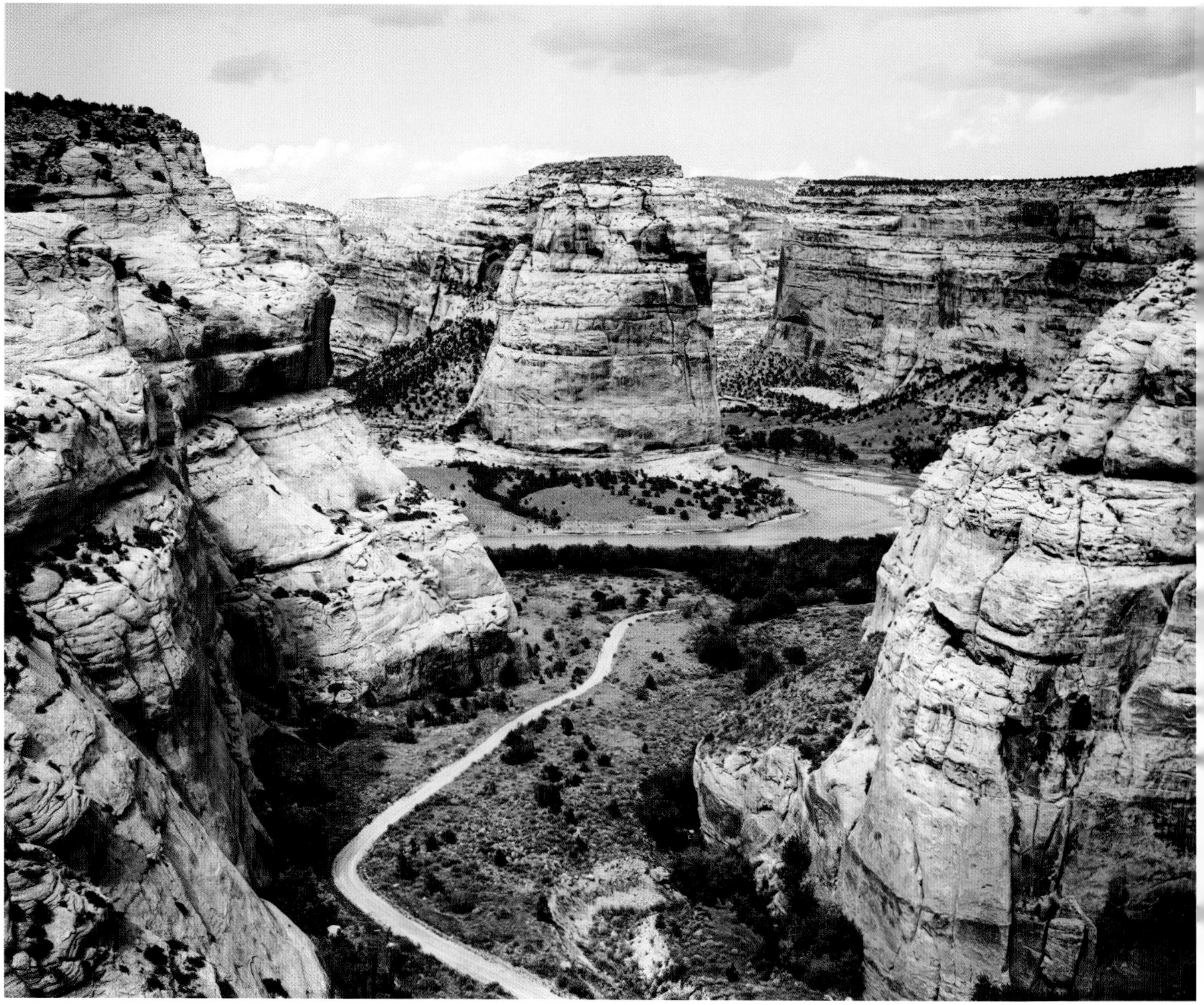

Echo Park (above) and Green River (right), Dinosaur National Monument
(elevation 4,500–7,000 feet), Colorado, 1992 and 1996.

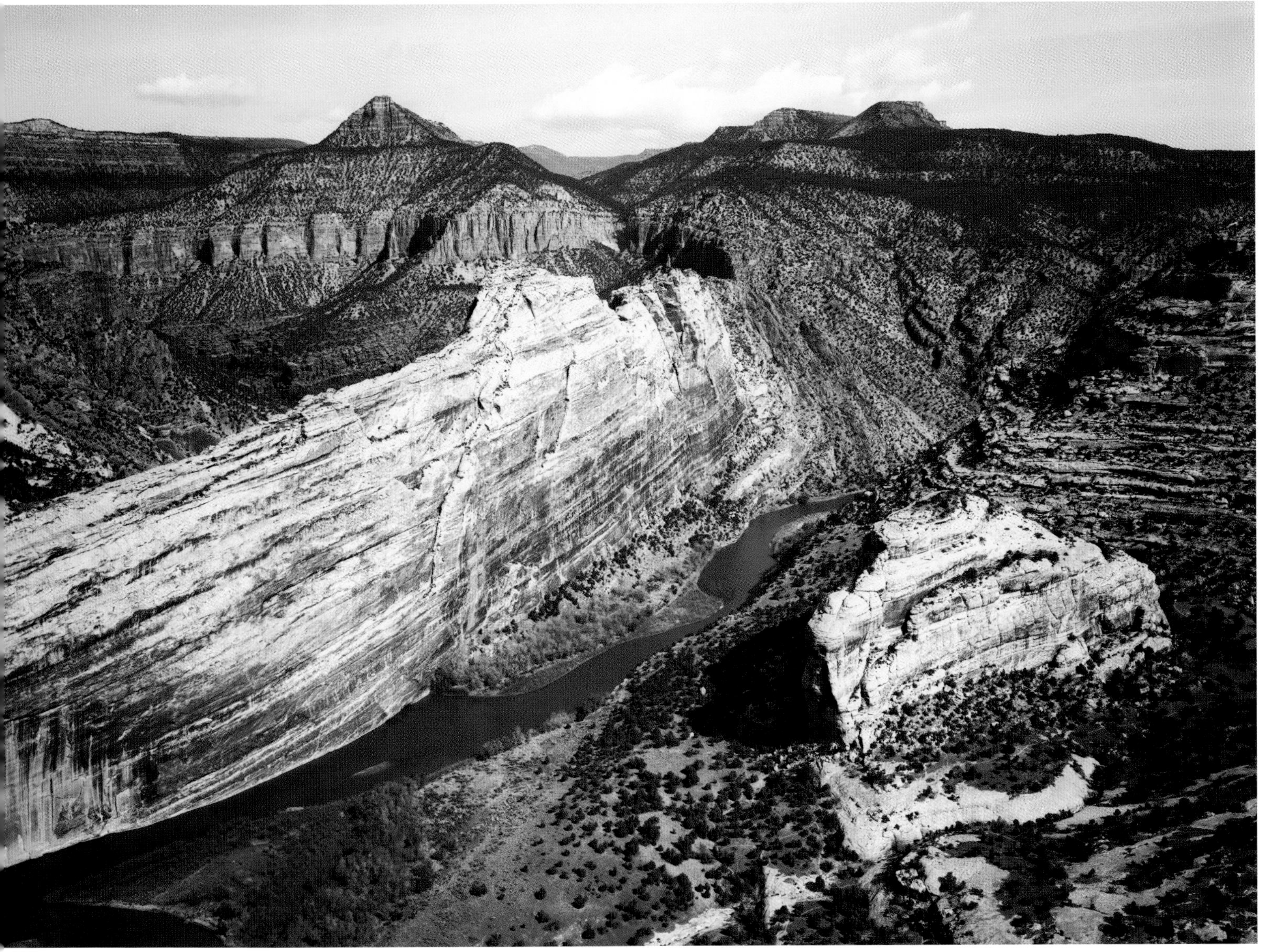

Steamboat Rock (elevation 5,800 feet), Dinosaur National Monument, Colorado, 1996.

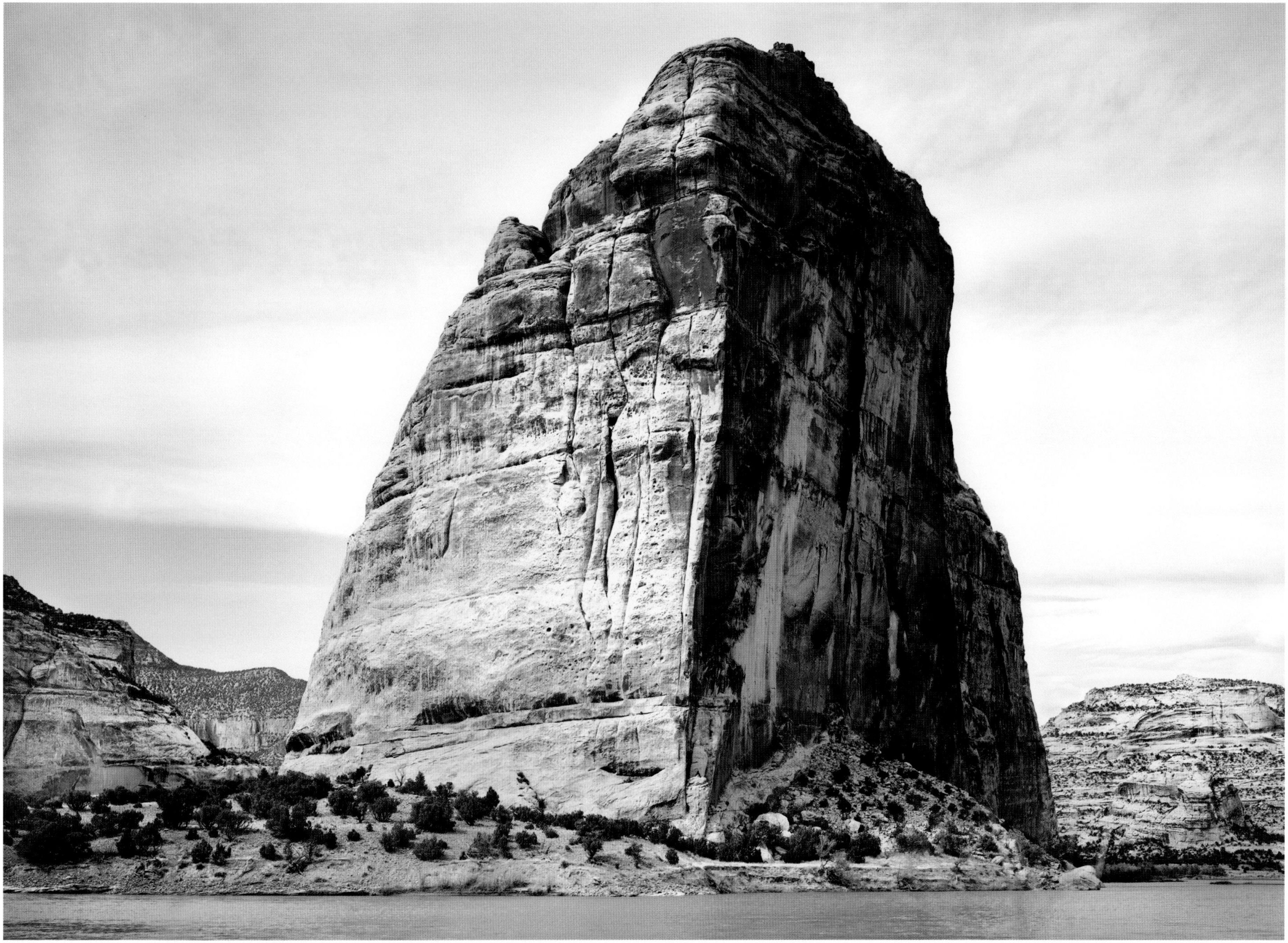

Chetro Ketl, Chaco Culture National Historical Park (elevation 6,000–6,800 feet), New Mexico, 1989.

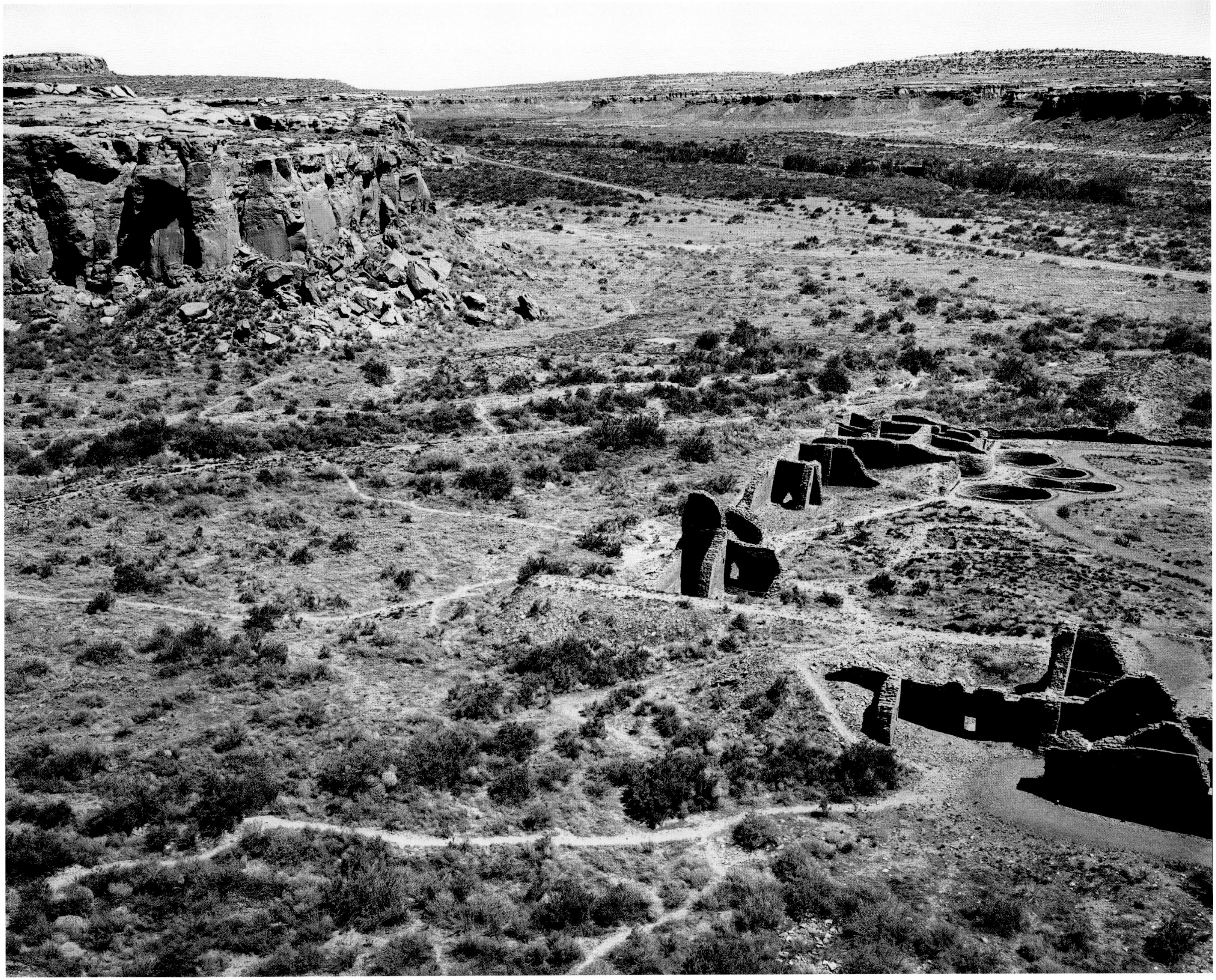

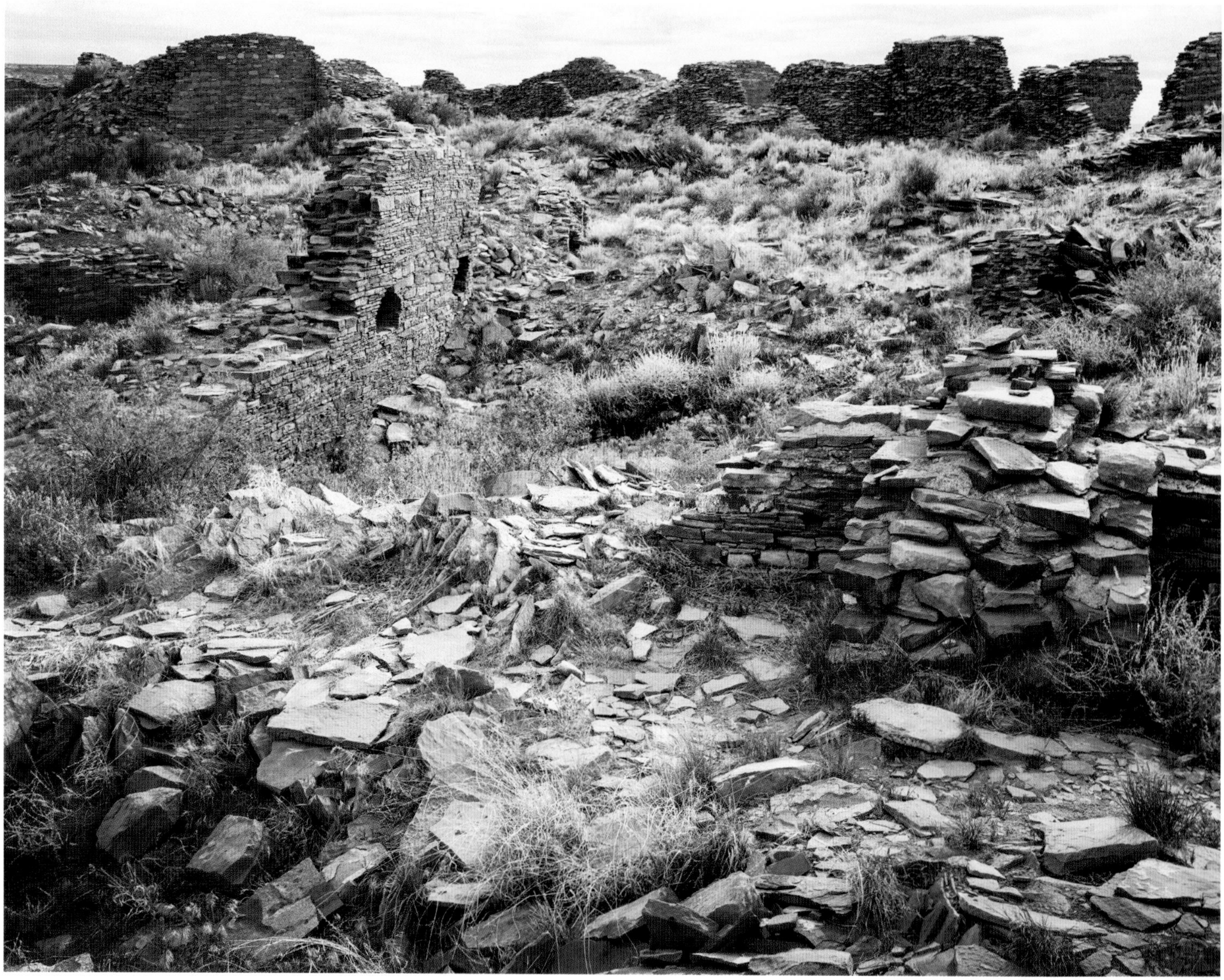

Pueblo Alto, Chaco Culture National Historical Park (elevation 6,000–6,800 feet), New Mexico, 1989.

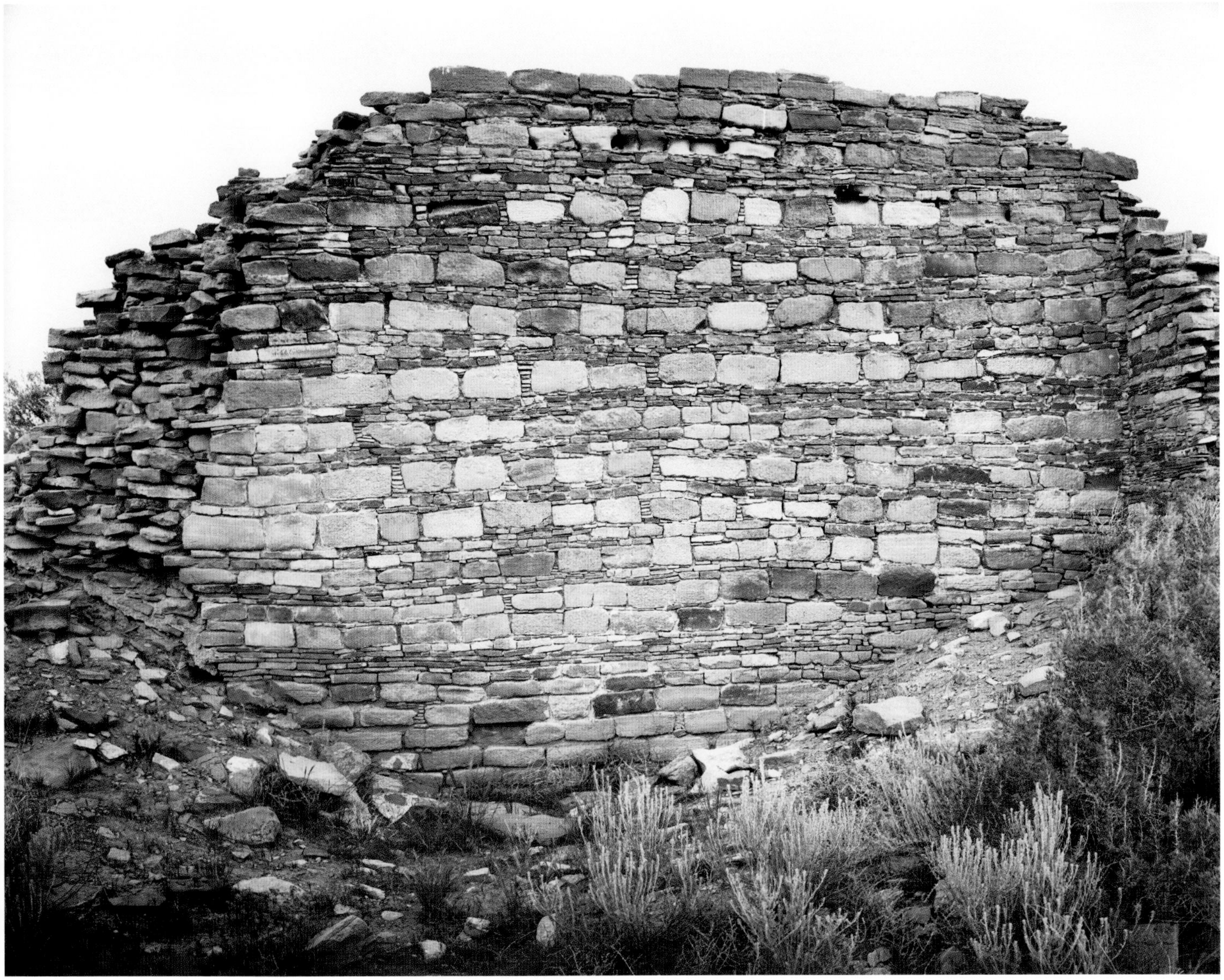

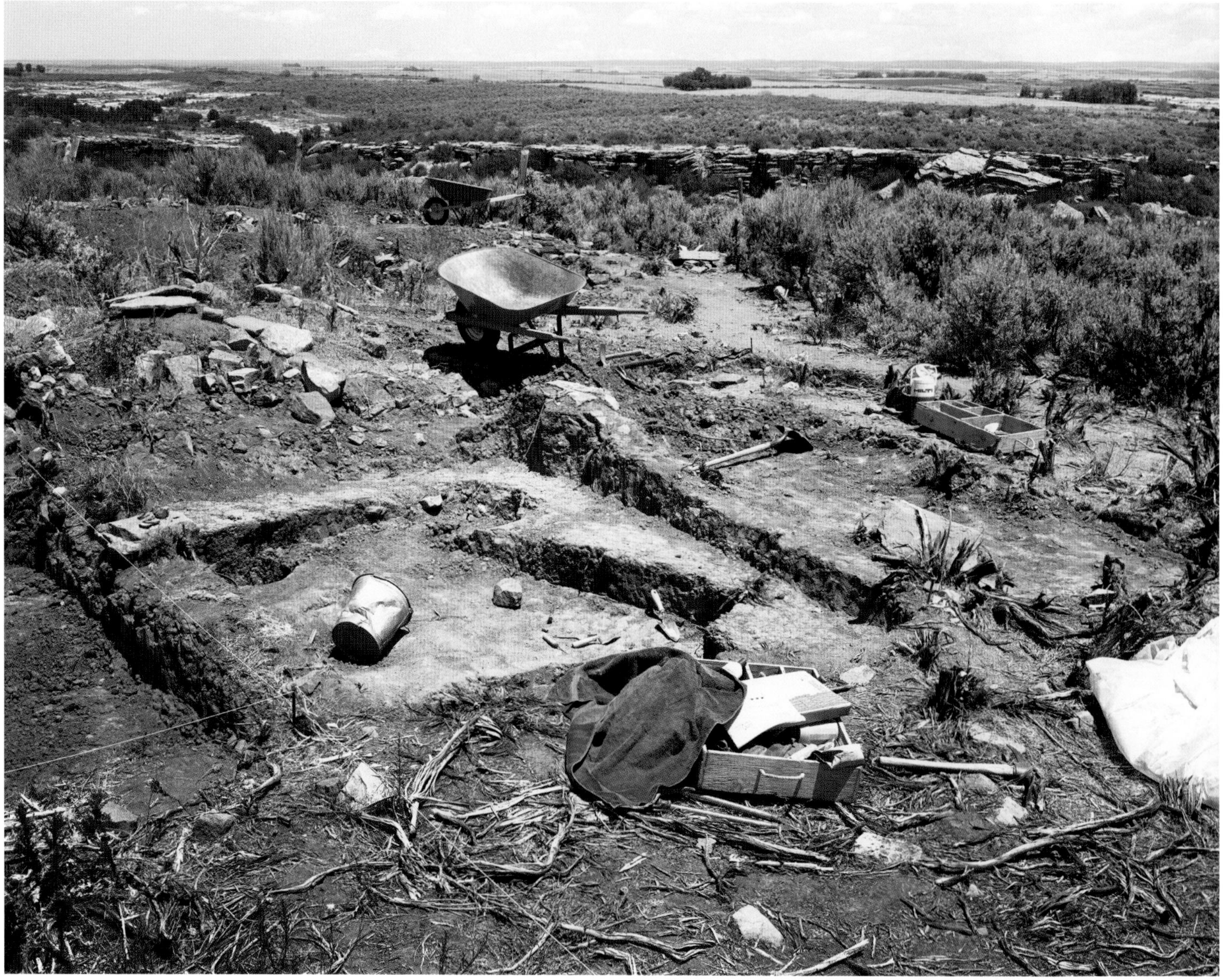

(Above) Yellow Jacket Pueblo Archeological Site (average elevation 6,900 feet), Canyons of the Ancients National Monument, Colorado, 1989, and (right) an unexcavated Pueblo ruin, Ute Mountain Ute Indian Reservation (average elevation 4,600 feet), Colorado, 1989.

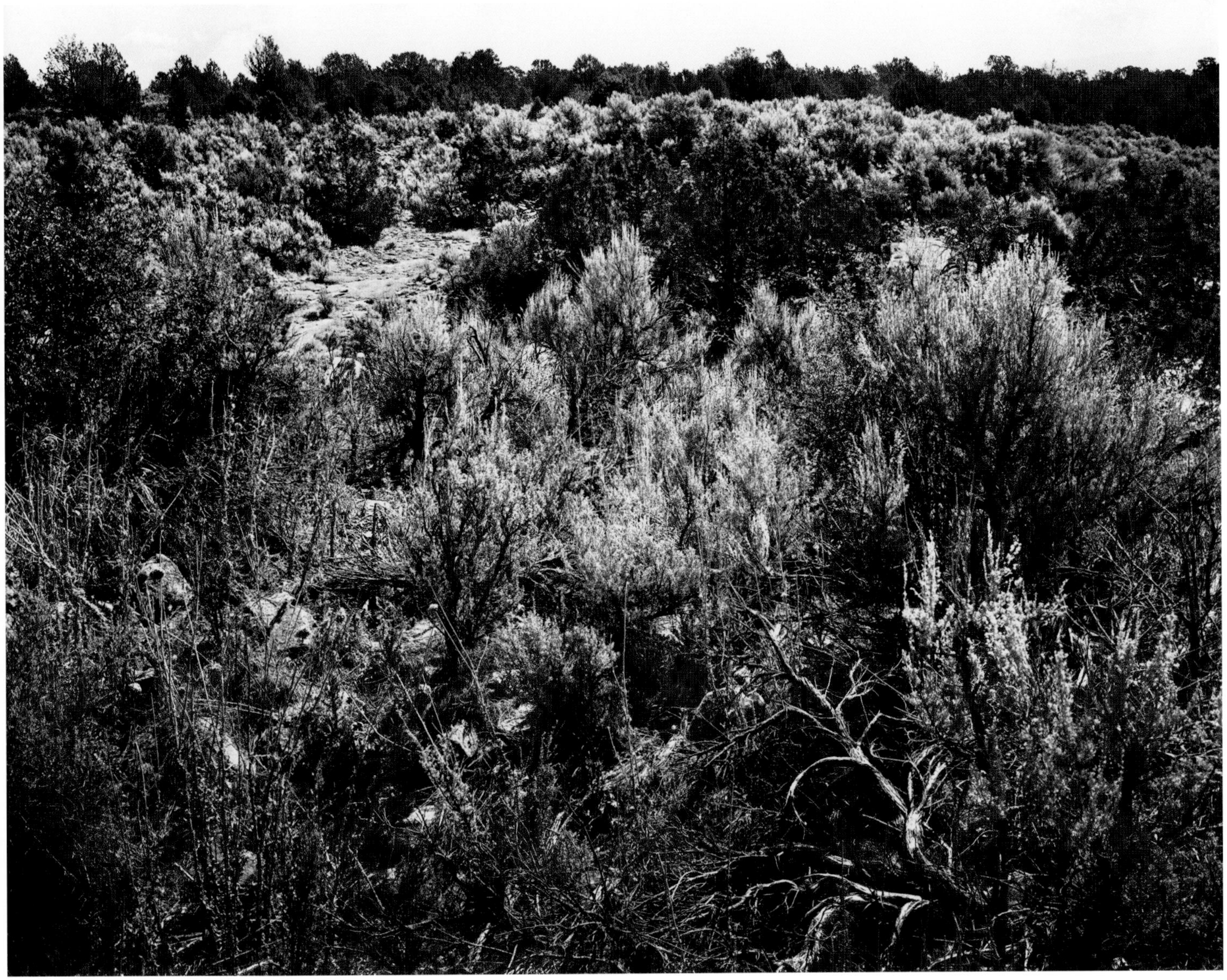

Stairway, Chaco Culture National Historical Park (elevation 6,000–6,800 feet), New Mexico, 1987.

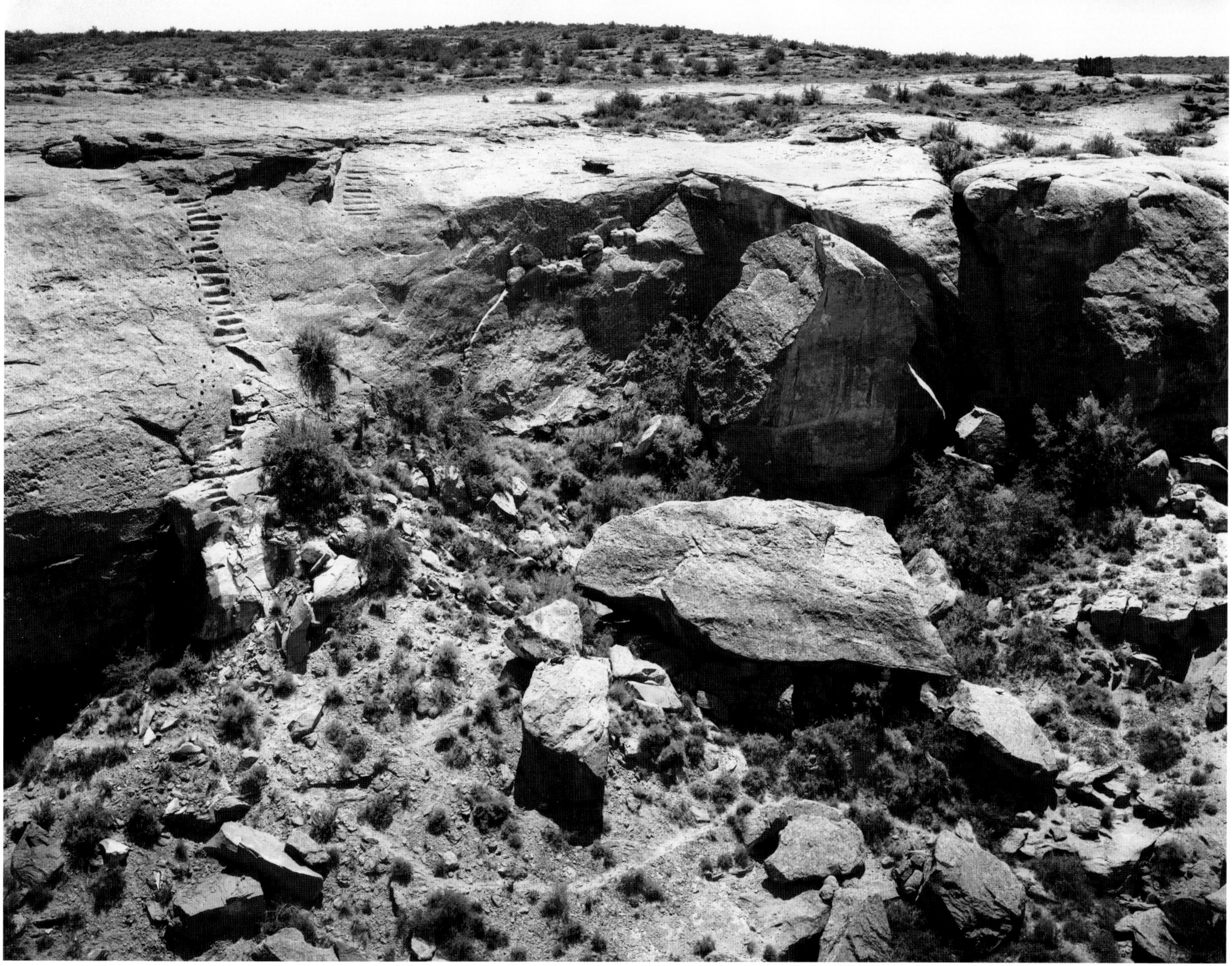

Super Nova Pictograph, Chaco Culture National Historical Park (elevation 6,000–6,800 feet), New Mexico, 1989.

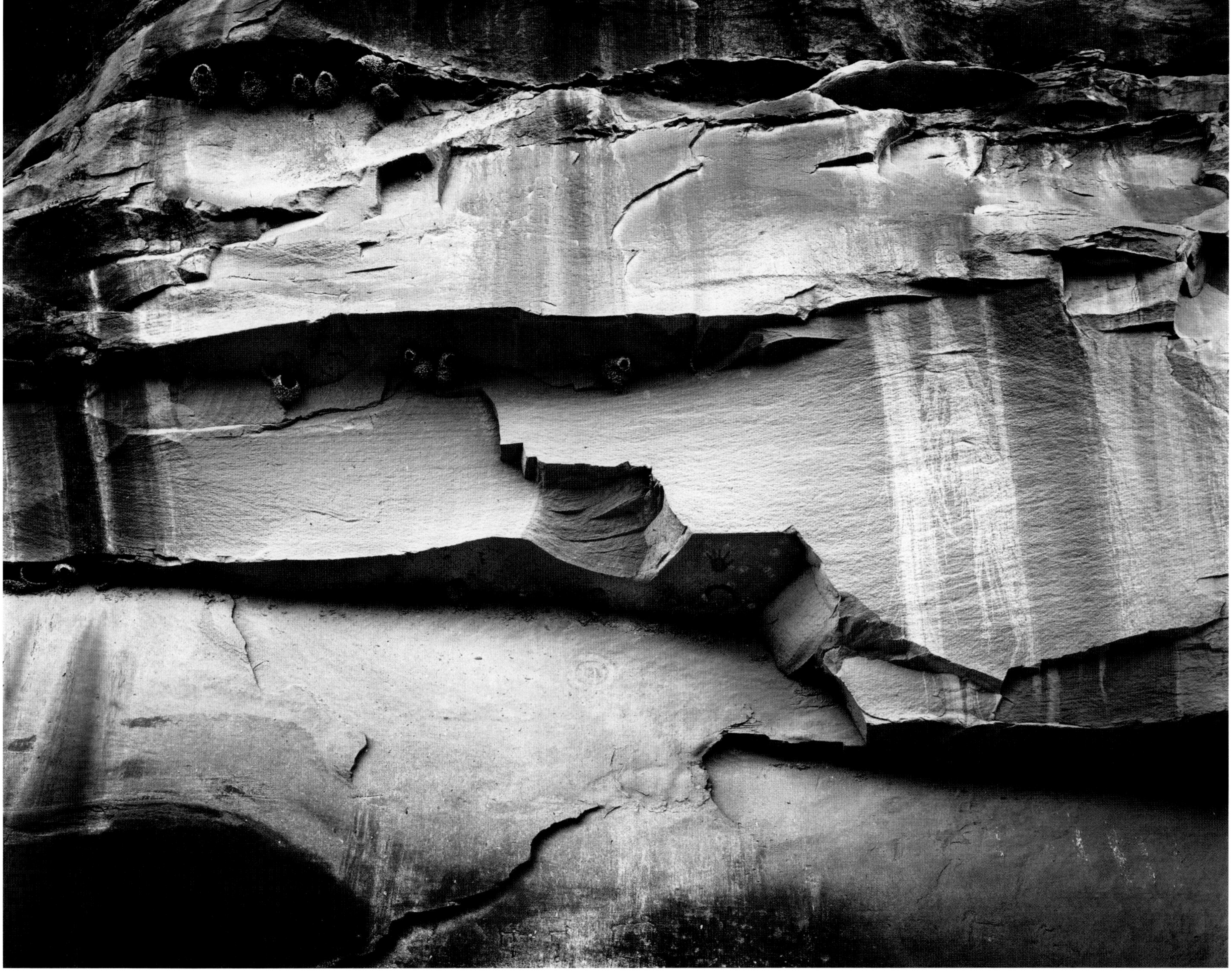

Crow Canyon Archeological District (elevation 5,295 feet at the center), New Mexico, 1989.

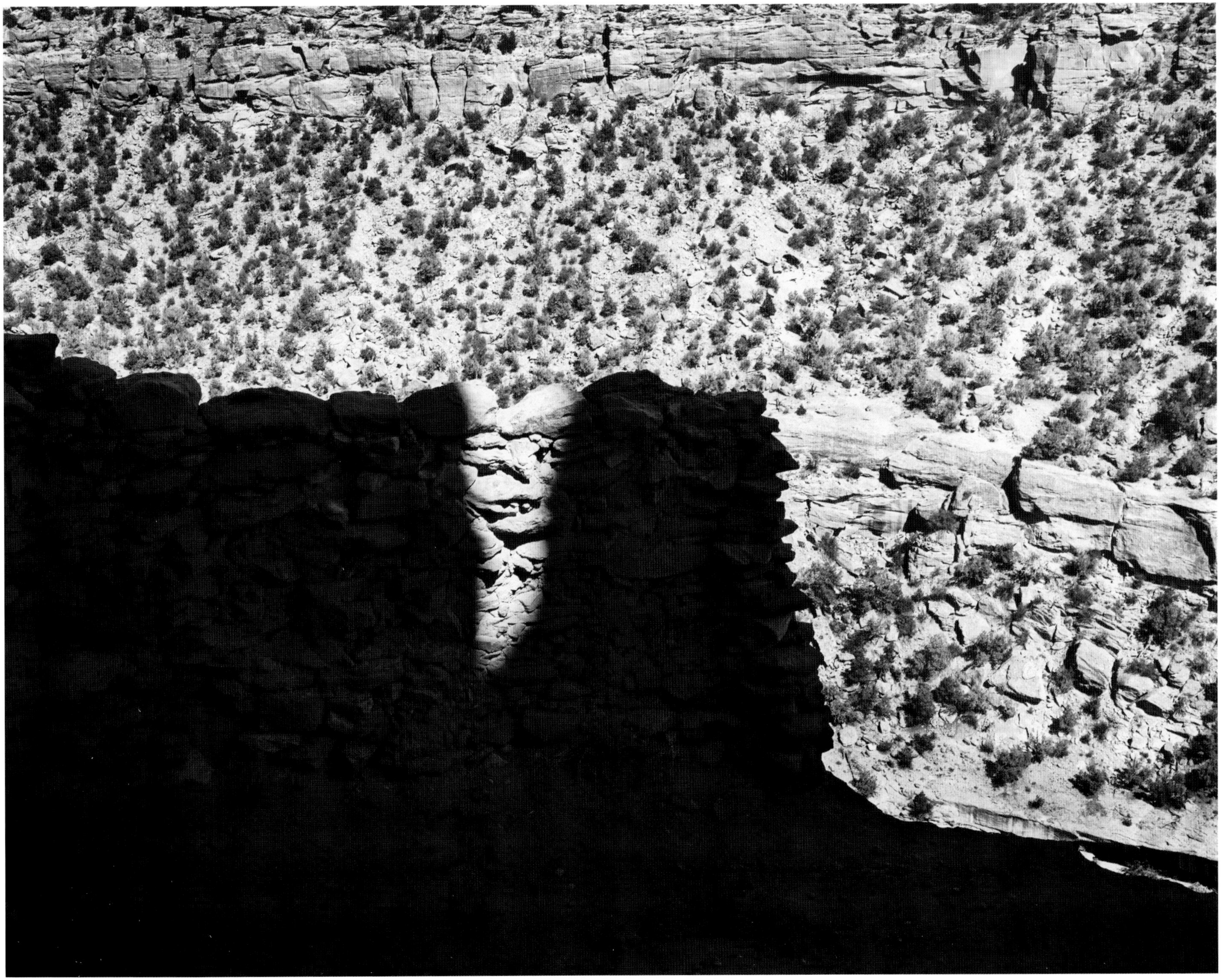

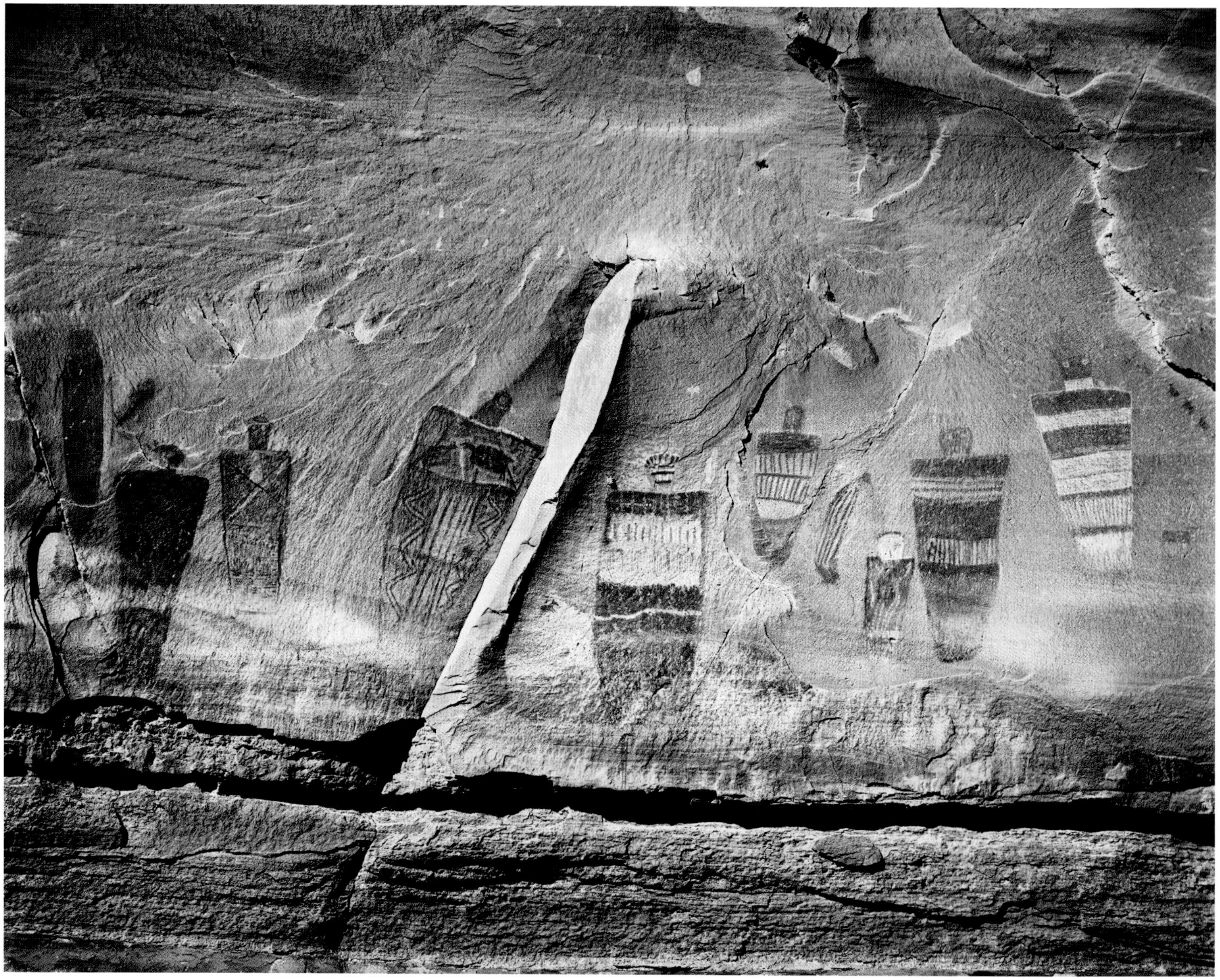

Great Gallery (above) and All-American Man (right), Canyonlands National Park (elevation 3,700–7,200 feet), Utah, 1989 and 1991.

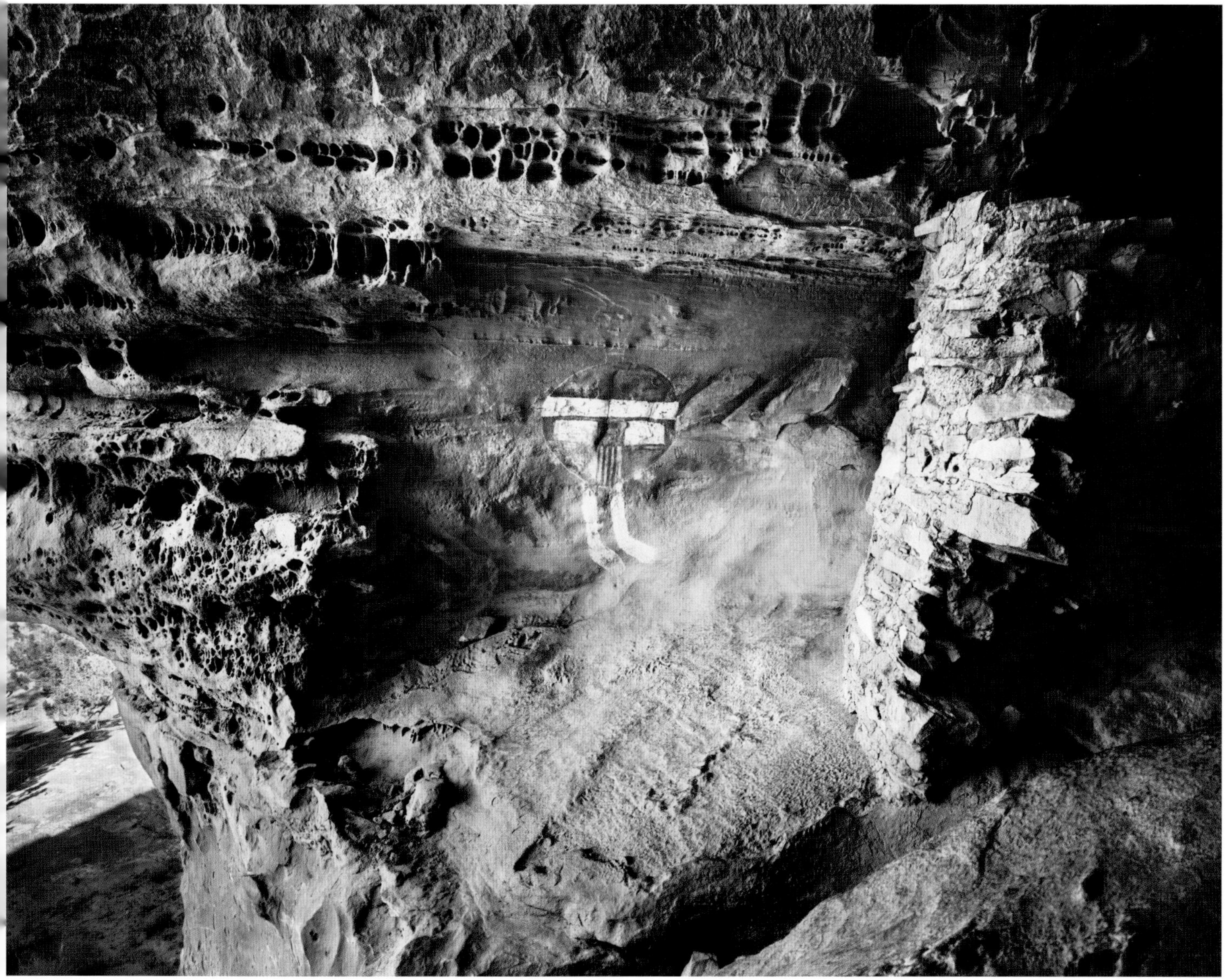

View of Mount Leidy (elevation 10,233 feet), Bridger-Teton National Forest, Wyoming, 1987.

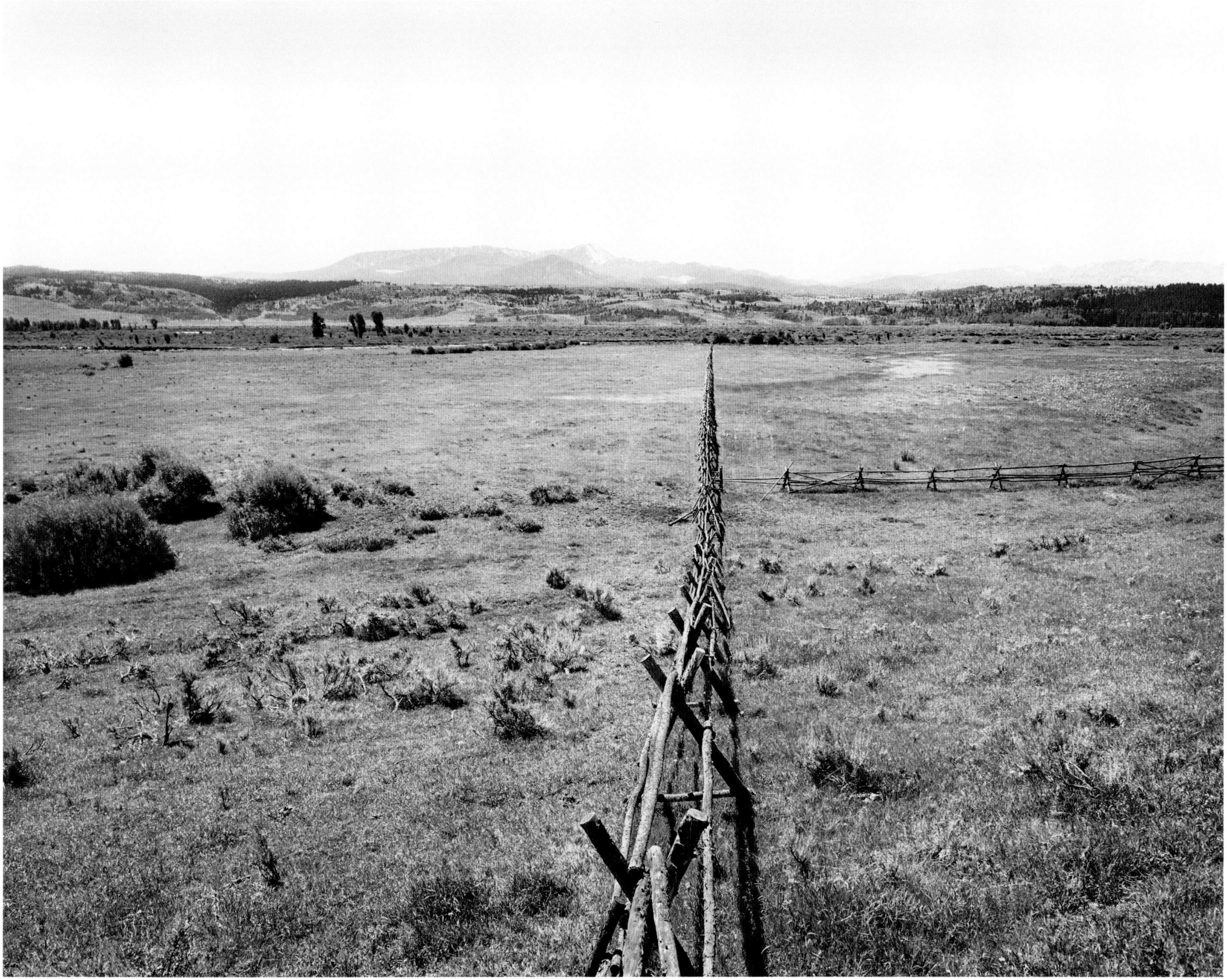

National Bison Range (elevation 2,585–4,885 feet), Montana, 1987.

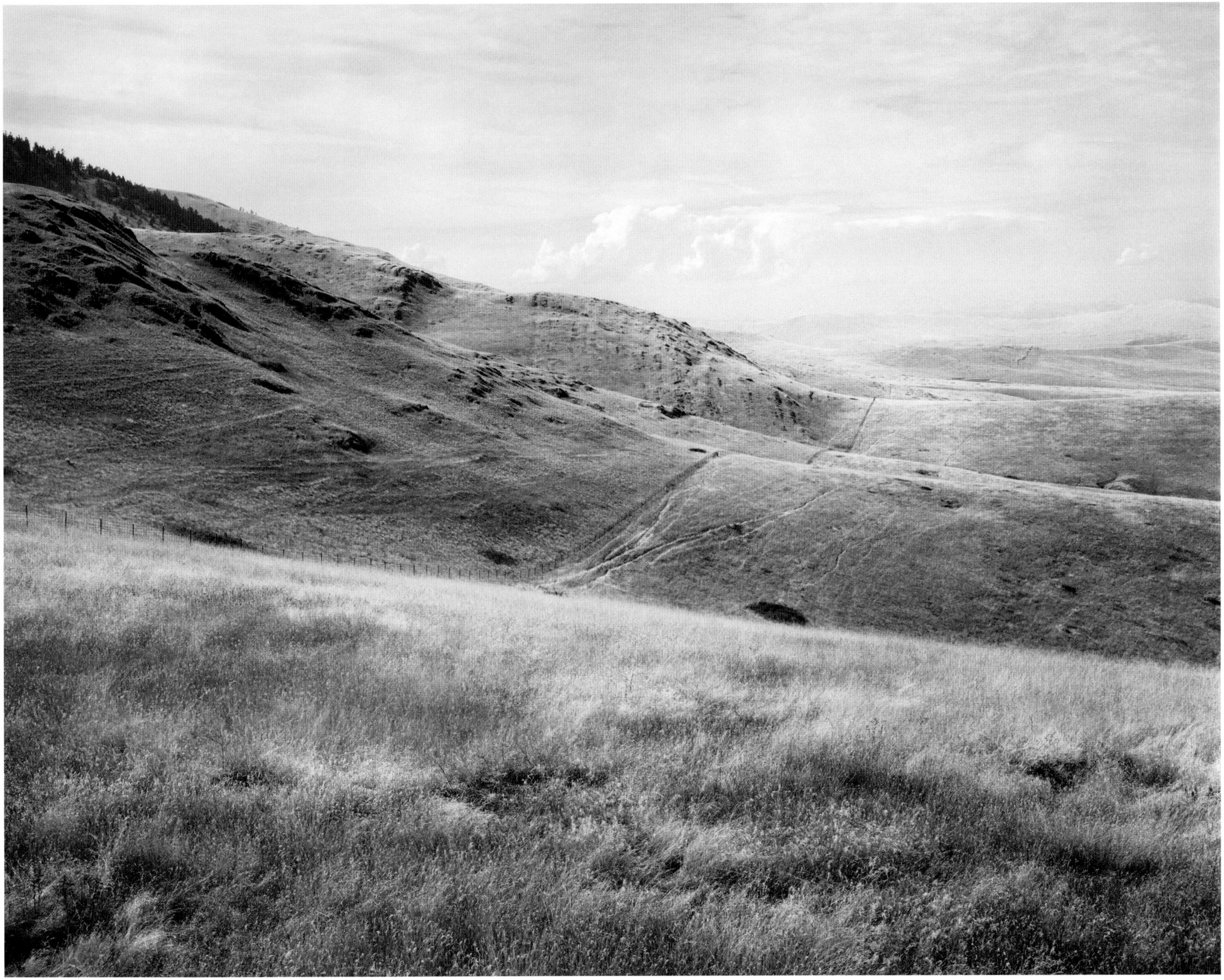

View of Skyline Drive from Warner Peak (elevation 8,017 feet), Hart Mountain National Antelope Refuge, Oregon, 2011.

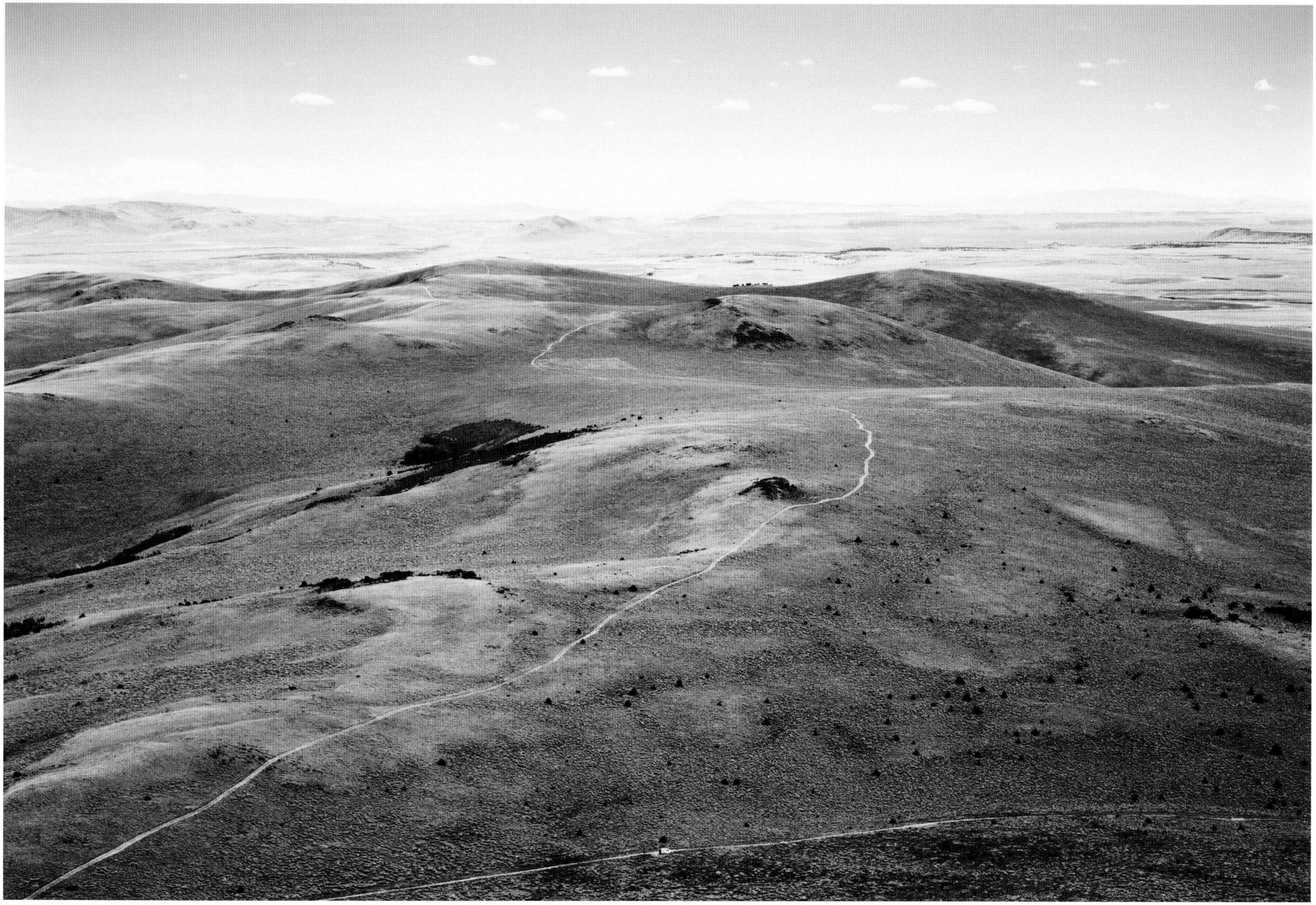

Owyhee River (average elevation 2,185 feet), Owyhee River Wilderness, Idaho, 1994.

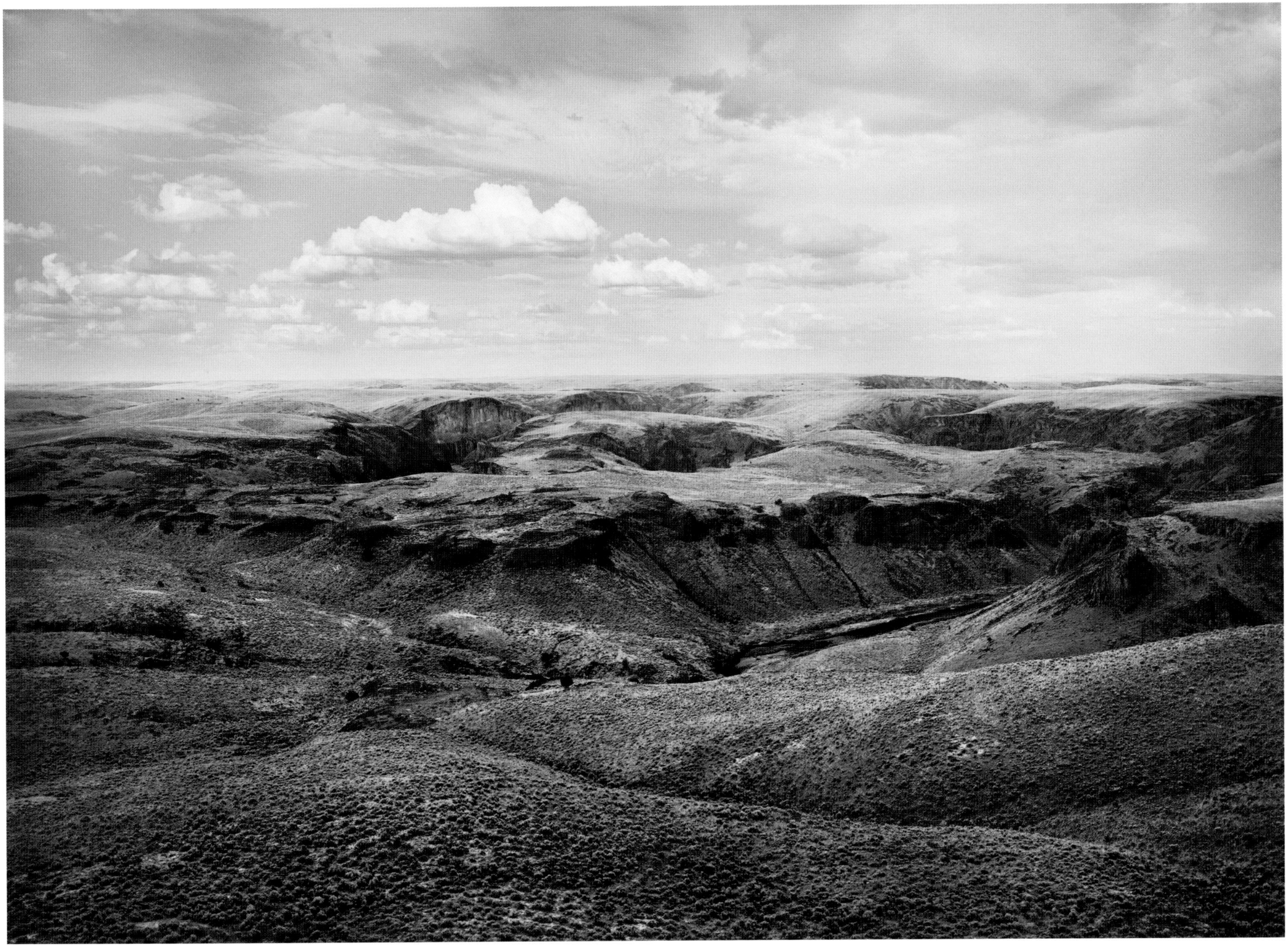

Middle Fork of the Salmon River, Salmon-Challis National Forest (elevation 2,800–12,662 feet), Idaho, 1994.

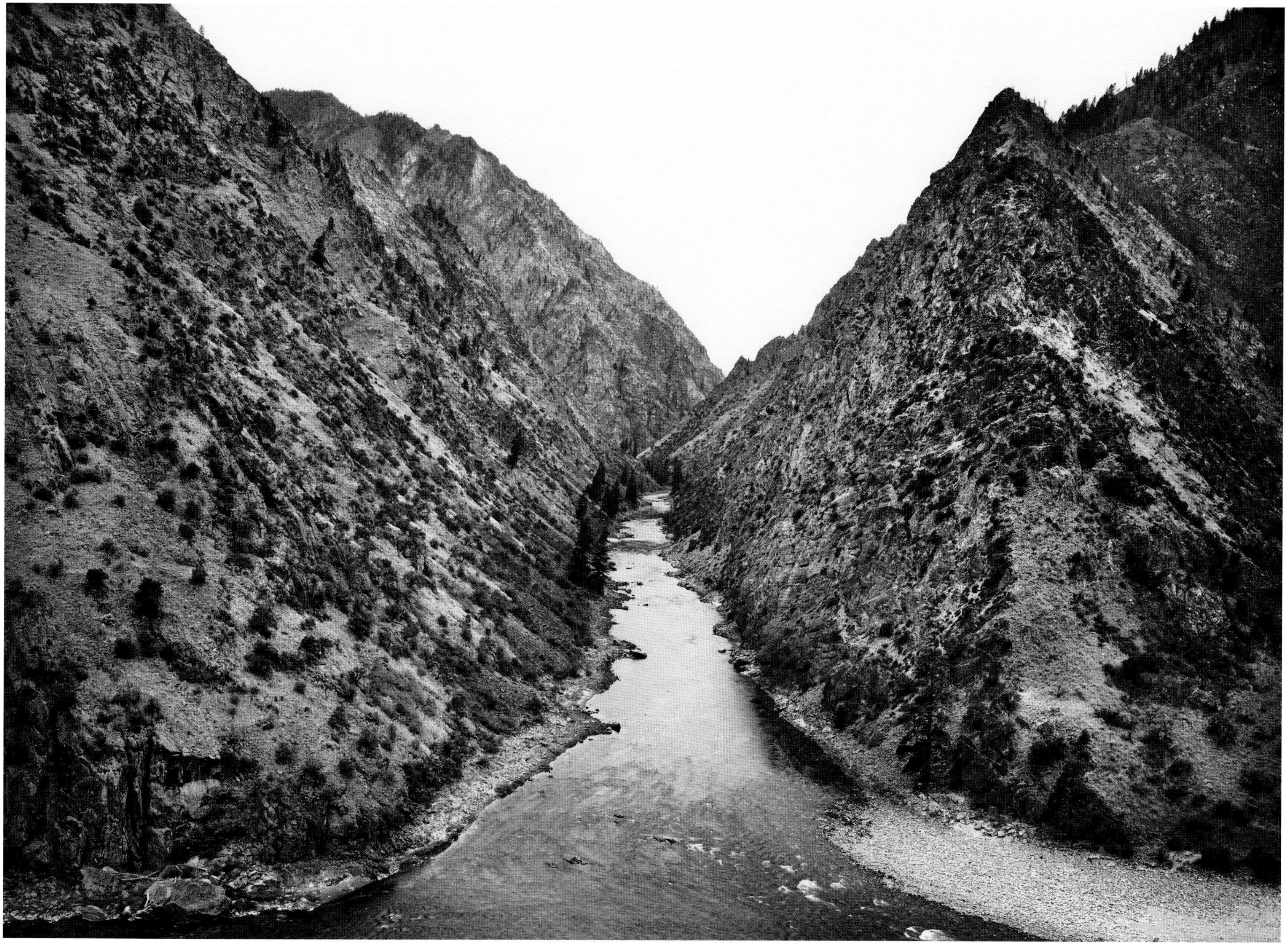

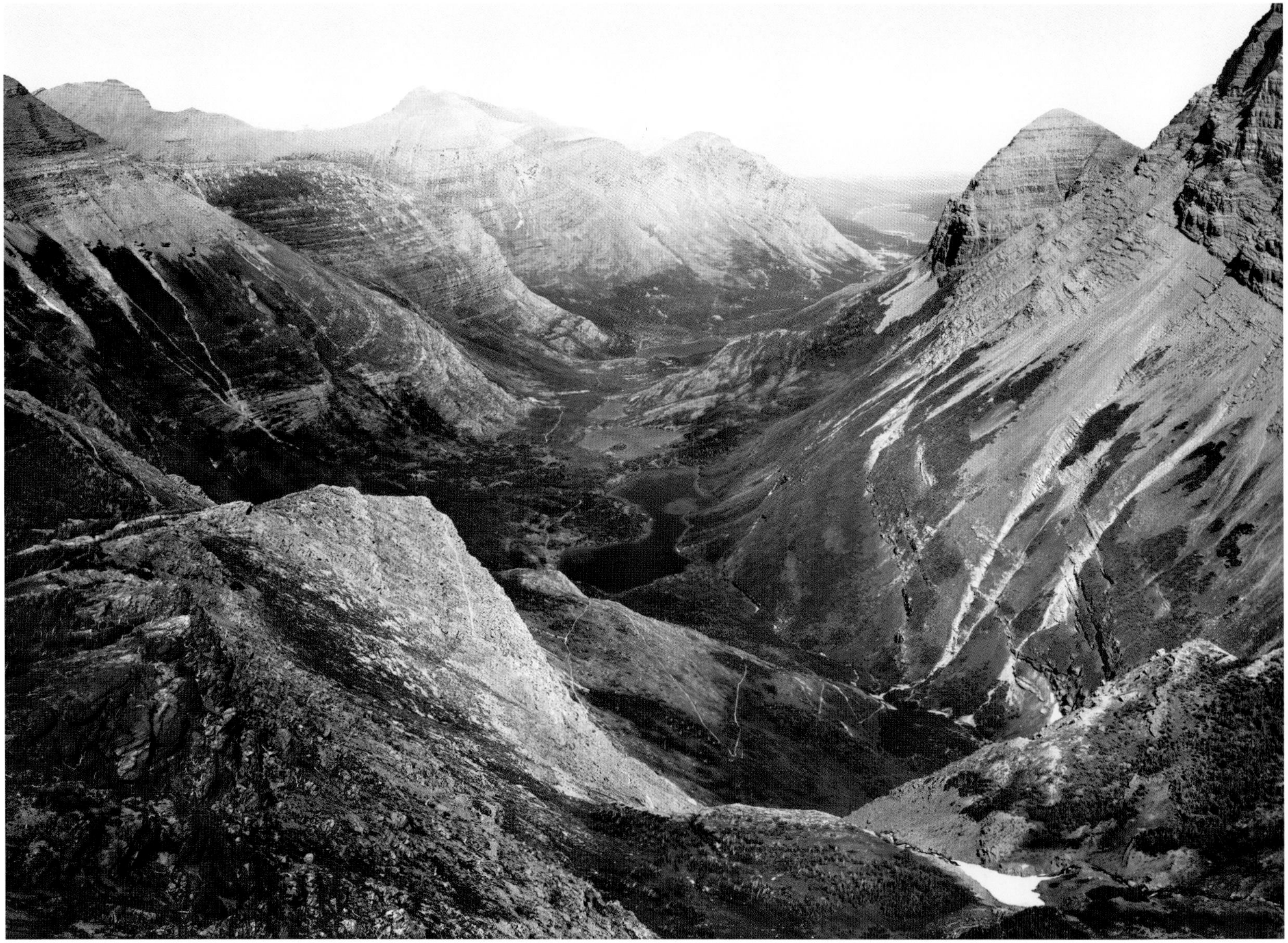

The valley floor (above) and Continental Divide (right), Glacier National Park (elevation 3,215–10,466 feet), Montana, 1994.

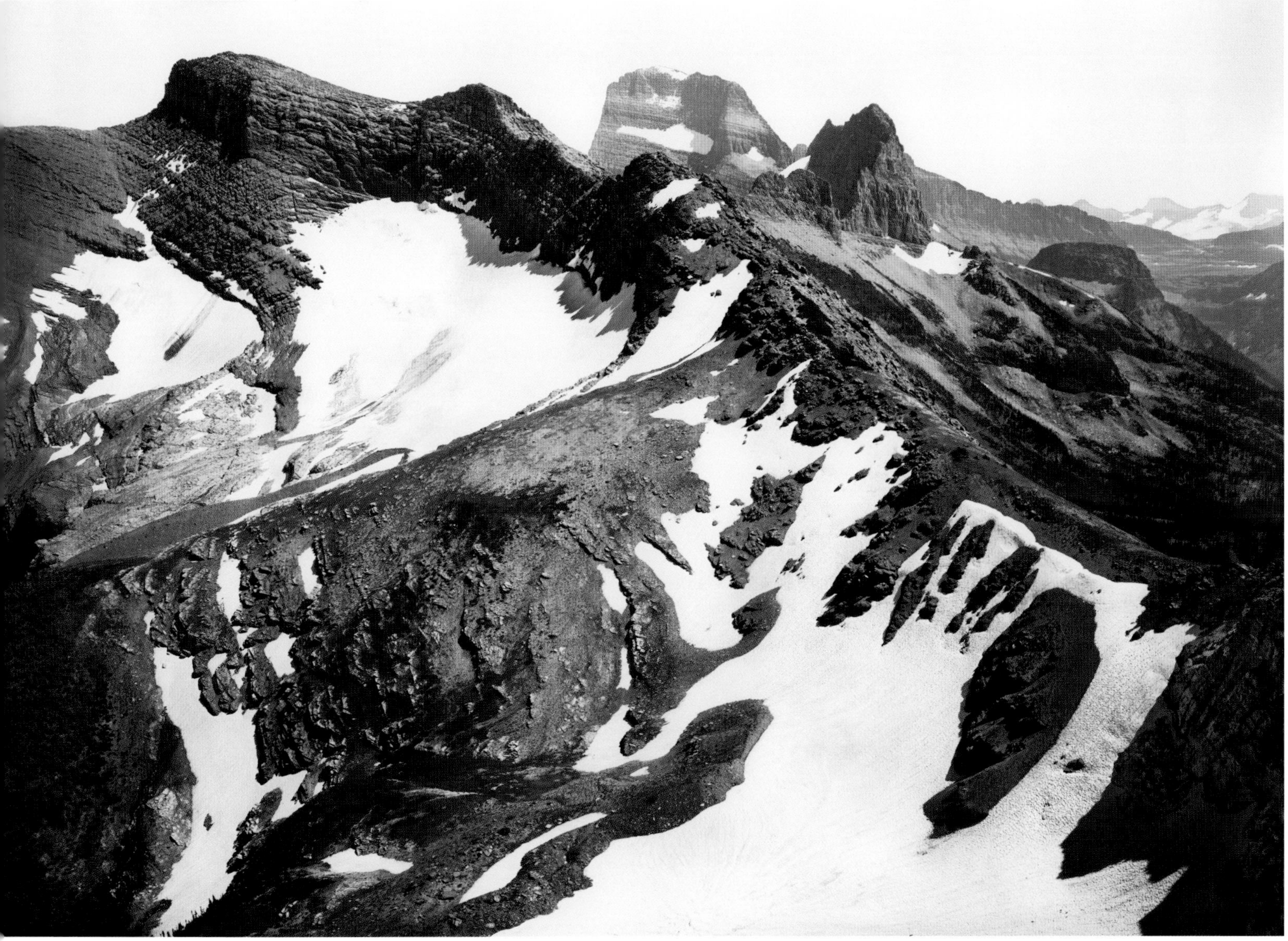

Above Gothic (elevation 9,485 feet), White River National Forest, Colorado, 1988.

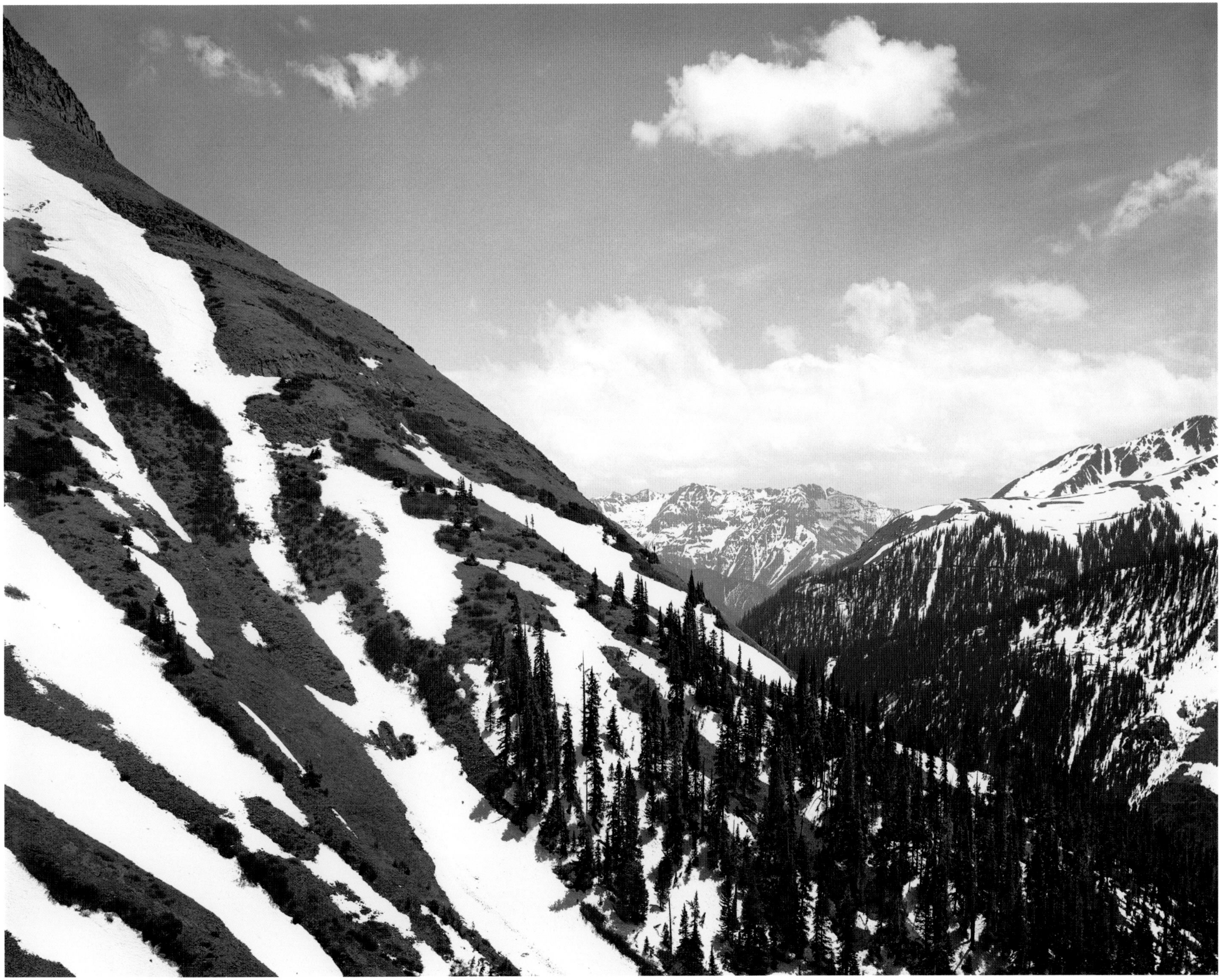

Mount Meeker (elevation 13,911 feet), Rocky Mountain National Park, Colorado, 1996.

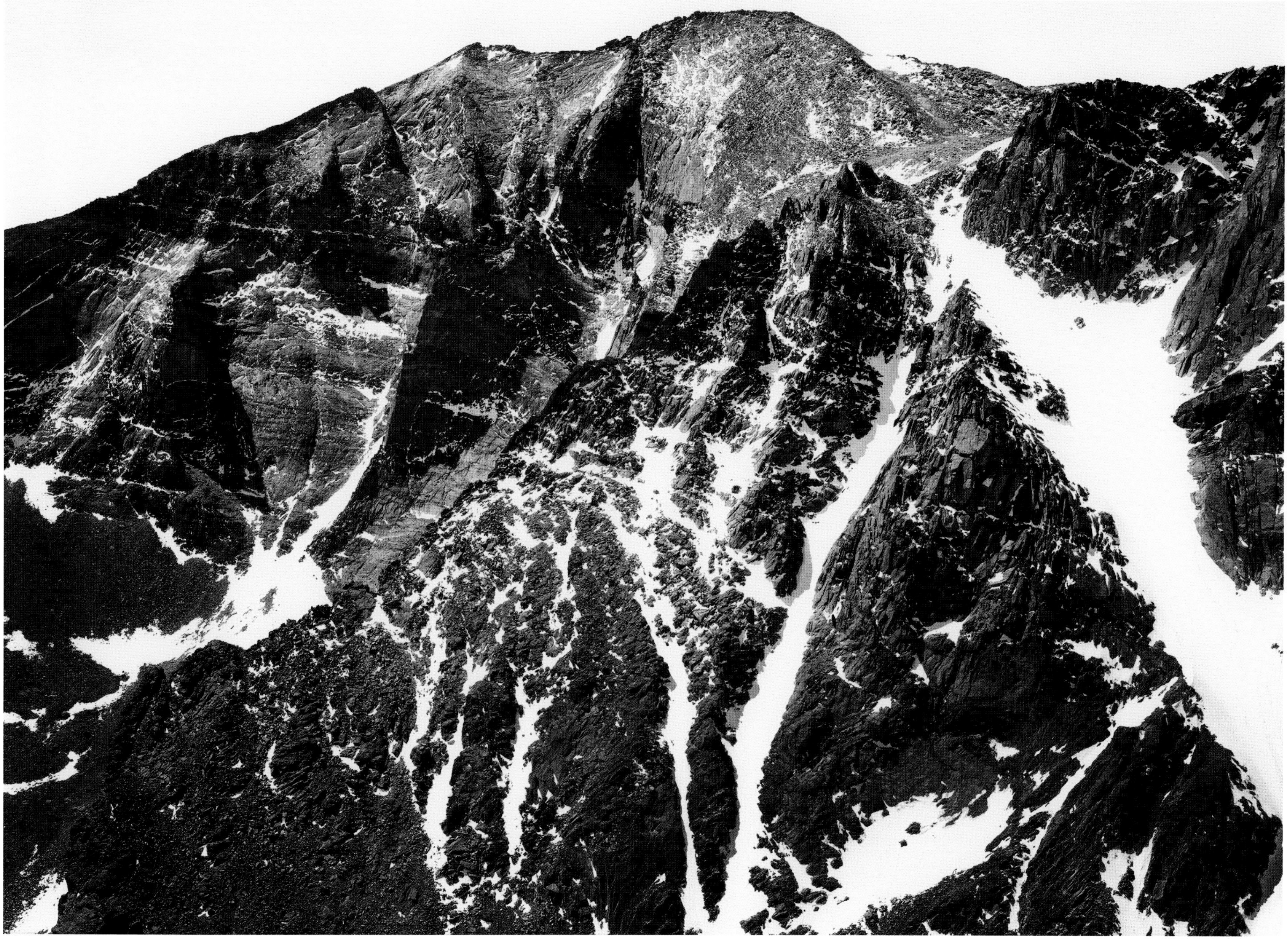

Sharkstooth Peak (elevation 11,686 feet), San Juan National Forest, Colorado, 1992.

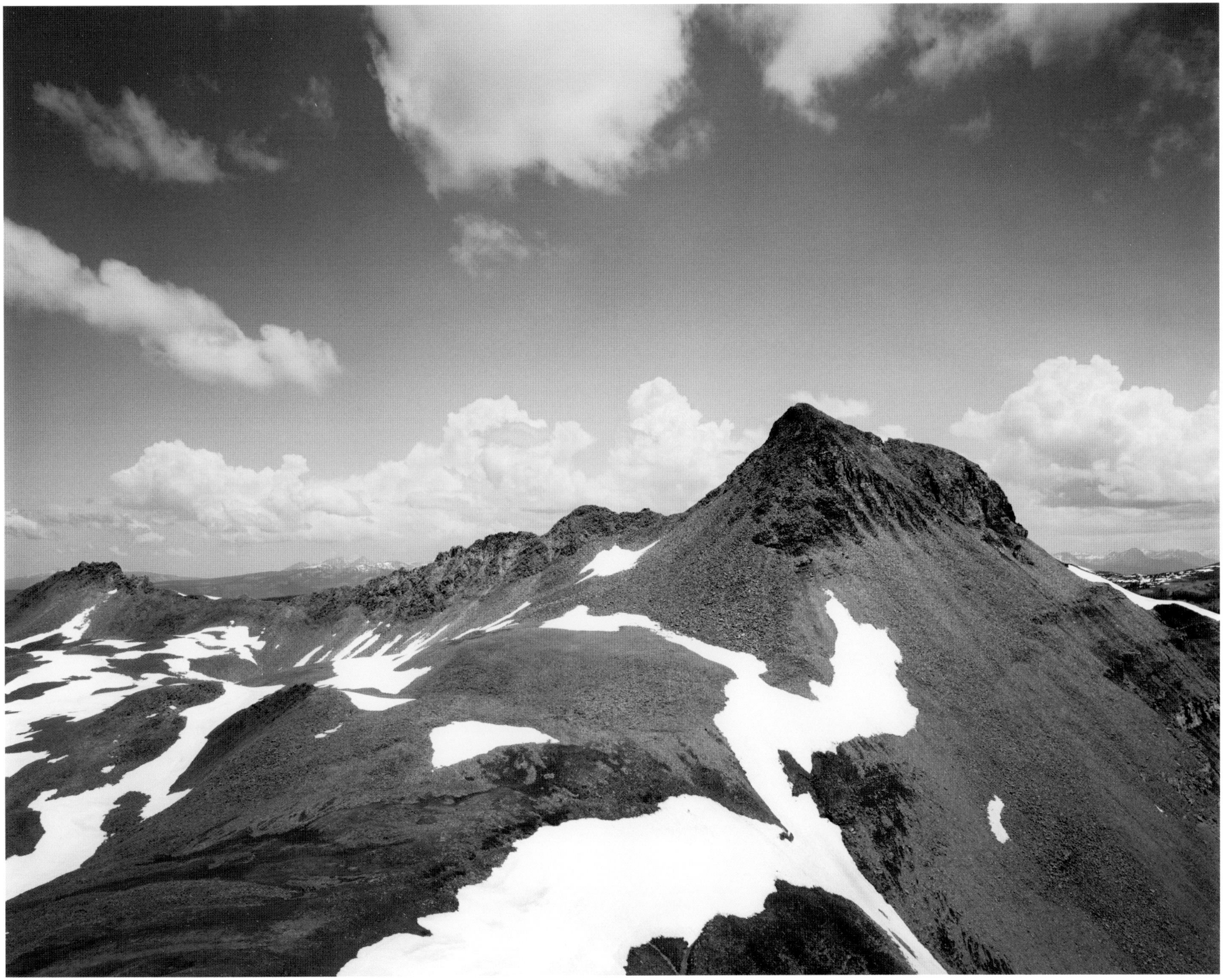

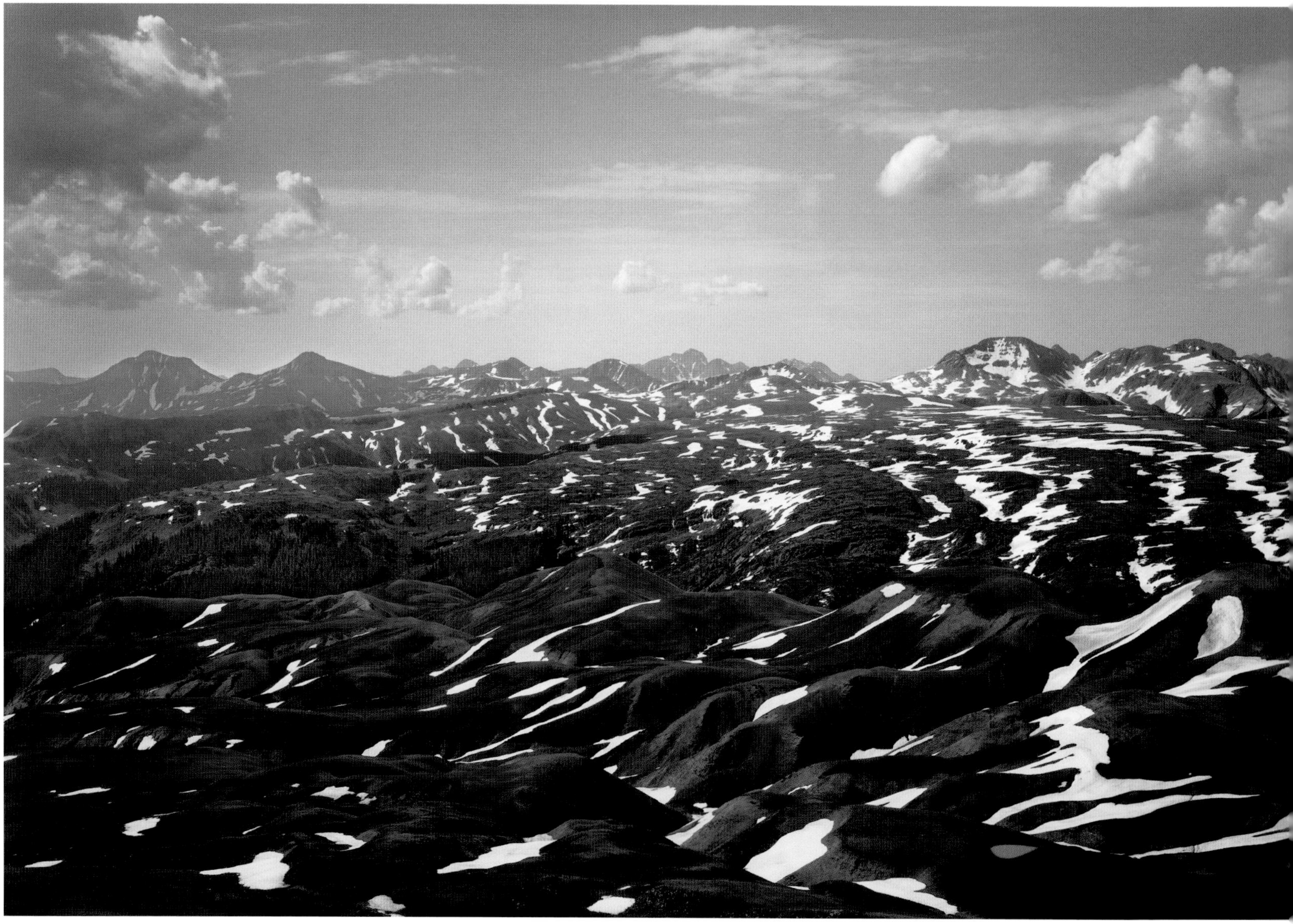

Views from near Stony Pass (elevation 12,588 feet), San Juan National Forest, Colorado, 1997 (above) and 1996 (right).

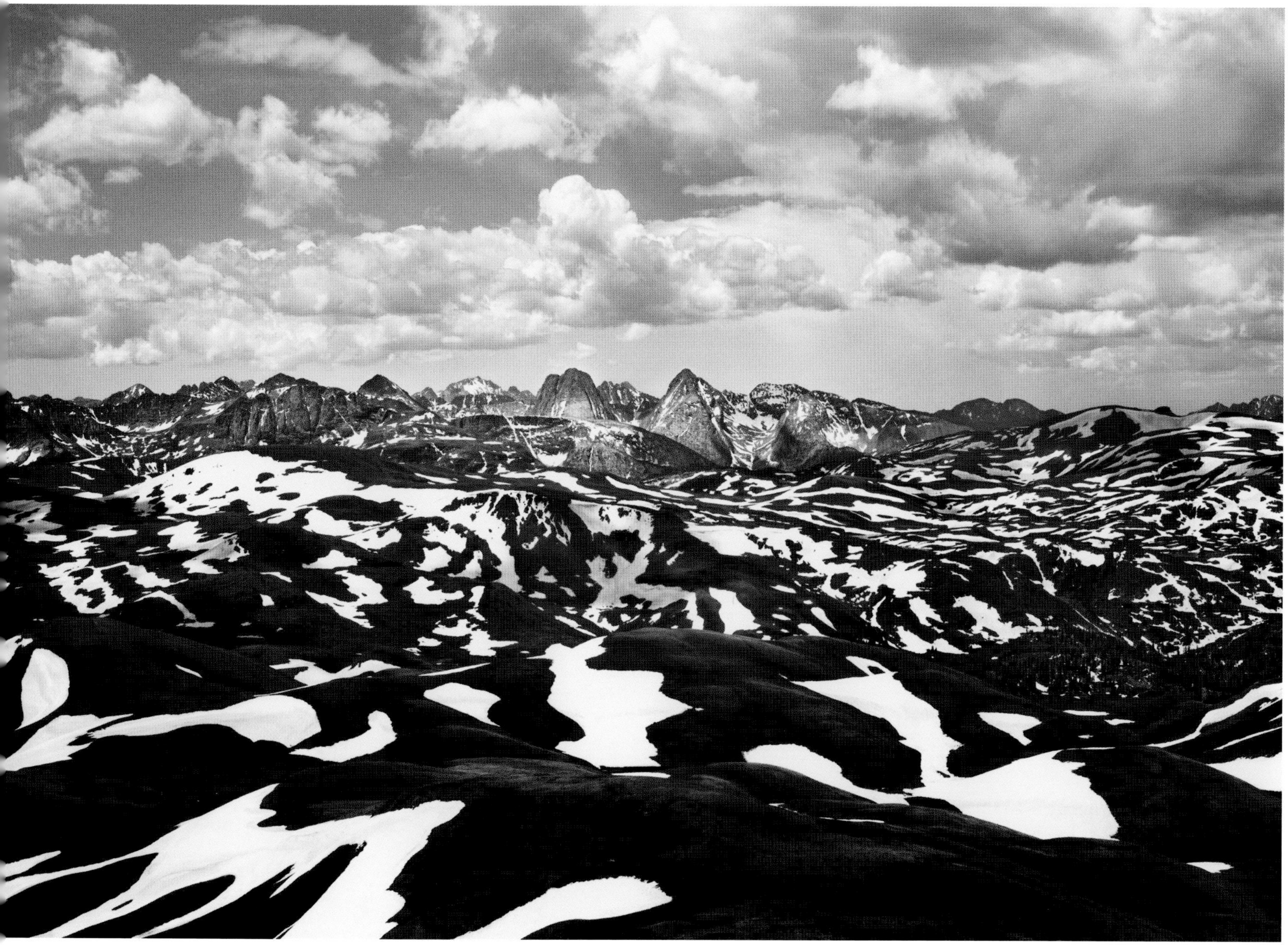

Great Sand Dunes National Park and Preserve (average elevation 8,200 feet) and Crestone Peak (elevation 14,294 feet) in Rio Grande National Forest, Colorado, 1996.

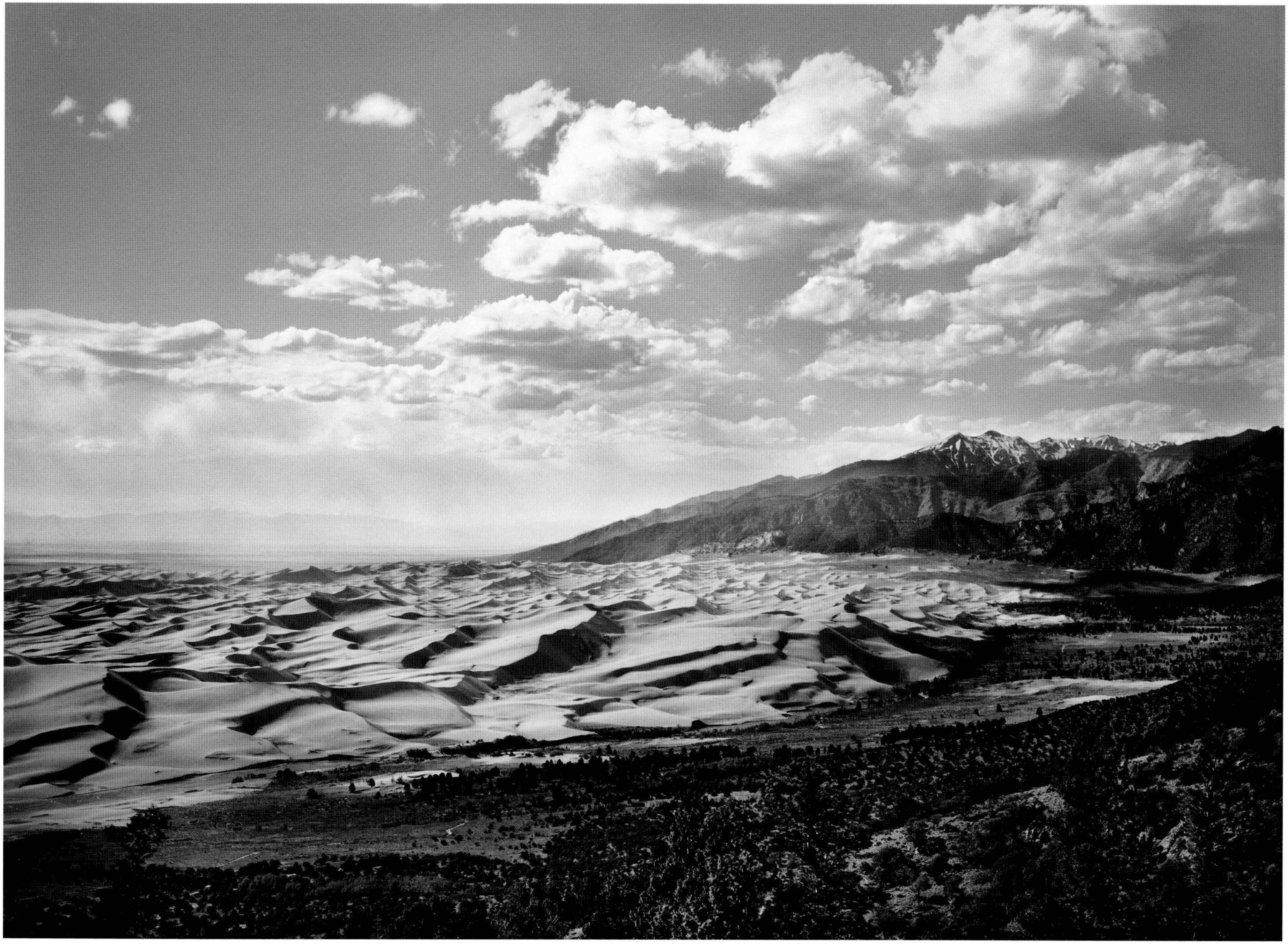

Great Sand Dunes National Park and Preserve (average elevation 8,200 feet), San Luis Valley, Colorado, 1996.

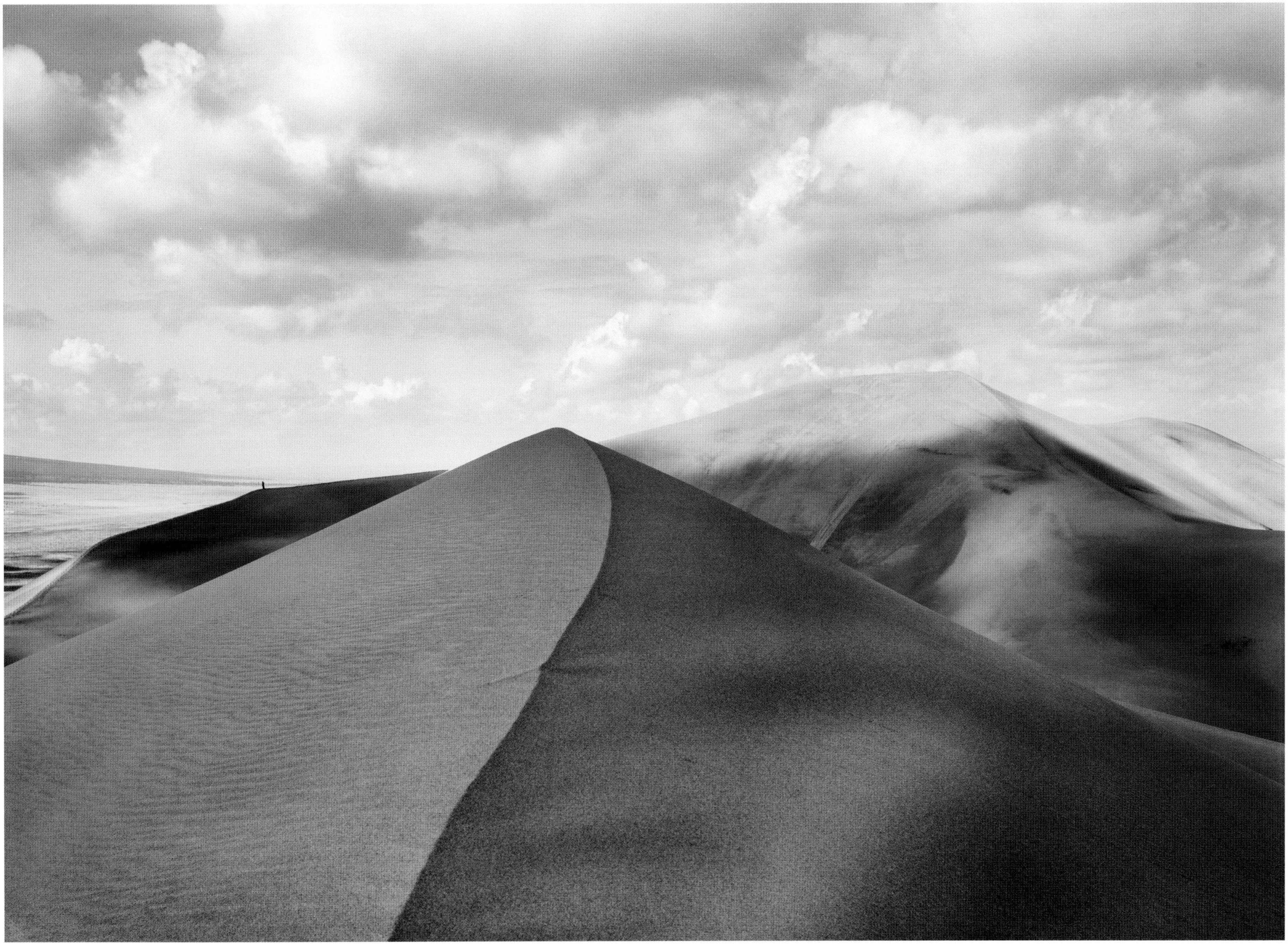

Mine tailings above Leadville (elevation 10,152 feet) and the Collegiate Peaks (elevation 13,745–14,440 feet), San Isabel National Forest, Colorado, 1989.

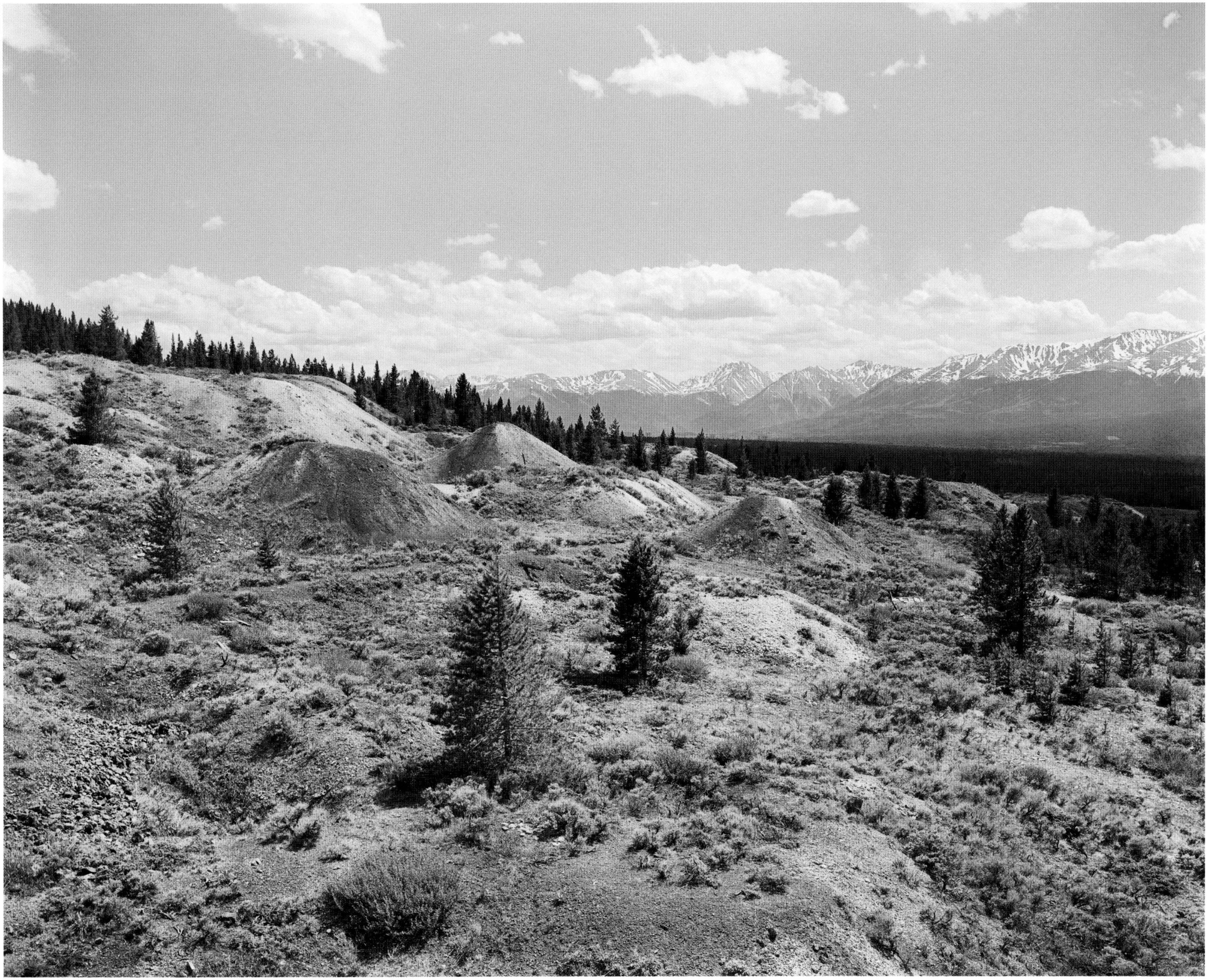

View of 14,163–foot Tabeguache Peak (upper left) from Mount Antero (elevation 14,269 feet), San Isabel National Forest, Colorado, 1995.

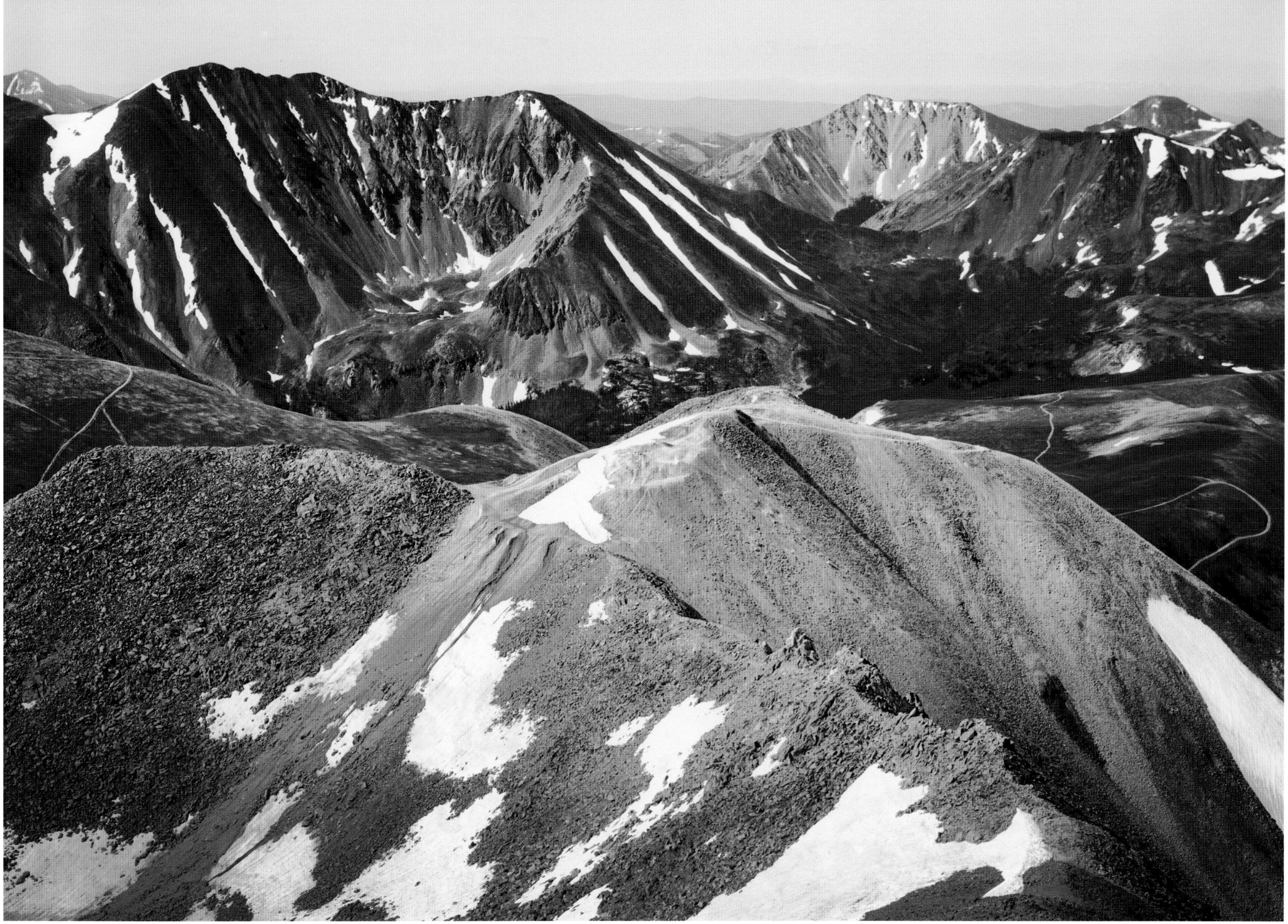

View of 13,524–foot Boulder Mountain (upper right) from Mount Antero (elevation 14,269 feet), San Isabel National Forest, Colorado, 1995.

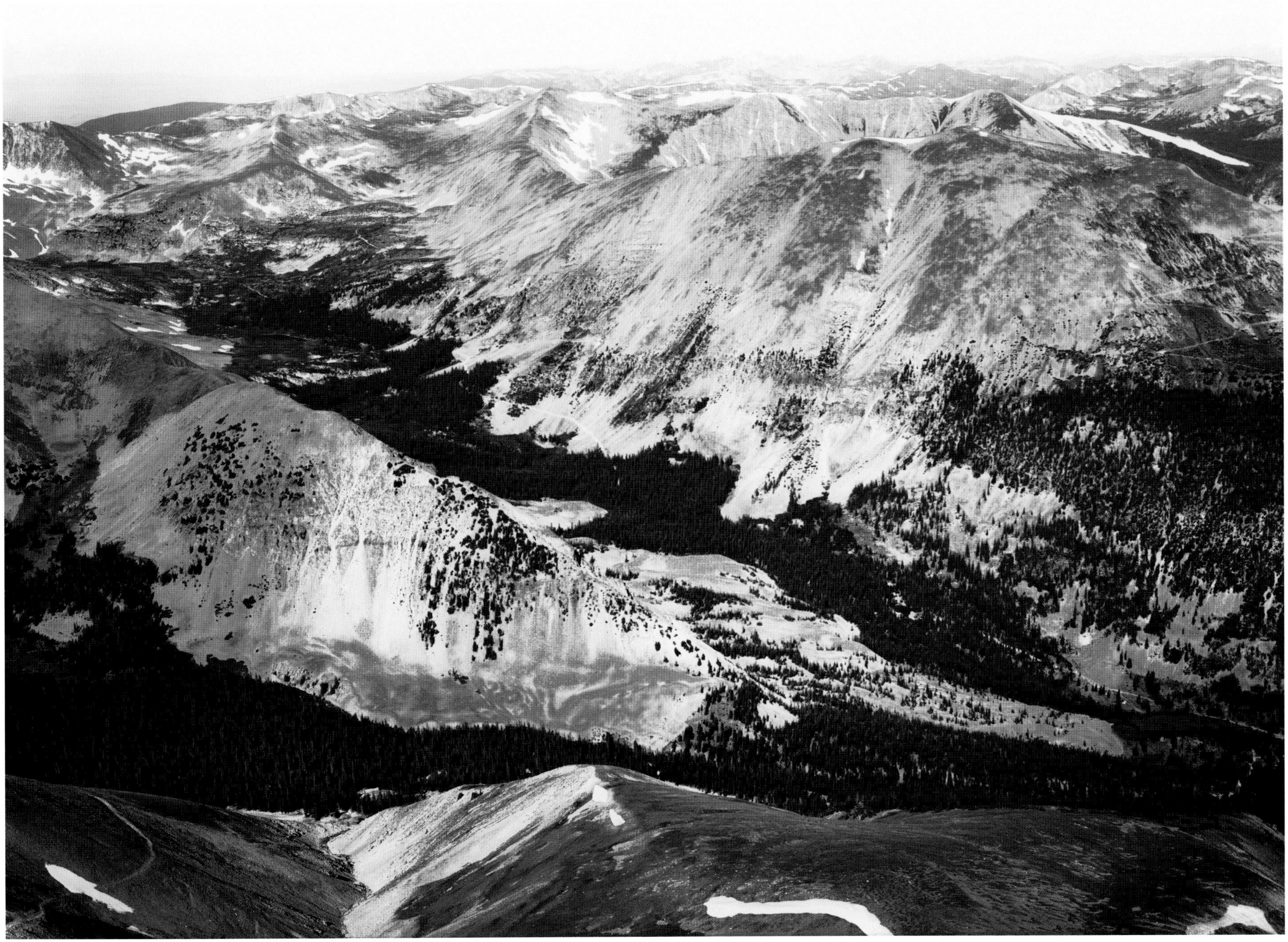

Sawmill, Lolo National Forest (elevation 3,205–9,096 feet), Montana, 1987.

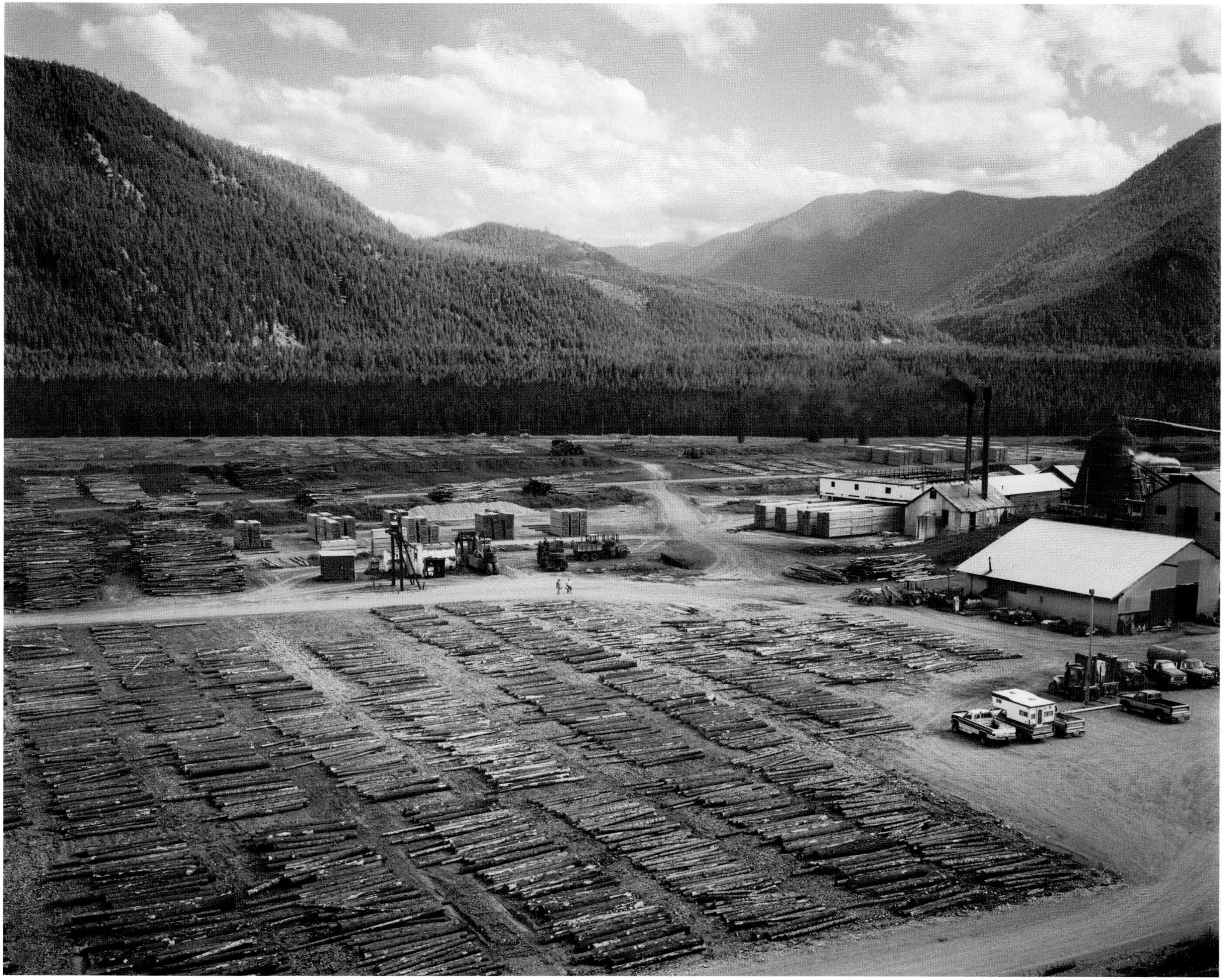

Tomboy Mine above Telluride (elevation 8,725 feet), Uncompahgre National Forest, Colorado, 1989.

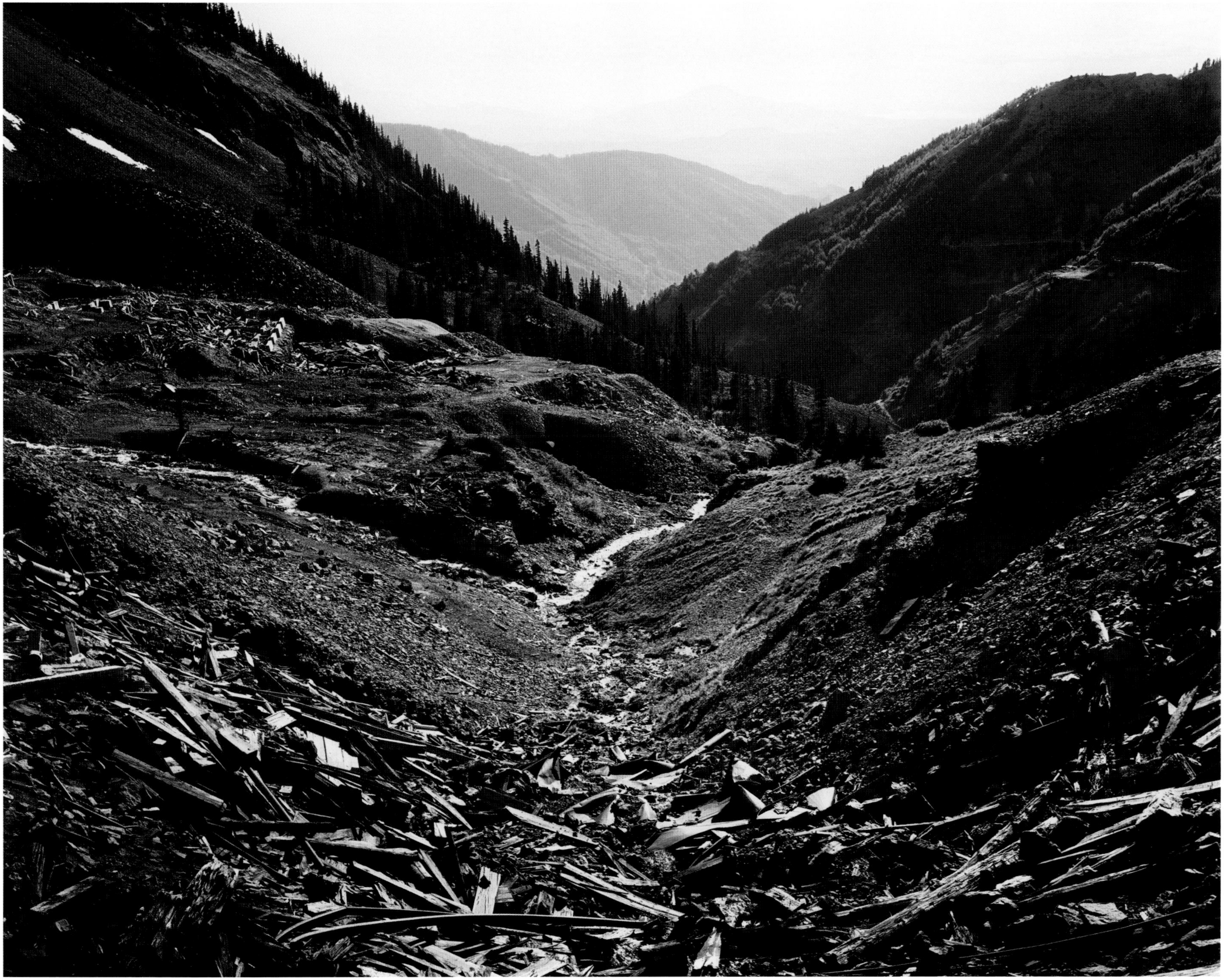

An orchard alongside Interstate 70, near Little Book Cliffs Wild Horse Range (elevation 5,000–7,421 feet), Colorado, 1989.

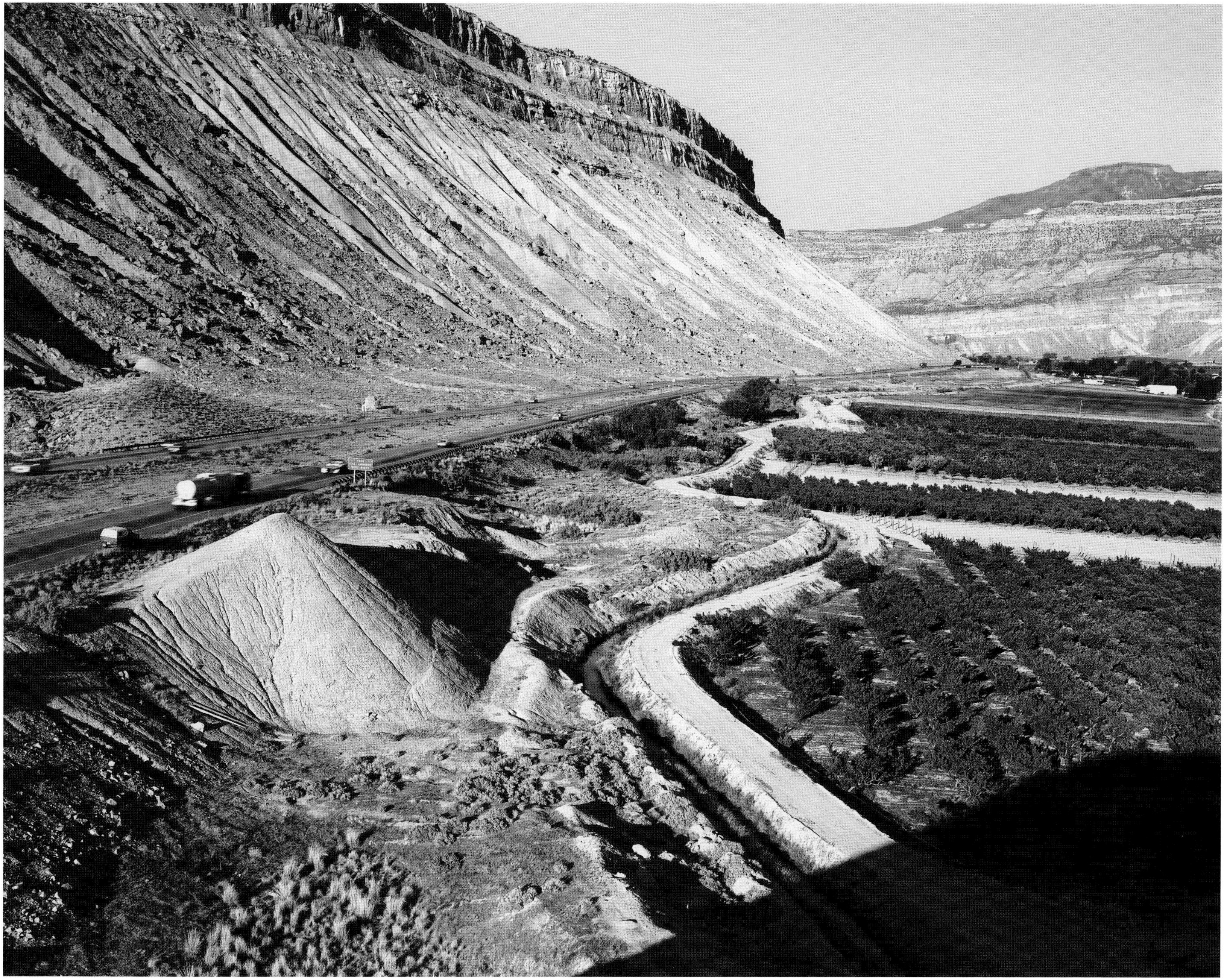

Narrows of the Big Thompson River, Roosevelt National Forest (elevation 5,800–13,392 feet), Colorado, 1986.

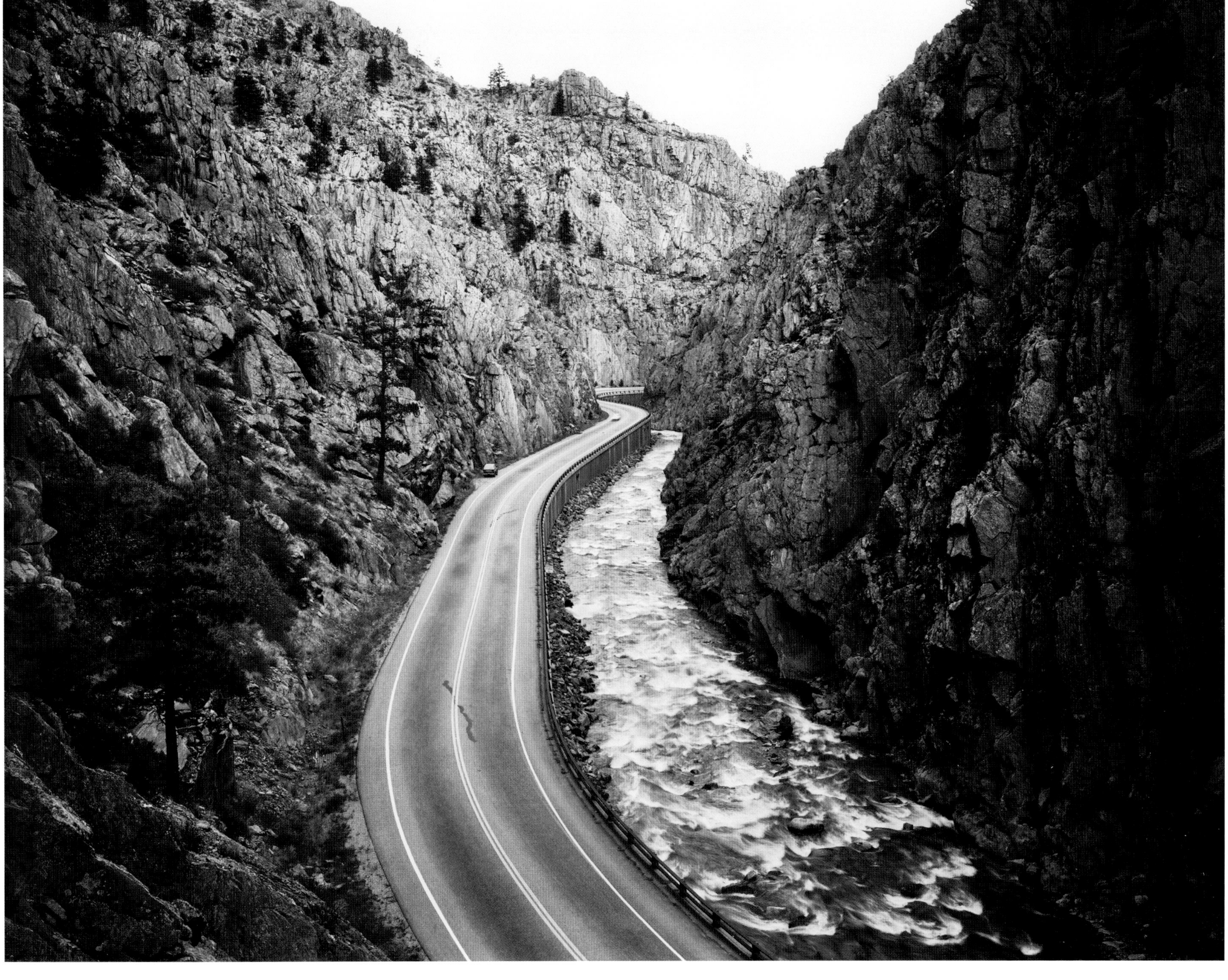

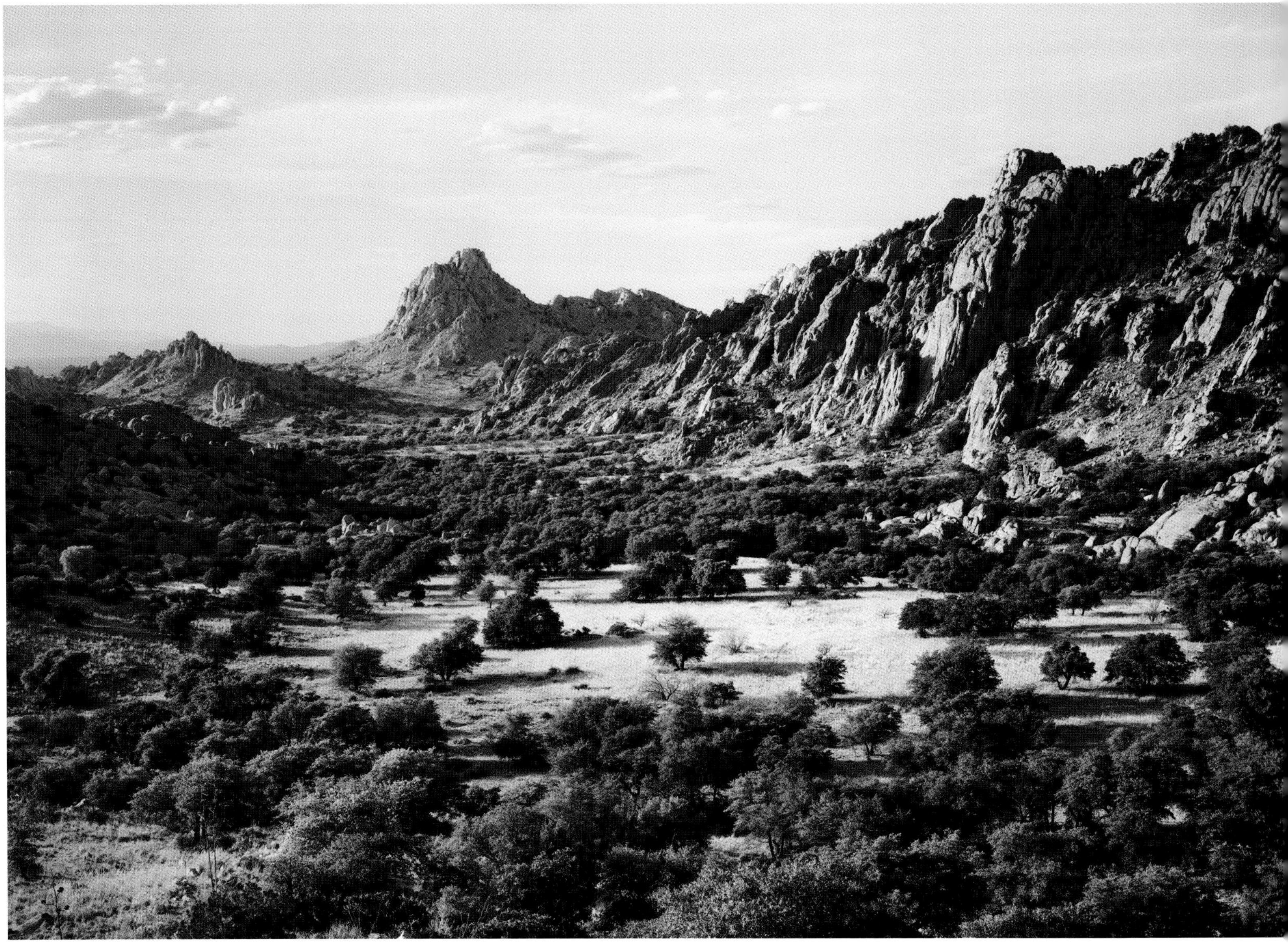

(Above) Dragoon Mountains (average elevation 7,520 feet) and (right) Skeleton Canyon (elevation 4,700–4,840 feet), Coronado National Forest, Arizona, 1994.

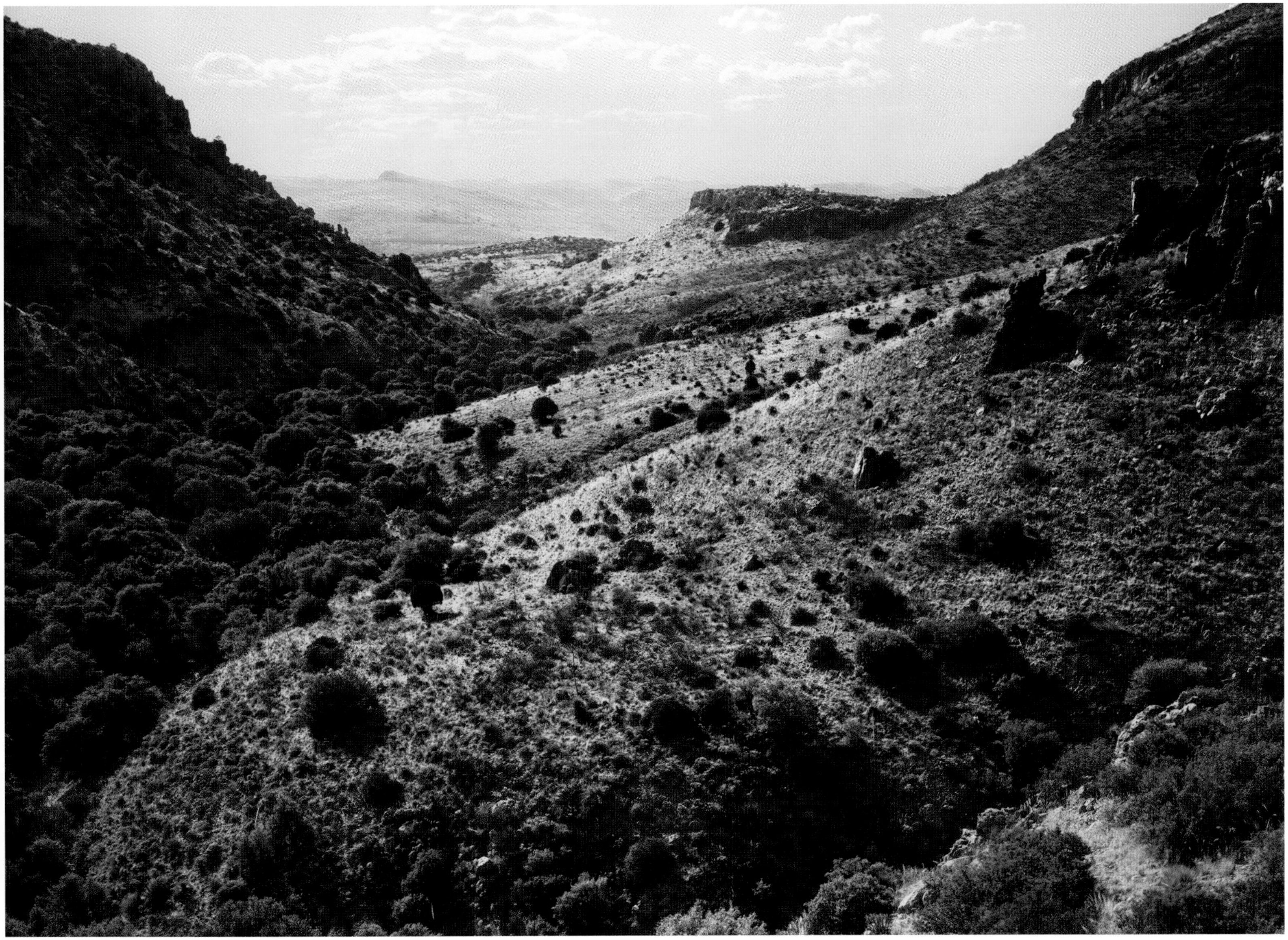

View of Mount Evans from its peak (elevation 14,264 feet), Arapaho National Forest, Colorado, 1990.

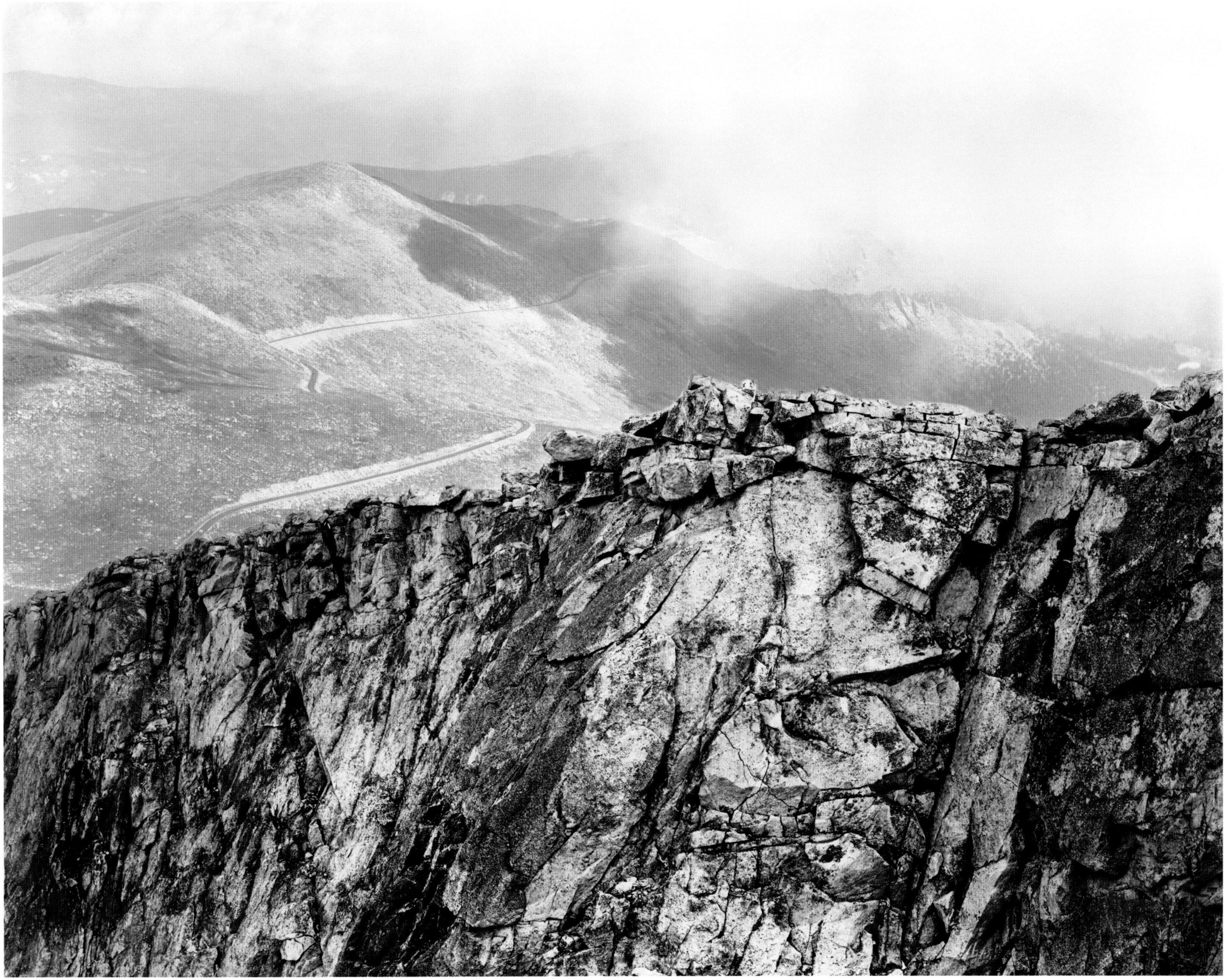

Boulder Canyon roadcut, Roosevelt National Forest (elevation 5,800–13,392 feet), Colorado, 1987.

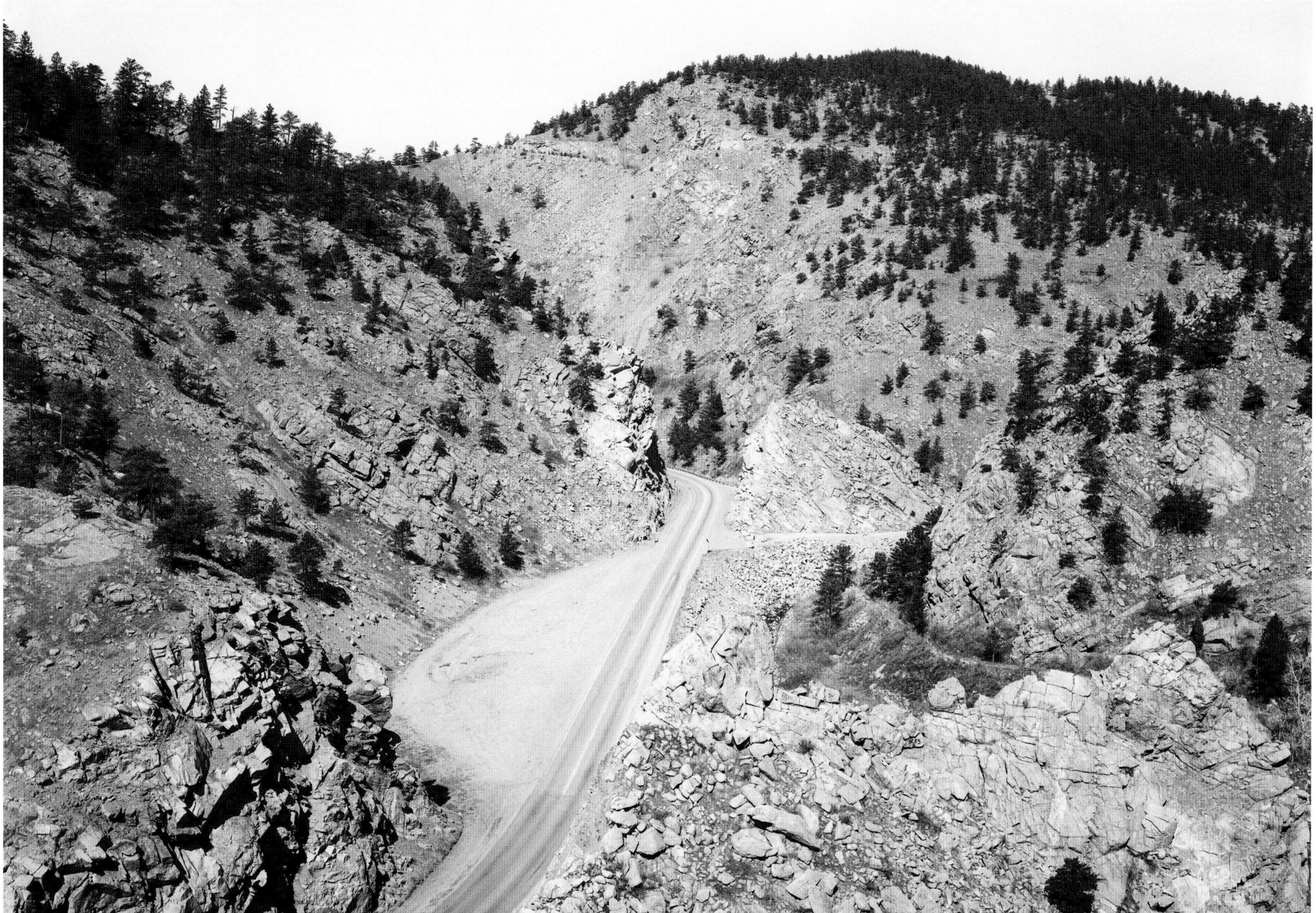

Ajo Mountain Road, Organ Pipe Cactus National Monument (elevation 1,670–4,808 feet), Arizona, 1987.

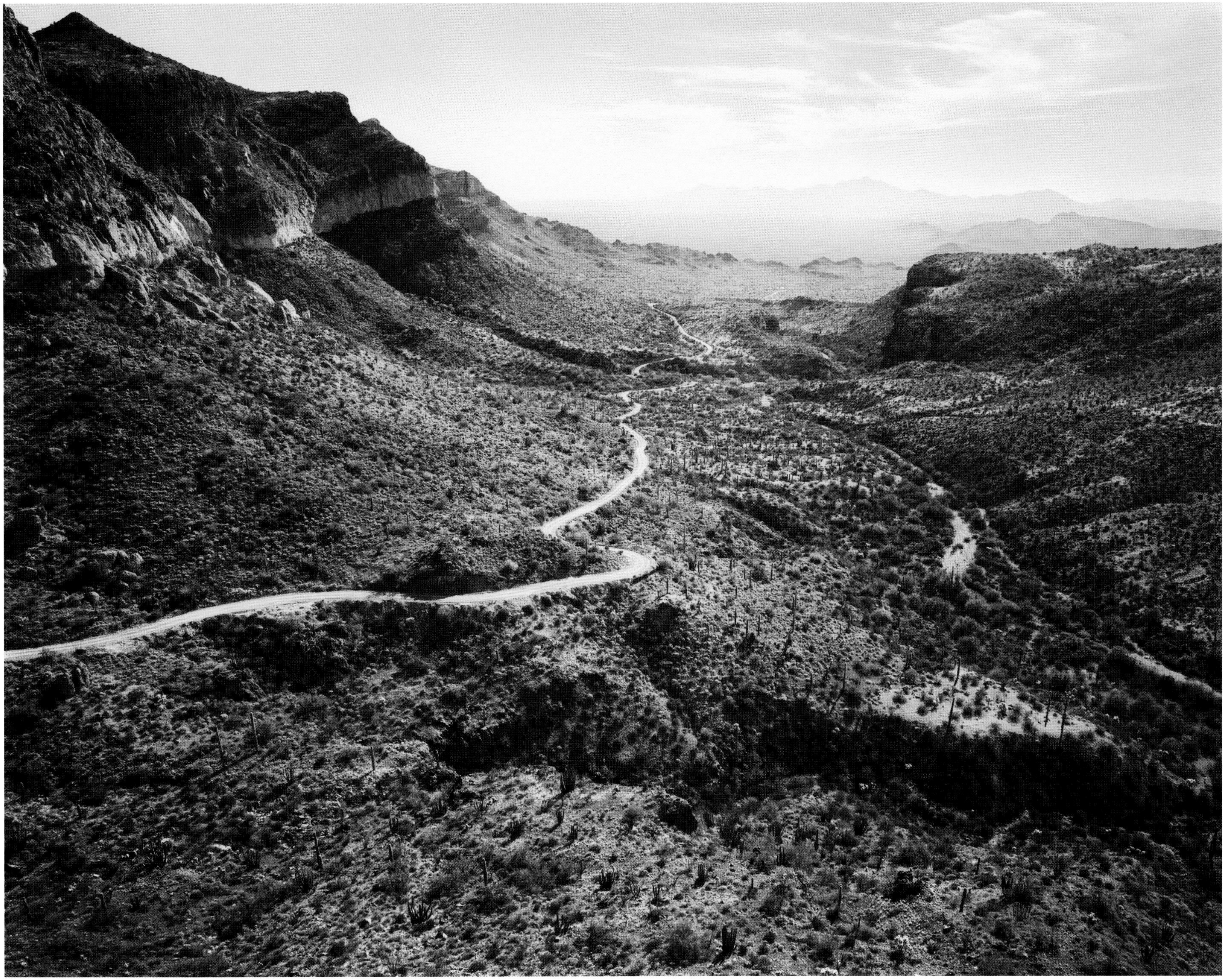

Organ Pipe Cactus National Monument (elevation 1,670–4,806 feet), Arizona, 1987.

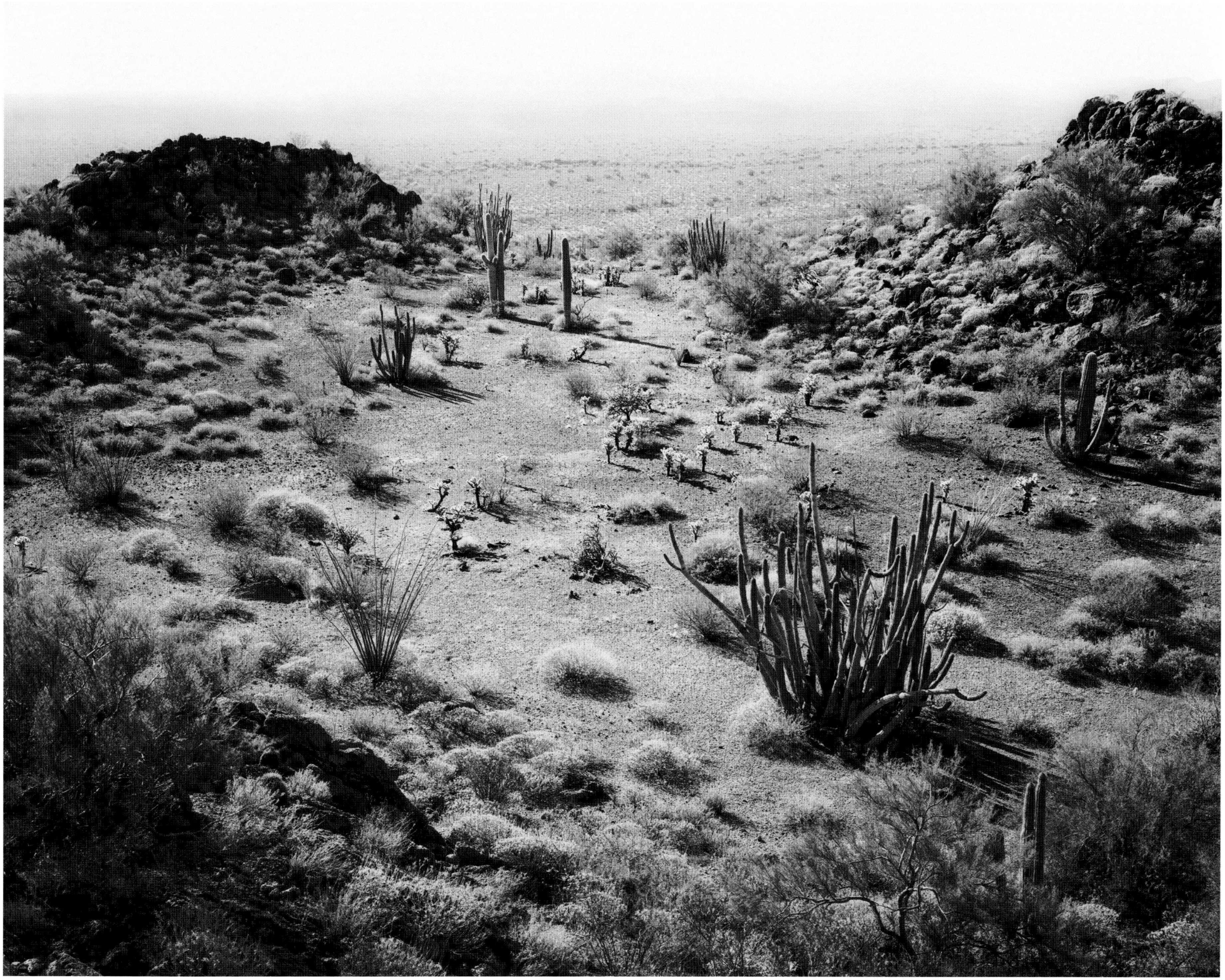

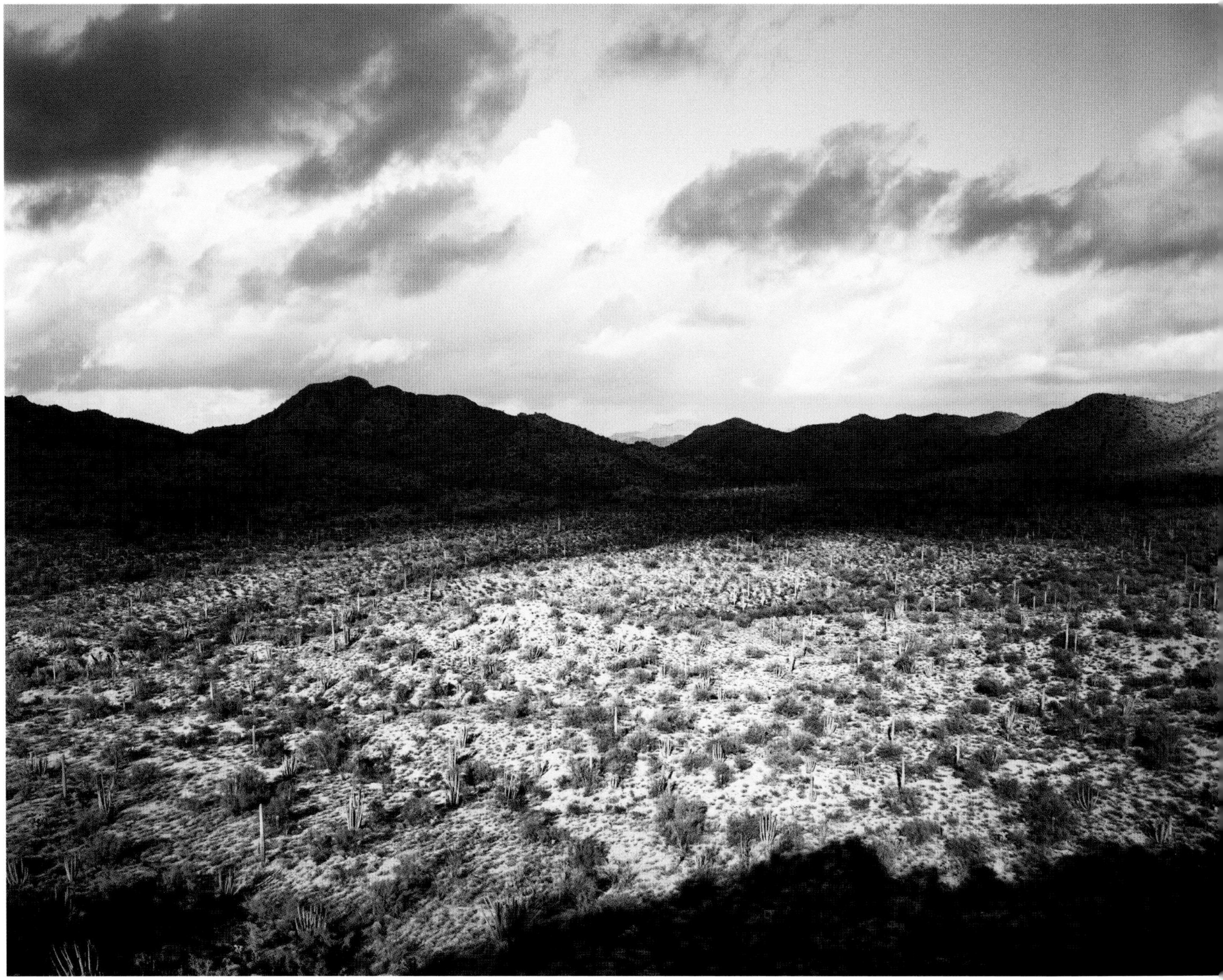

Senita Basin (average elevation 1,670 feet), Organ Pipe Cactus National Monument, Arizona, 1987.

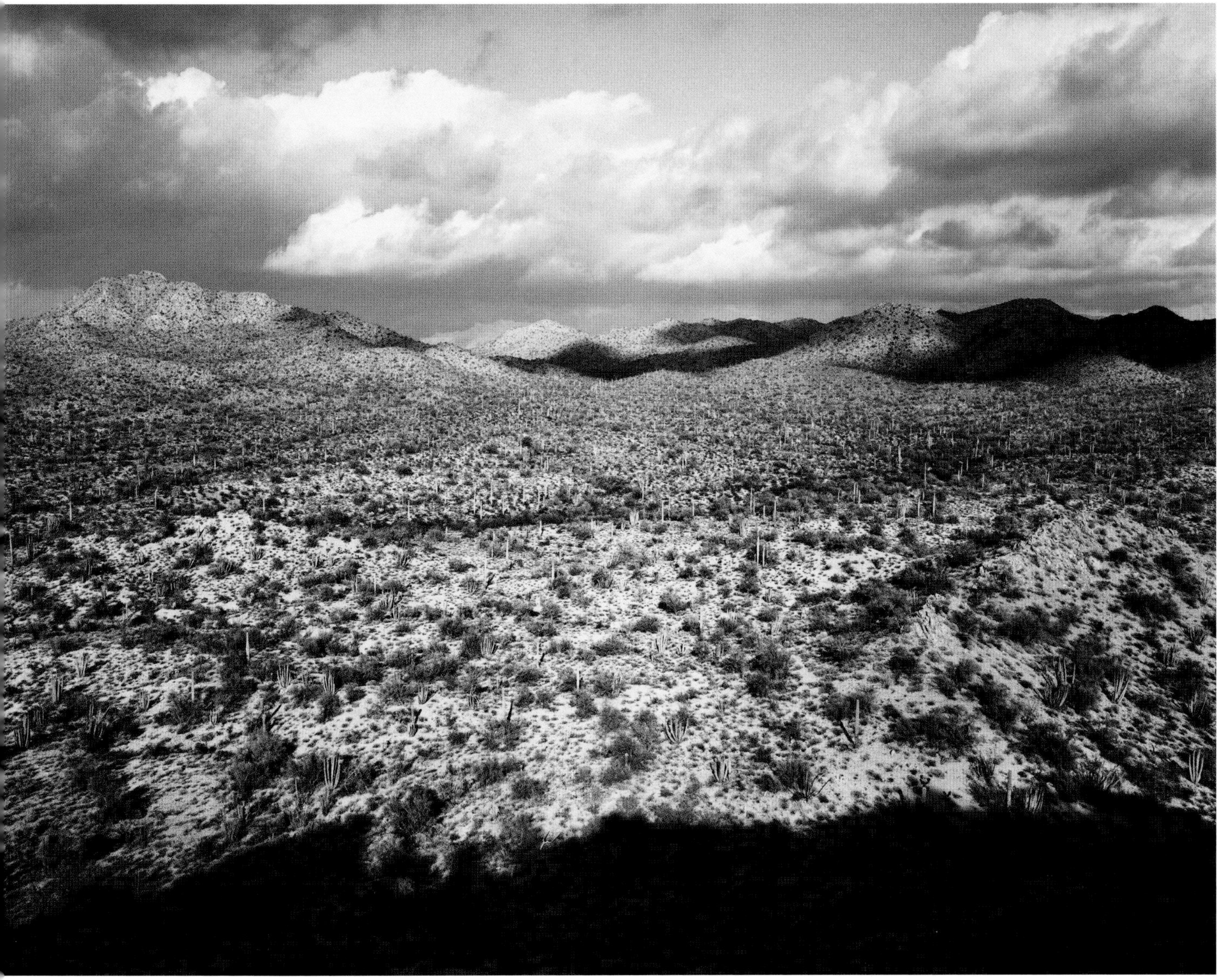

View from Kitt Peak (elevation 6,880 feet), Tohono O'odham Indian Reservation, Arizona, 1987.

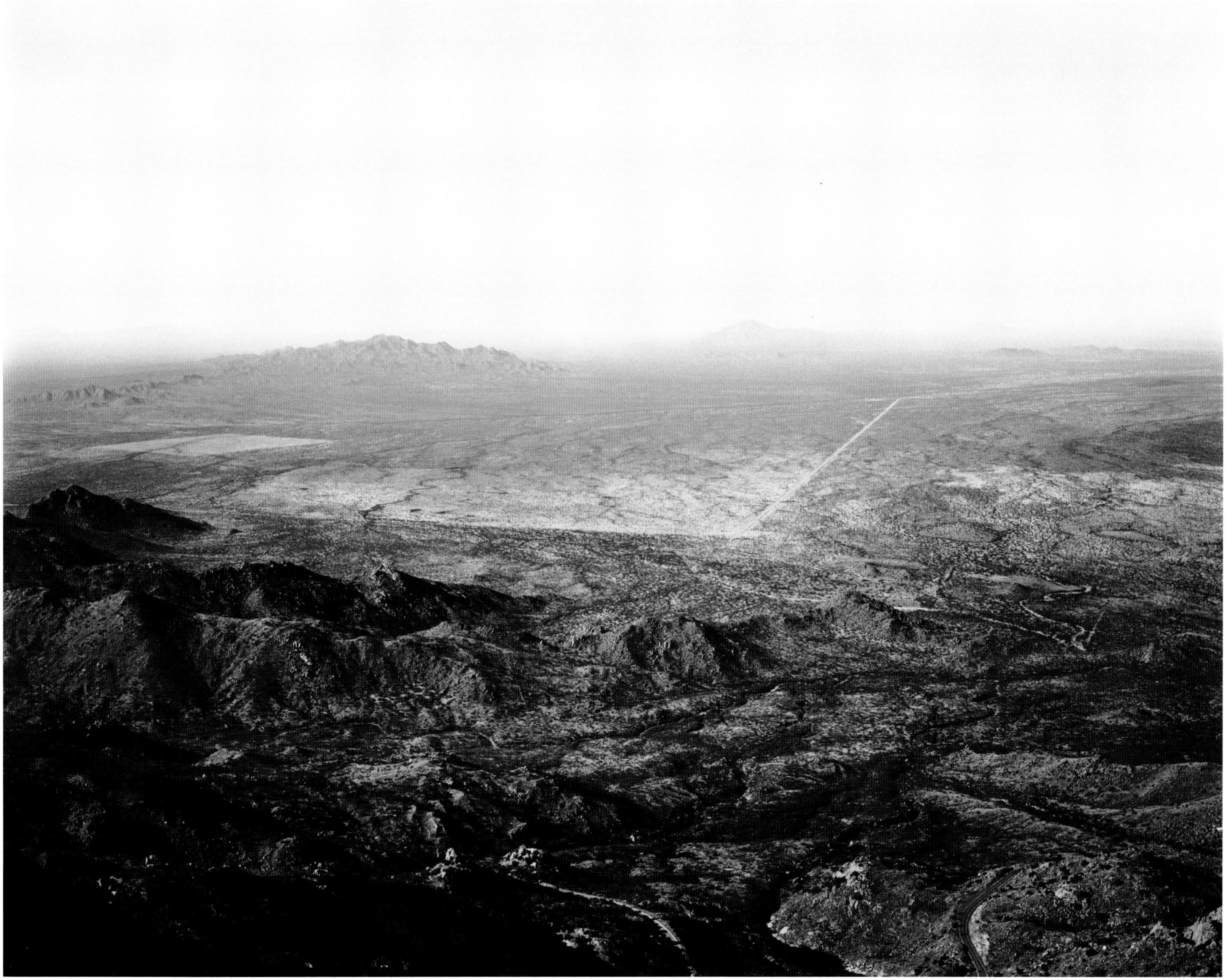

Warner Lakes (average elevation 4,475 feet), Hart Mountain National Antelope Refuge, Oregon, 2011.

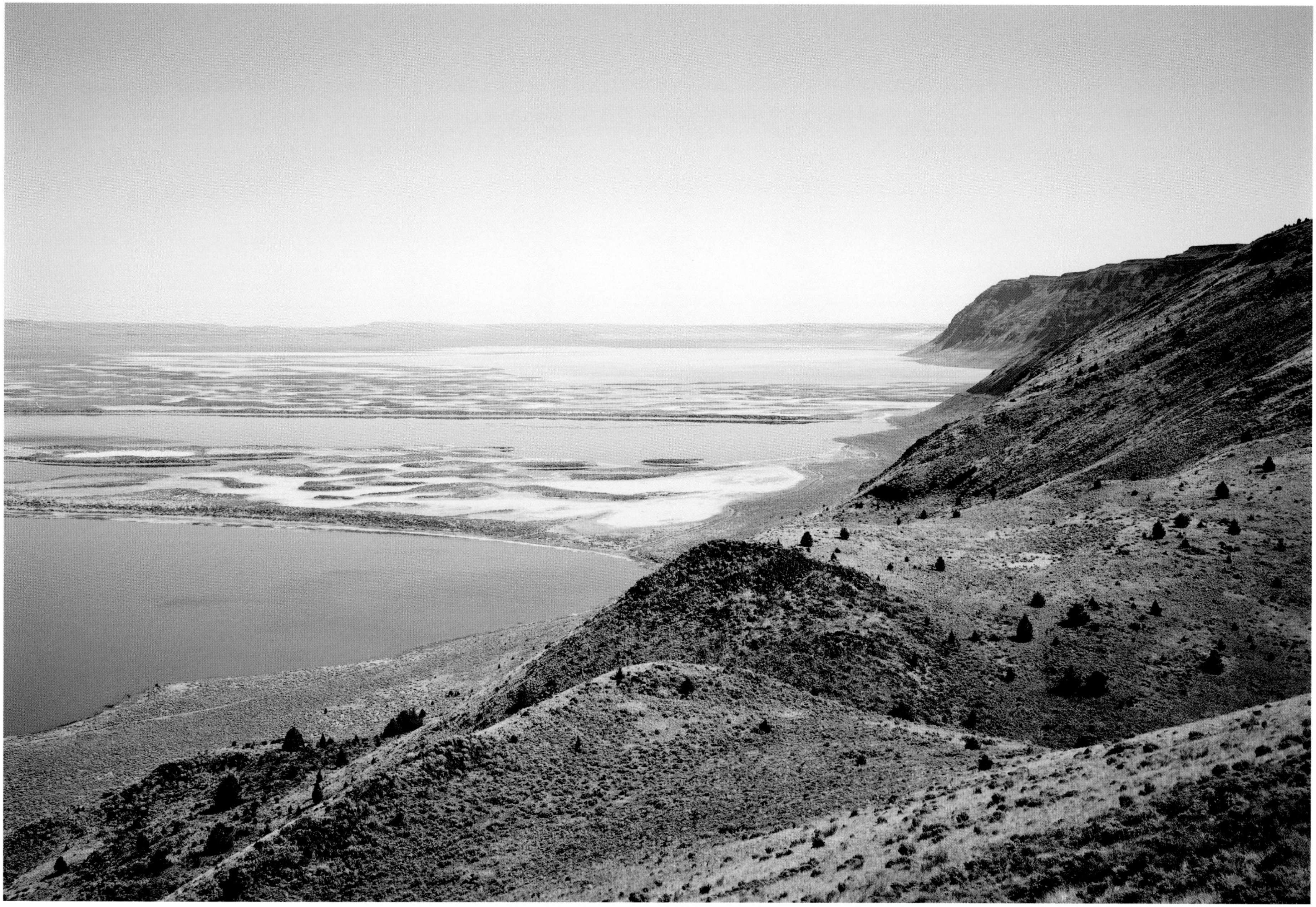

Columbia River, near Saddle Mountain National Wildlife Refuge (elevation 486–3,283 feet), Washington, 1987.

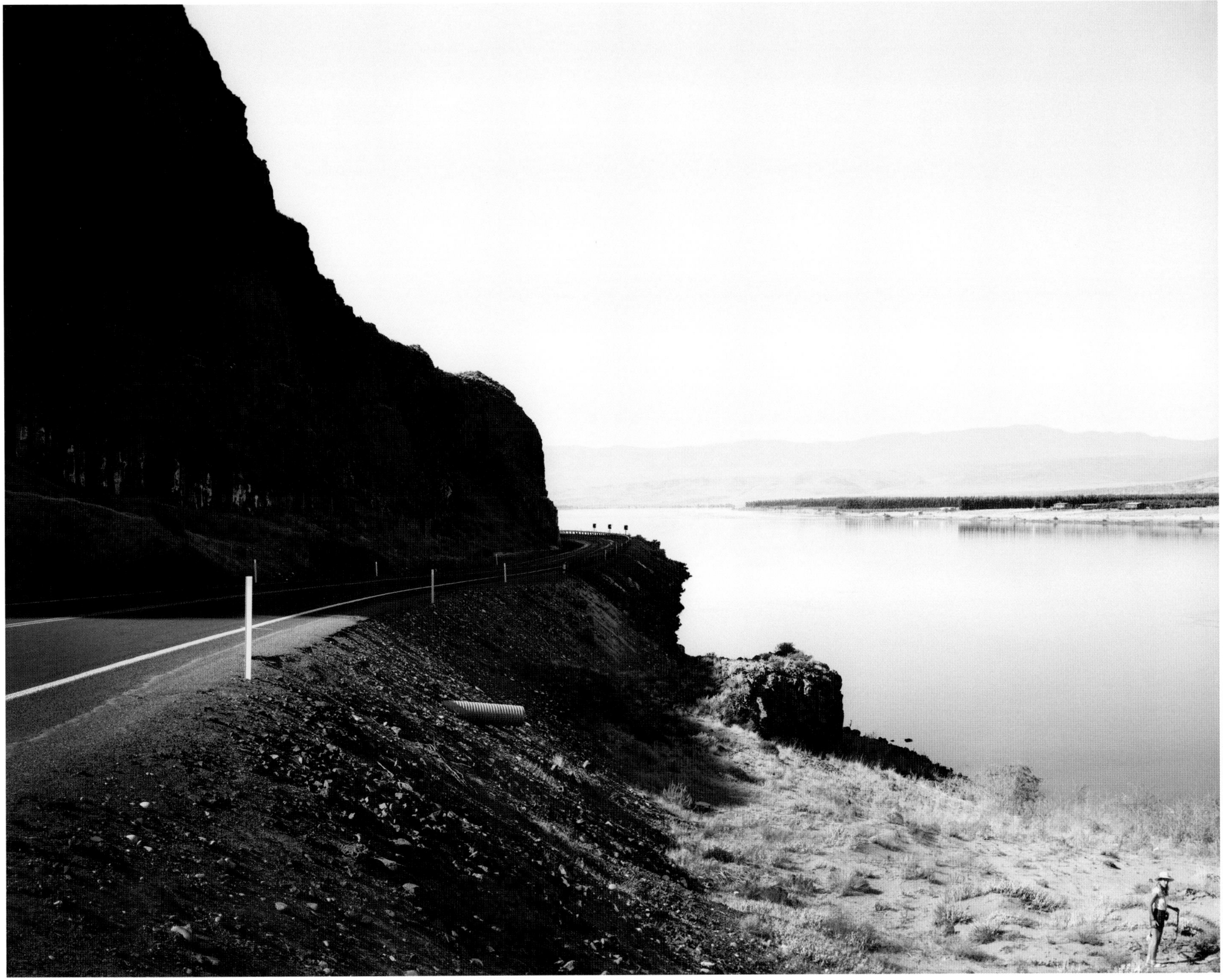

Mount St. Helens National Volcanic Monument (elevation 4,605–8,363 feet), Washington, 1987.

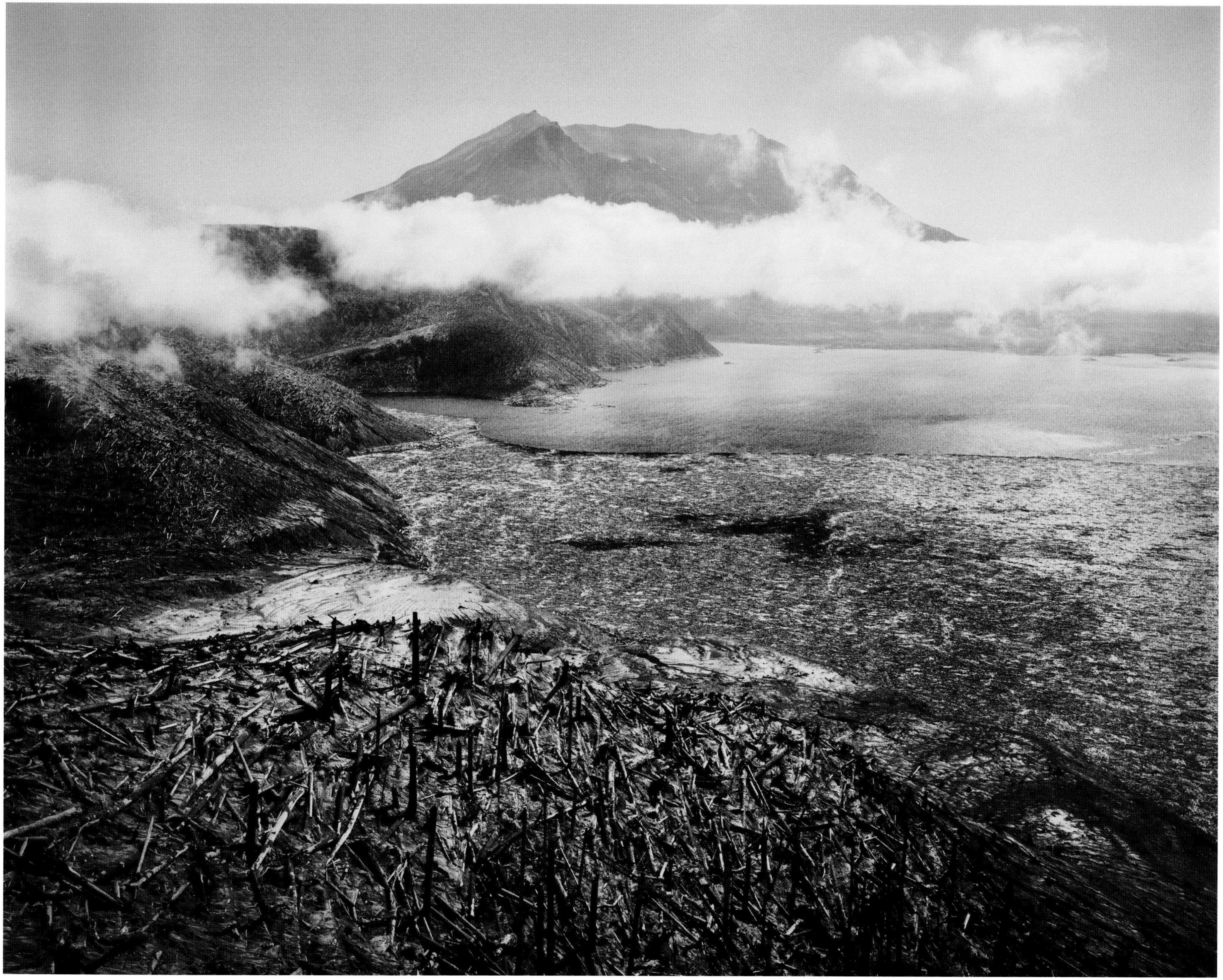

Death Valley National Park (lowest elevation –286 feet), California, 1991.

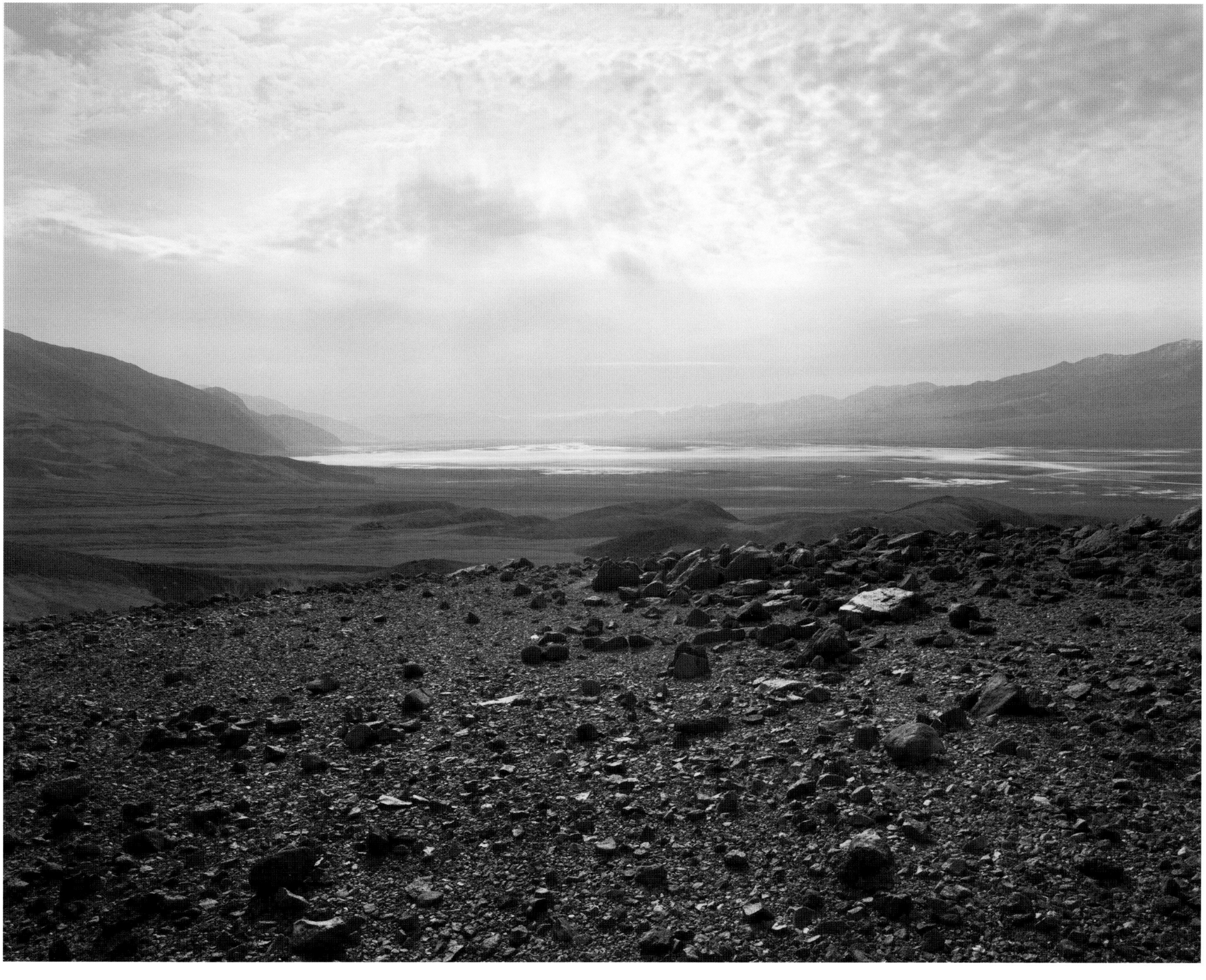

View of the (upper left) Kern Mountains (elevation 9,680–9,720 feet) and (upper right) Snake Range (peak elevation 10,879 feet) from near 11,883–foot North Schell Peak (foreground), Humboldt-Toiyabe National Forest, Nevada, 2011.

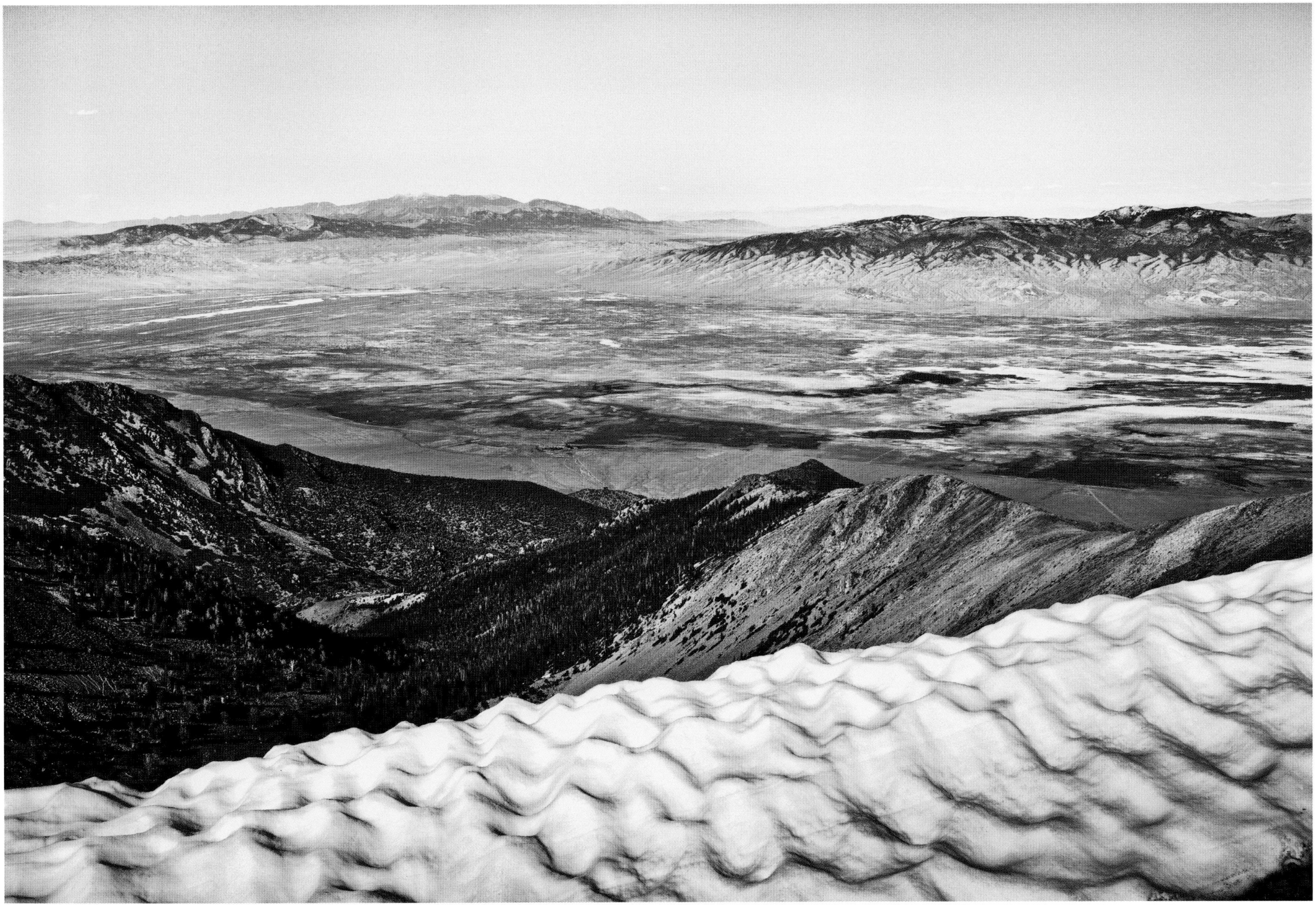

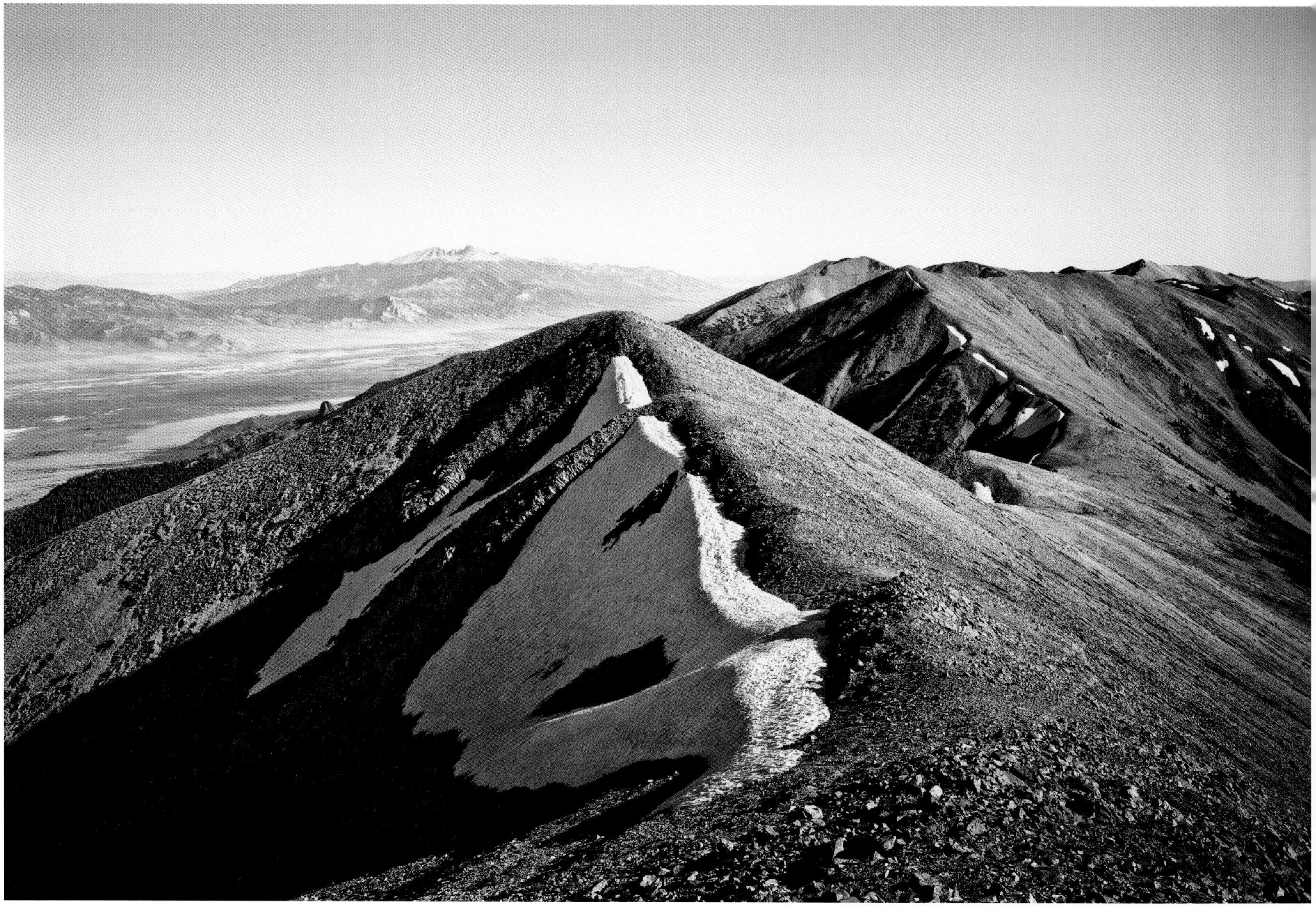

(Above) Great Basin National Park from North Schell Peak (elevation 11,883 feet) and (right) 11, 215–foot Mount Fitzgerald (upper left) and 11,137–foot Snow Lake Peak (upper right), Humboldt-Toiyabe National Forest, Nevada, 2011.

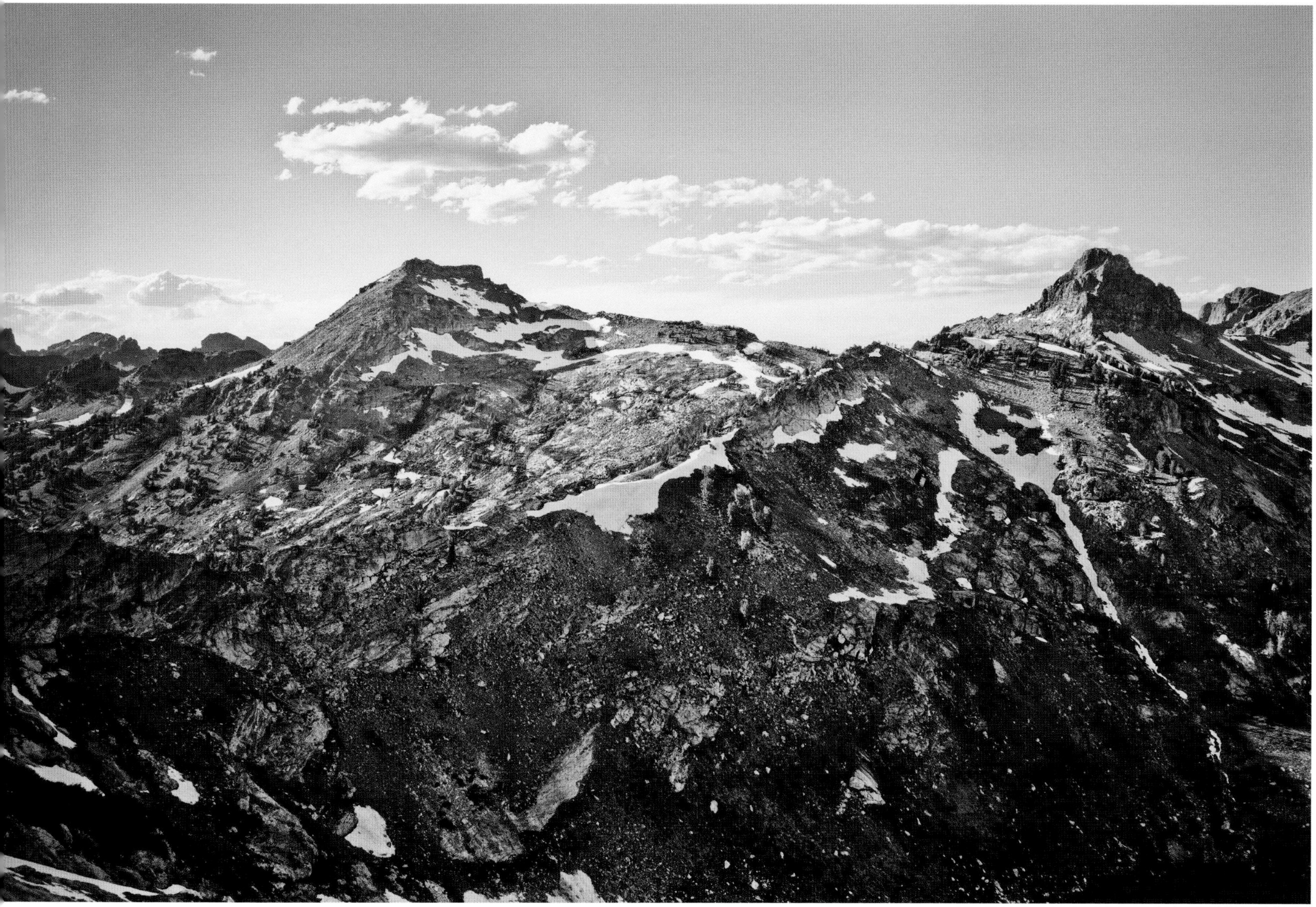

View from Mount Scott (elevation 8,934 feet), Crater Lake National Park, Oregon, 2011.

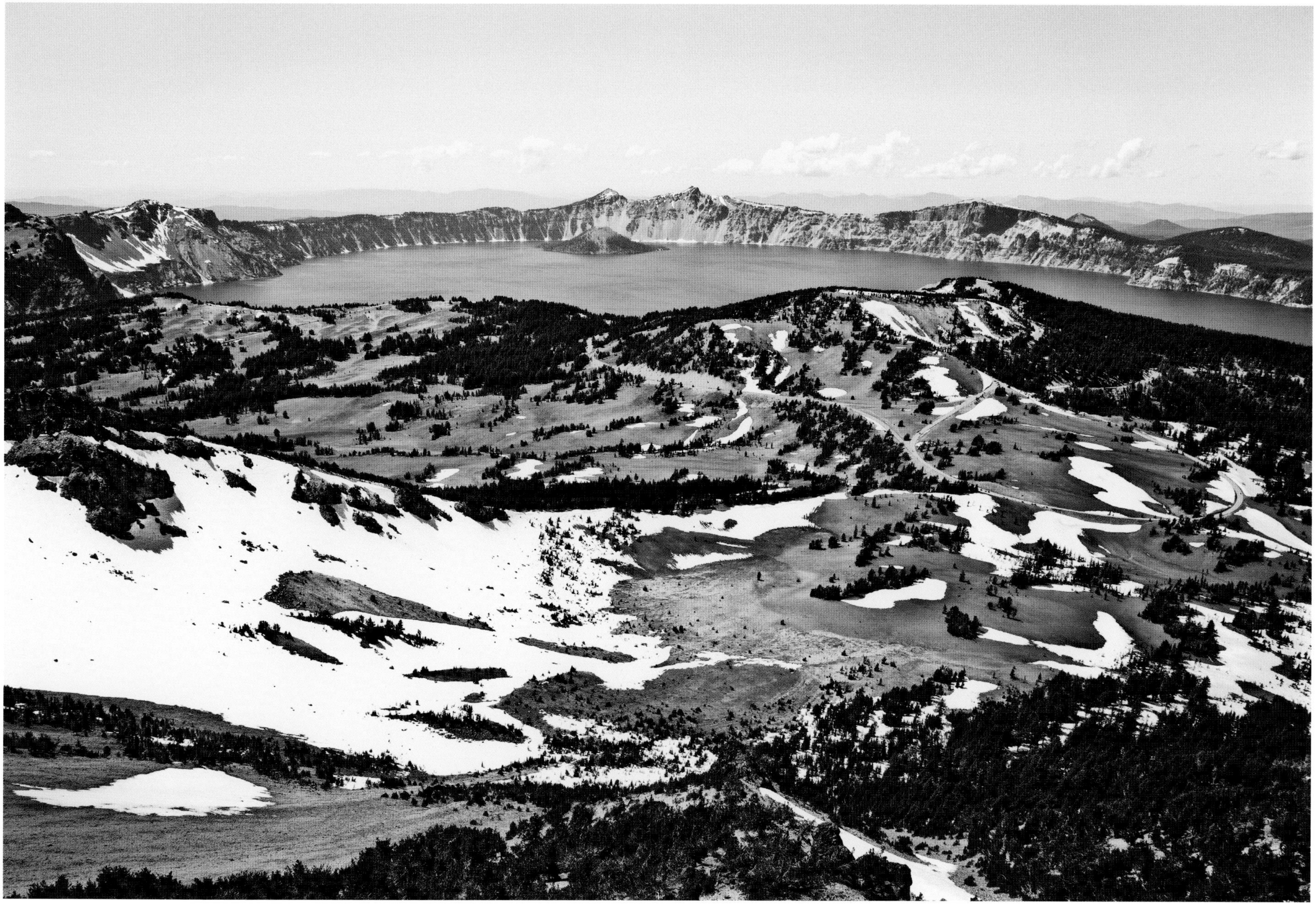

Jeff Davis Peak (elevation 12,777 feet), Great Basin National Park, Nevada, 2011.

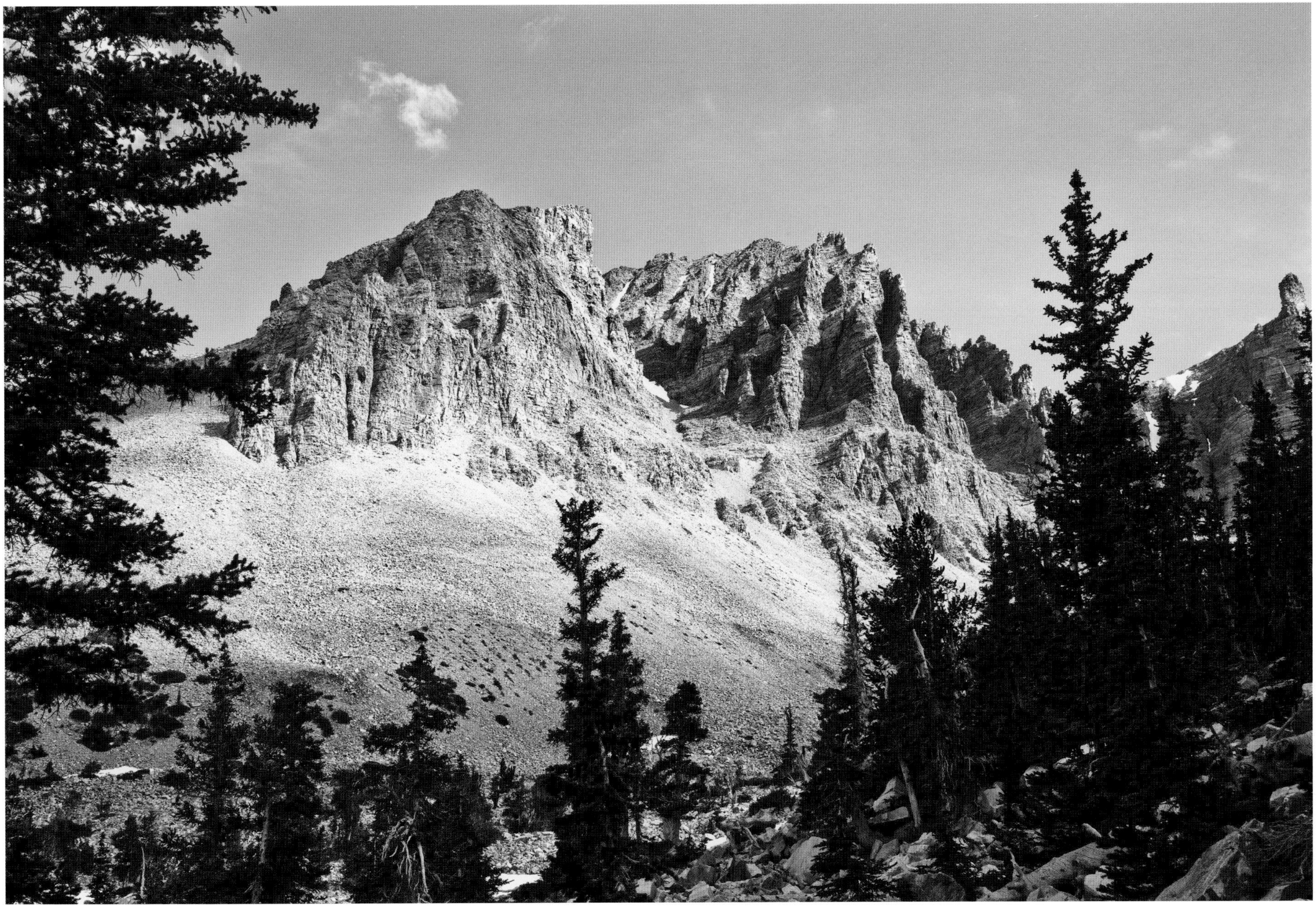

Yosemite Valley, Yosemite National Park (elevation 2,127–13,114 feet), California, 1979.

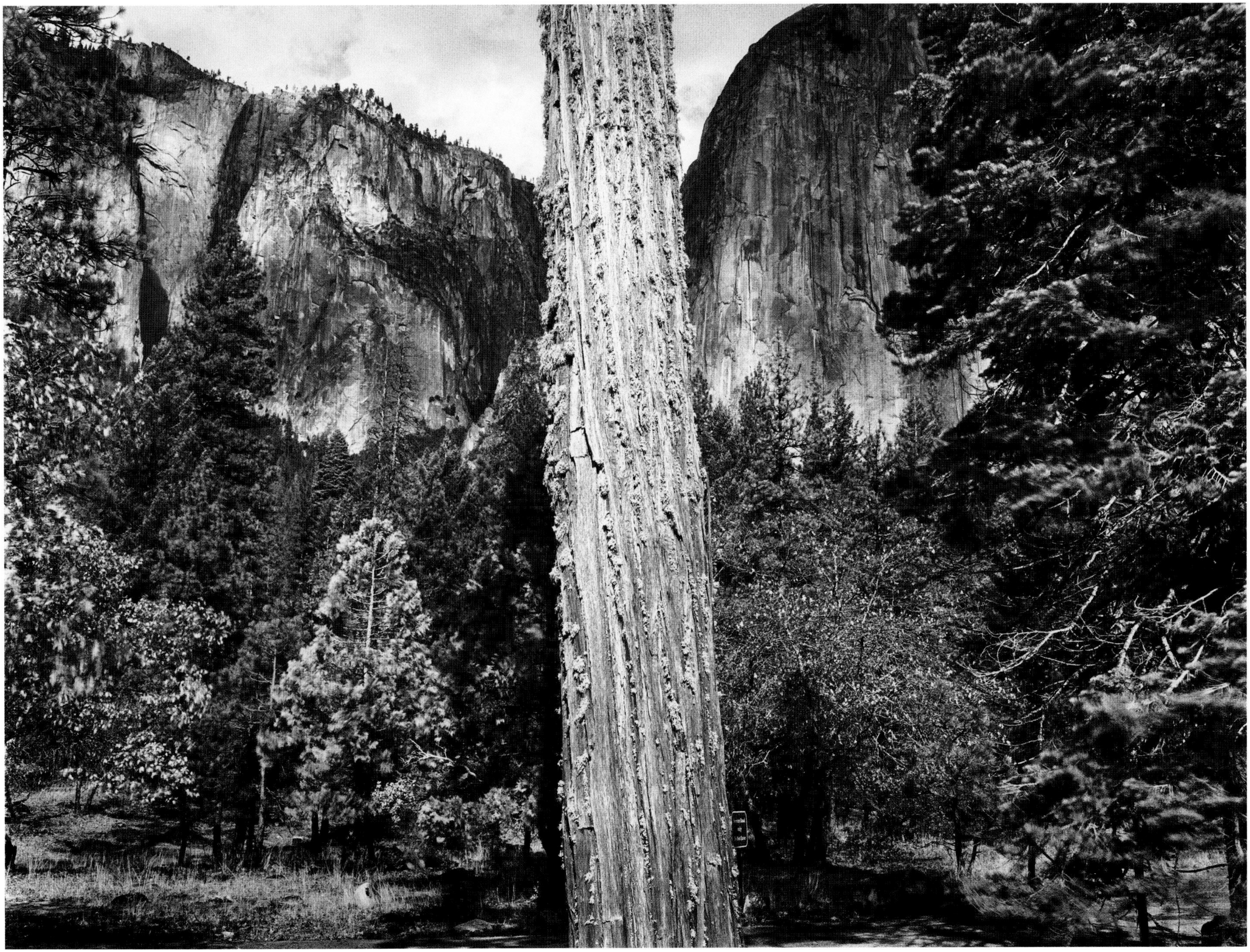

Wolverine Petrified Forest on the western side of the Circle Cliffs area, Grand Staircase-Escalante National Monument (elevation 3,873–8,616 feet), Utah, 1992.

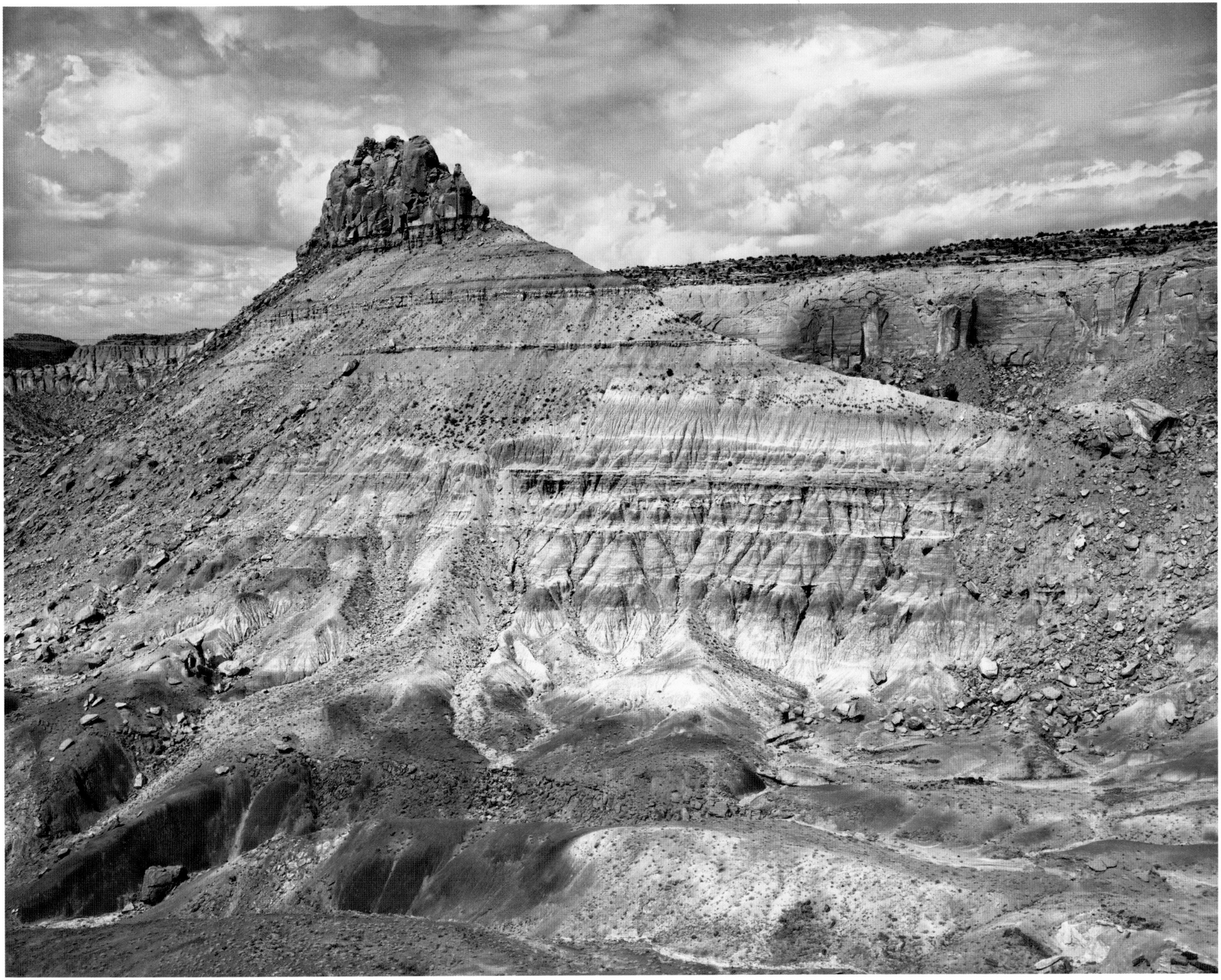

Painted Desert, Petrified Forest National Park (elevation 5,300–6,235 feet), Arizona, 1987.

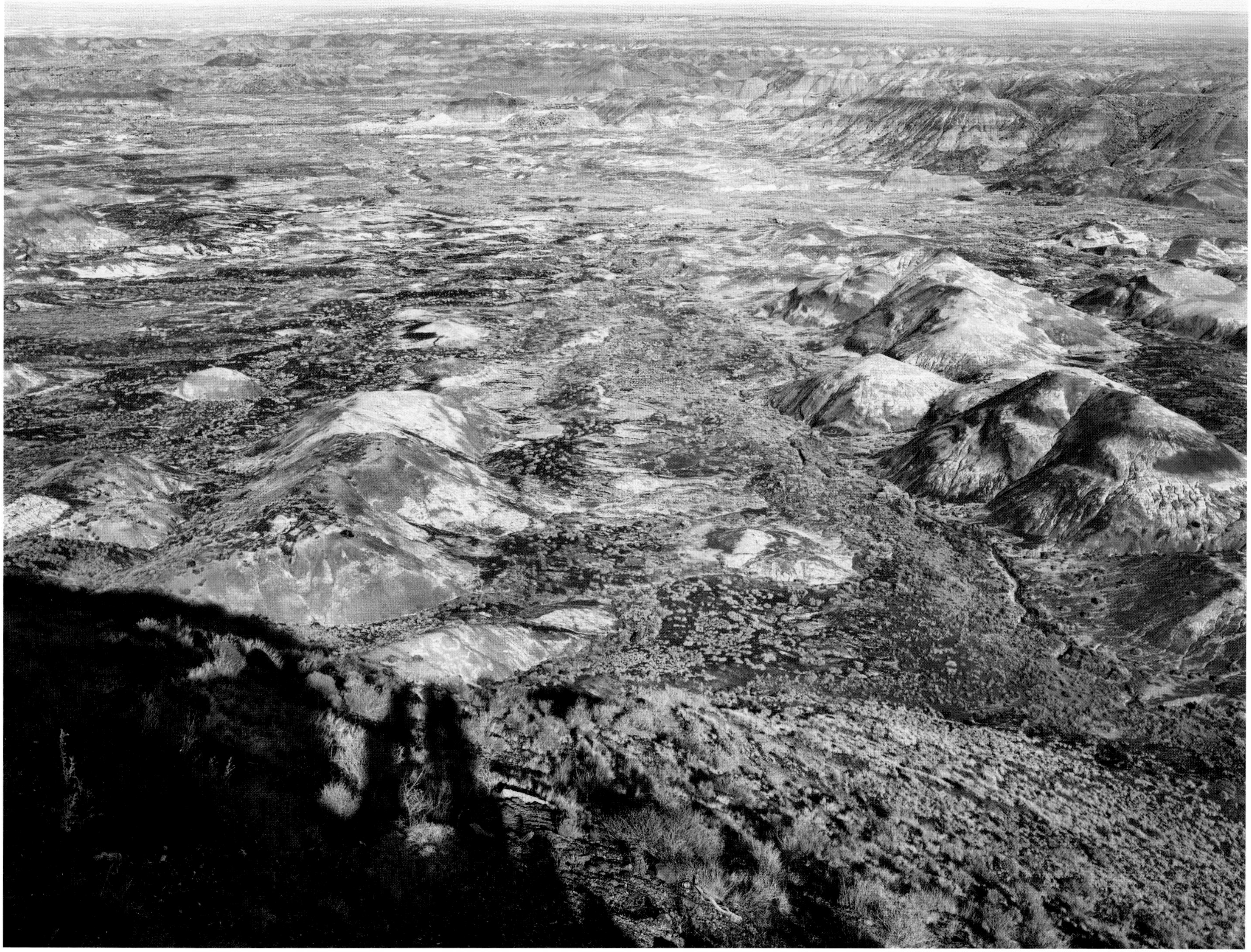

Hinkey Pass Road, Santa Rosa Mountains, Humboldt-Toiyabe National Forest (elevation 6,000–10,839 feet), Nevada, 2011.

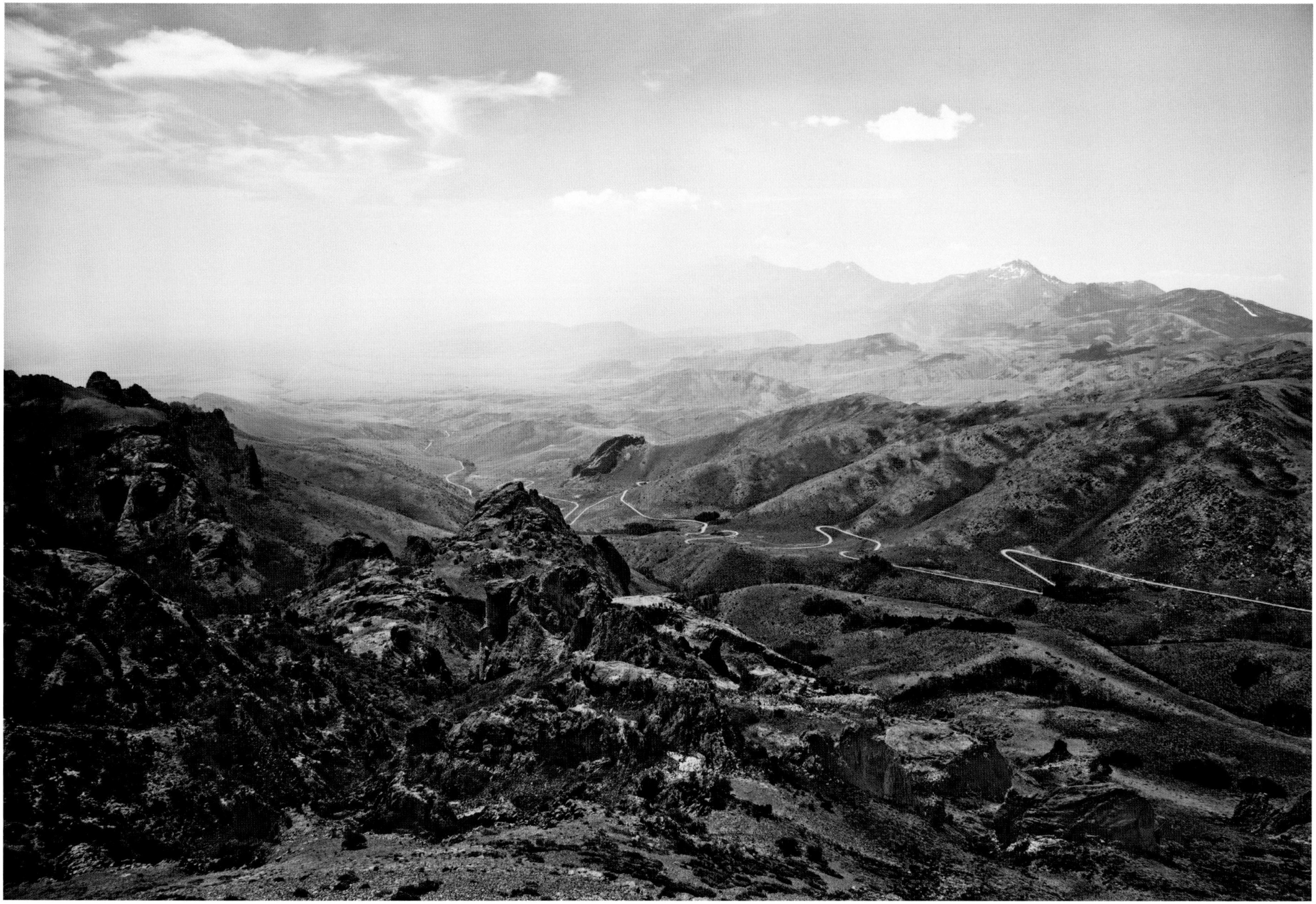

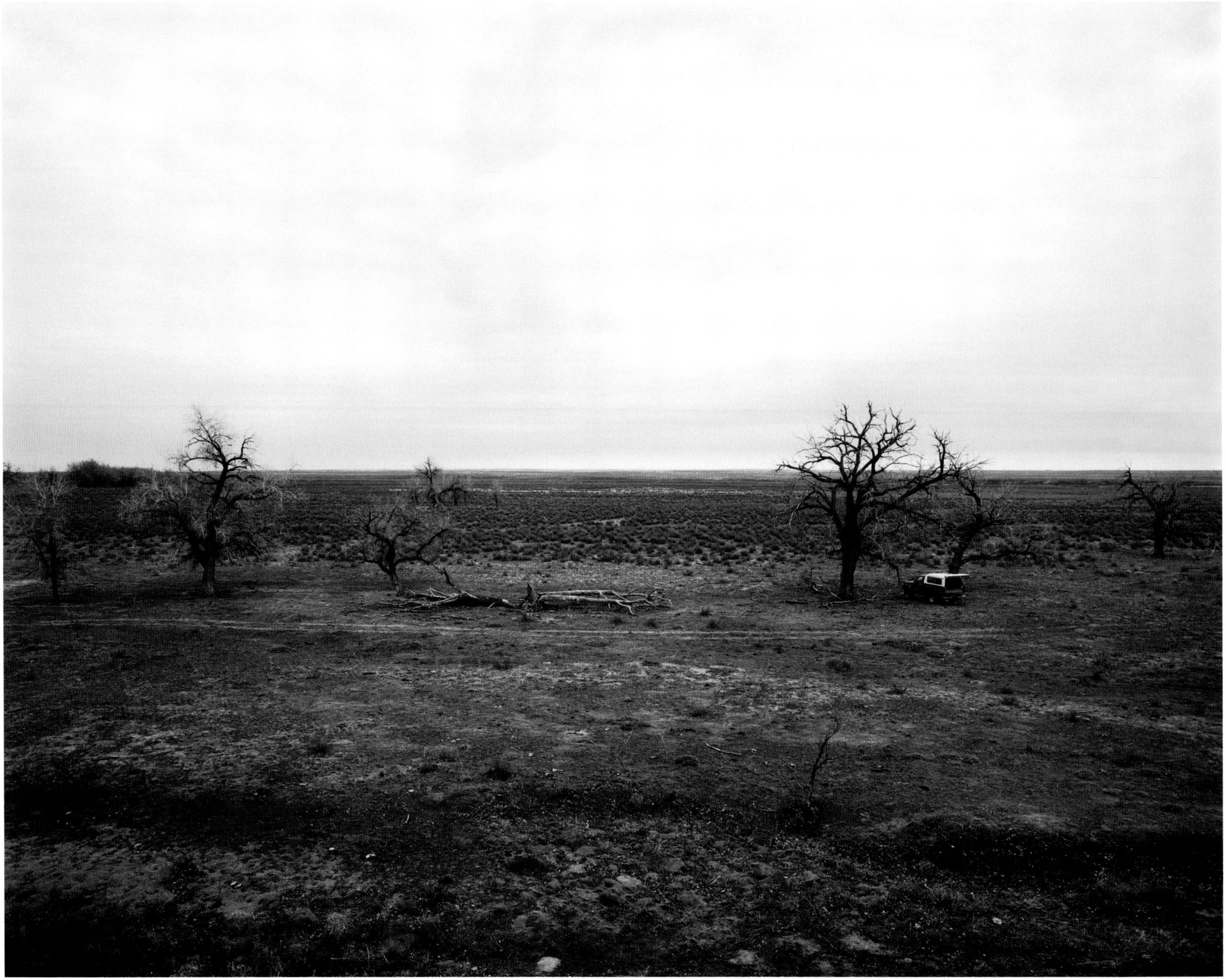

Four-Wheel Drive

by Toby Jurovics

MOST LANDSCAPE PHOTOGRAPHERS, when recounting their artistic development, bring up their first truck at one point or another. There is almost universal faith in a Toyota four-wheel drive. Beyond allowing you to navigate a rocky two-track without getting high-centered, a truck also delivers the possibility of disconnecting for a few days or a few hundred miles. As Willy Sutton notes in his introductory essay, "I stowed food, a stove, backpacking gear, and at times more than twenty gallons of water. My original truck had an additional gas tank, allowing me to drive an extra 400 miles. I could camp almost anywhere. In my pickup, I was temporarily self-sufficient." Little spells *opportunity* more clearly than a full tank of gas, a sleeping bag, and a good set of tires, and many of us know the excitement of loading our gear, shutting the tailgate, and being ready to go.

Several years ago, I drove with Sutton from his home in Boulder to the North Platte River in central Wyoming. *Let It Bleed* was playing over the hum of the tires as we rolled to a stop at an intersection in the middle of nowhere particular, a place where a pair of roads just happen to cross. Scanning the landscape through the windshield, I remember thinking at that moment there was no better way to see the West and no better person to do so with. Make no mistake—this was hardly the same as being out on the King Survey (1867–1872), and I am equally certain that photographer Timothy H. O'Sullivan (1840–1882) and his companions would have encamped at the nearest Comfort Inn had they been given the chance. But there

(Left) Willy Sutton's pickup truck, Sand Creek Massacre National Historic Site (elevation 3,940–4,018 feet), Colorado, 1986.

are still moments when the landscape feels like it is full of promise, and we step out of the cocoon of the cab and stretch, and look in every direction, and feel that all is well.

This enthusiasm for the open landscape fills Sutton's photographs, and, turning from page to page, we share not only the excitement of recognizing places we, too, have been, but also the anticipation of discovering new places we have yet to visit. At the same time, Sutton has deliberately set himself apart from most of his contemporaries. He subscribes to an idea about landscape photography that is, within the context of contemporary practice, unpopular: he remains a committed advocate of nature and wilderness.

New Topographics: Photographs of a Man-altered Landscape—the 1975 exhibition curated by William Jenkins (b. 1944) and assisted by Joe Deal (1947–2010) at the International Museum of Photography at the George Eastman House—is noted by most photographers and critics as the pivotal moment in defining how the camera described the American landscape during the late twentieth century. We find places that are mostly urban or suburban, overbuilt, and laden with what appears to be disregard, if not outright contempt, for the land itself—the banal culmination of Manifest Destiny's march to the Pacific Ocean and the nation's subsequent doubling back to consume itself less than a century later. Robert Adams (b. 1937), a participant in the exhibition who later became a mentor and colleague of Sutton's, wrote, a few years later, "This leaves photography with a new but not less important job: to reconcile us to half wilderness."[1] This was a big pill to swallow but one that gradually came to be understood as true: since, presumably, there was little left of the wild, perhaps the most helpful thing photography could do was to find moments of grace or affection in a compromised place.

It is clear that Sutton was never entirely comfortable with this idea. "I really am more interested in nature and processes of nature, rather than in the man-made environment," he told me. "I don't think that *New Topographics* really cares about nature."[2] I would argue this last point but agree that the photographs made under its general rubric *look* to most people like the photographers don't care about nature.[3] So, caught in that pull between the "New West"

1. Robert Adams, "Inhabited Nature," *Aperture*, Vol. 81 (1978): 31.

2. Conversation with the author, June 13, 2010.

3. See Toby Jurovics, "Same as It Ever Was: Re-reading *New Topographics*," in Greg Foster-Rice and John Rohrbach, eds., *Reframing the New Topographics* (Chicago: The Center for American Places at Columbia College Chicago, 2010), 1–12.

of Robert Adams and the romanticized West of the other famous Adams of photography—Ansel (1902–1984)—Sutton held firm on the importance of nature and wilderness, to the possibility of an unbroken horizon.

This might make Sutton's photographs seem like an anachronism, although one can also make that argument about landscape photography itself. As we become further and further removed from the natural world, it is reasonable to ask why photographs like these still matter. One answer can be found in Edward Abbey's introduction to *Desert Solitaire*:

> It will be objected that the book deals too much with mere appearances, with the surface of things, and fails to engage and reveal the patterns of unifying relationships which form the true underlying reality of existence . . . For my own part I am pleased enough with surfaces—in fact, they alone seem to me to be of much importance. Such things for example as the grasp of a child's hand in your own, the flavor of an apple, the embrace of a friend or lover, the silk of a girl's thigh, the sunlight on rock and leaves, the feel of music, the bark of a tree, the abrasion of granite and sand, the plunge of clear water into a pool, the face of the wind—what else is there? What else do we need?[4]

Abbey quickly travels from the personal and intimate to the world at large, each "surface" laden with affection and emotion and excitement. Whether fingertips tracing the back of a neck or turning a smooth river stone over and over again in your hand, these were experiences he understood to have the same direct, piercing meaning and connection. Sutton, too, believes in a world connected to itself and to us by bonds that can be made visible as easily as those Abbey described—that seemingly straightforward and direct images can be revelatory of deeper truths.

The core of Sutton's photographic work is his ongoing series, "Public Lands of the American West," a survey that describes the expanse of open land between Canada and Mexico,

4. Edward Abbey, *Desert Solitaire: A Season in the Wilderness* (New York: McGraw-Hill, 1968), xiii.

from the 100th meridian west to the Pacific Ocean: "Two-thirds of the land in the West is open and accessible and ours. The idea for the pictures is that we hold all this land in common, and what we decide to do with it is an expression of our values and who we are."[5] It is a noble proposal and mirrors the words of novelist and environmentalist Wallace Stegner (1909–1993), who wrote that, perhaps one day, we will have "a chance to create a society to match its scenery."[6]

Unlike many of the best-known photographs by Stegner's friend, Ansel, however, Sutton didn't always set his tripod within the recognizable—and easily accessible—confines of the national parks. The majority of the images in this book were made on lands under the jurisdiction of the Bureau of Land Management and the U.S. Forest Service—"The Land of Many Uses"—who together control more than ten times the area managed by the National Park Service. Home to roads, clear-cuts, gravel pits, mines, and grazing cattle as well as hunting, fishing, skiing, snowmobiling, and camping, they are places that, unlike the national parks (barring some fundamental change in federal policy), could easily be logged or turned over to a mining company. They comprise the great majority of federal land in the West and are the most contested.

Public lands are something else the national parks are not—they are, for the most part, empty of tourists, motor homes, snack shops, and souvenir stands. Their landscapes can be just as picturesque, rugged, and inspiring as those found at a designated scenic viewpoint in a national park, but these are the kind of places most people don't go to, unless they are willing to forgo restaurants, and a room in the lodge and—for at least a day or two—be self-sufficient.

In many ways, the history that Sutton's "Public Lands of the American West" is closest to is that of the photographers who first surveyed the West in the decades following the American Civil War (1861–1865). Their images pictured the Western landscape as an expression of varied interests: the geologic history of the Rocky Mountains, when Timothy H. O'Sullivan was working with Clarence King (1842–1901) on the U.S. Geological Exploration of the Fortieth Parallel; or territorial expansion and the wealth of natural resources, when O'Sullivan

5. Conversation with the author, June 13, 2010.

6. Wallace Stegner, *The Sound of Mountain Water* (Garden City, NY: Doubleday & Company, 1968), 38.

and William Bell (1830–1910) photographed for Lieutenant George M. Wheeler's Geographical and Geological Explorations and Surveys West of the One Hundredth Meridian; or William Henry Jackson's (1843–1942) 1872 photographs of Yellowstone's sublime and curious landscapes, made in the company of geologist Ferdinand Vandeveer Hayden (1829–1887); or industrial conquest, as revealed by Andrew J. Russell (1829–1902) in *The Great West Illustrated* (1869), the most literal photographic document of national and corporate Manifest Destiny, published to mark the Union Pacific Railroad's triumphant run from Omaha to Promontory Summit in Utah Territory. Each of these photographers fulfilled an assignment, making images that met the needs of a client, whether the War Department or the railroad. But their images also reveal that they were inspired by the same characteristics of the Western landscape that move us today, the same rugged silhouettes and challenging emptiness. Not that they would have seen the need to argue for preservation or elected to go camping for recreation, but that the particular narrative of Western space did not go unnoticed.

Sutton's photographs sit squarely within all of these traditions, from the wonder and fascination and potential of the West during the nineteenth century to elegiac reflections of the modern landscape, heavy under the weight of highways and smog and housing developments. On another drive, this time along I-70 heading to the Frying Pan River near Aspen, I challenged Sutton to elaborate on his reticence to be more direct, to engage the mining scars and truck stops and condominiums rising up the slopes of the Continental Divide. He answered, "One of the reasons these pictures are important is because the world no longer looks this way."[7]

We know this, too. What Sutton hopes we might do is to locate what we believe is most important and defend it—to shape our future rather than simply sit back and wait for its inevitable decline. Will it matter if a place we have never seen, and aren't likely to, is leased to an energy conglomerate or opened to development? Or is it important that some places still require you to lock the hubs of your four-wheel drive and get out the atlas, because Google Maps still has no idea where you are or where you want to go?

7. Conversation with the author, August 6, 2006.

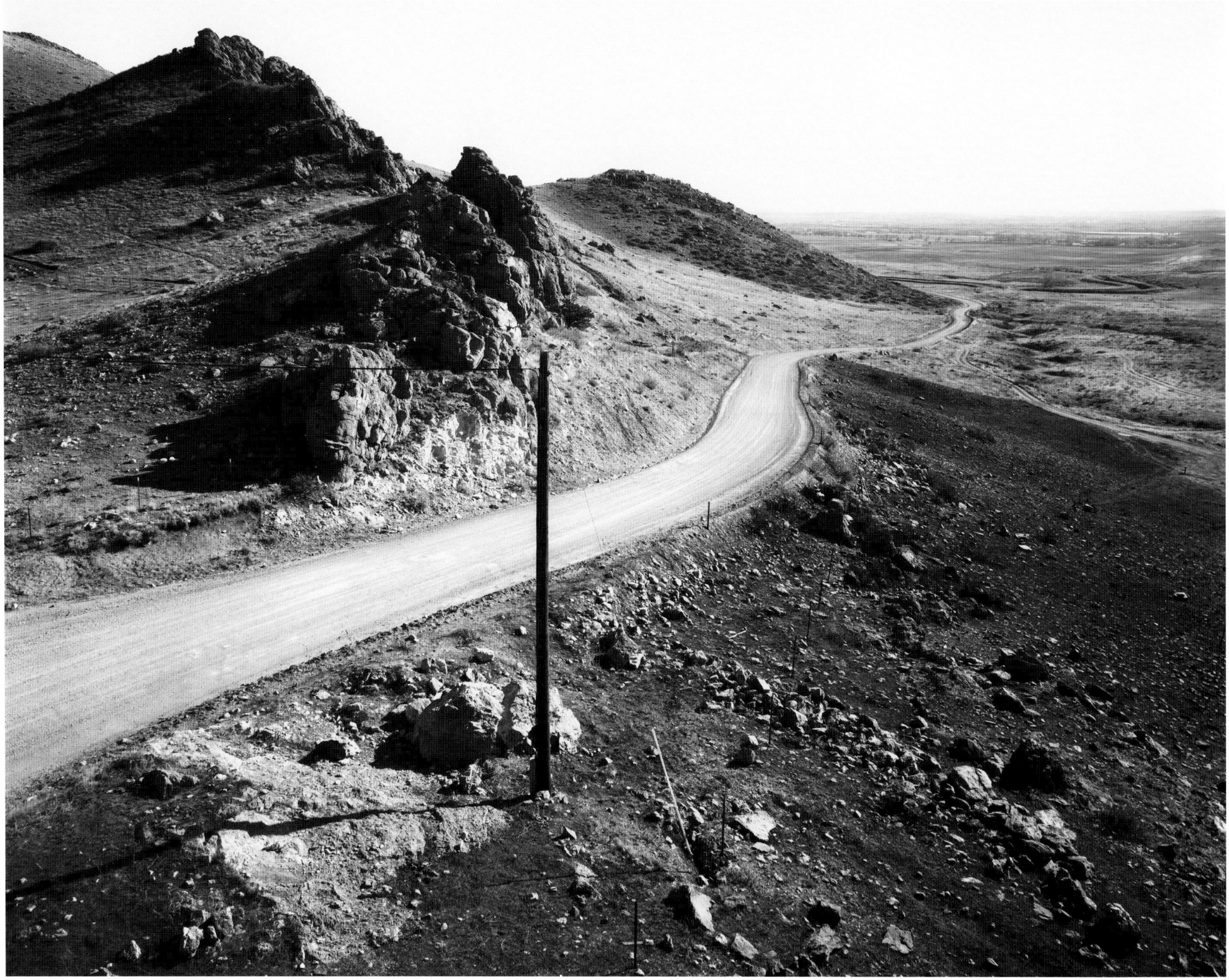

Willy Sutton's West

by Susan B. Moldenhauer

WILLY SUTTON'S EVOCATIVE IMAGES of the American West document lands held in the public trust and explore their importance through a sensitive eye, a passion for landscape, and an interest in understanding *place* through photography. For Sutton, the American West is an enormous region: everything west of the 100th meridian—the approximate but historically significant dividing longitude that separates the semi-arid West from the humid East of the United States.

Sutton is not the first photographer to focus on public lands as the geographic boundary for his work, but he is certainly the only one to attempt to photograph the complexity and enormity of it single handedly. His contemporaries—Gregory Conniff, Robert Dawson, Joe Deal, Peter Goin, Wanda Hammerbeck, Mark Klett, and Martin Stupich, among others—have focused their work on the American West through projects, often collaborative in nature, that have explored, in varying degrees and ways, the environmental, political, and social issues of the time. This awareness of the modern, post-World War II American landscape and the effect of its intersection with civilization follows a fundamental shift in landscape photography that came to the fore with the seminal 1975 exhibition, *New Topographics: Photographs of a Man-altered Landscape* (curated by William Jenkins and assisted by Joe Deal for the International Museum of Photography at the George Eastman House), and, more specifically, with three photographers in the exhibition: the American Robert Adams (b. 1937) and the German couple, Bernd (1931–2007) and Hilla (b. 1934) Becher. A year earlier, Adams's path-breaking book, *The*

(Left) Road near Rabbit Mountain (elevation 5,400–6,000 feet), Boulder County Parks and Open Space, Colorado, 1985.

New West: Landscapes along the Colorado Front Range, was published, an unsentimental view of the juncture of land and urban sprawl between Denver and Colorado Springs. Objective, cool and formal, Robert Adams both challenged the romantic view of the landscape, as made known by Ansel Adams (1902–1984), and signaled a rethinking of landscape photography.

Like Robert Adams did for many years, Sutton has made his home in Colorado. He has quietly and deliberately pursued his work, traveling alone in the national parks and monuments, national forests and grasslands, archeological sites and Bureau of Land Management parcels, scenic rivers and wildlife refuges that dominate an increasingly urbanized Western landscape. Criss-crossing the West from Montana to Arizona and from Nebraska to California, he creates poetic but often grand images of views captured at a particular moment when light, line, and texture combine with geology, history, and the human presence. His pursuit is personal: to experience, understand, and acknowledge the land in his time and in its present condition, and his approach seeks the "magic" of the moment of his presence in a place.

Sutton's photographs in this book convey the diverse landscapes of the American West and his passion for them. If there is any neutrality about the images, it is Sutton's embrace of the pristine, unaltered landscape interwoven with views that reflect both prehistoric and modern-day impacts of our presence. And there is a playfulness about the images in Sutton's use of scale and the overarching power of nature. *Bison in Lamar Valley, Yellowstone National Park, Wyoming, 1995* (page 31) is anchored on a sunlit, meandering creek in the shadowy foreground that plays off the side-lit land rising across the middle and is offset by the distant, darker mountains. A peppering of bison that seem to defy their size emphasizes the grandeur of the place. It is an interesting counterpoint to the strict geometry of fence lines that bisect the landscape in *View of Mount Leidy, Bridger-Teton National Forest, Montana, 1987* (page 65). The dramatic vanishing point creates a tension between the distance of the view and the figure-ground structure of the image, simultaneously referencing the patchwork of public and private land ownership in the West.

The power of nature is evident as Sutton transforms sand dunes into a massive, tsunami-like wave in *Great Sand Dunes National Park and Preserve, San Luis Valley, Colorado, 1996* (page 87) or makes the rolling lands of the westernmost Great Plains appear as an undulating surface of dark water in *The Sandhills, Samuel R. McKelvie National Forest, Nebraska, 1989* (page 29). The upthrust of the massive, 800-foot-high rock form in *Steamboat Rock, Dinosaur National Monument, Colorado, 1996* (page 49) defies logic, as if it landed there from outer space. In *Green River, Dinosaur National Monument, Colorado, 1996* (page 47), the rock face that skirts the river below seems to be torn away, leaving a scar upon the land. All of these images reveal the forces of geological events that form the diverse, unique lands of the American West.

Occasionally, automobiles are a reference for the scale of what we are observing. *Campground, Chaco Canyon National Historical Park, New Mexico, 1986* (page 19) shows a diminished, off-road camping location near a long, rock cliff, and, opening to the distance, a myriad of pathways scramble in all directions. The entire composition rests on the camper's pickup truck at the edge of the dirt loop road that comes from and returns to the horizon. In *Narrows of the Big Thompson River, Roosevelt National Forest, Colorado, 1986* (page 101), the vehicle is pushed to the side as the road winds up the canyon, mirroring the river's downward, whitewater flow.

Sutton is also cognizant of the ancient people who inhabited the region centuries, even millenia, ago, playing the human-scale architectural ruins against the vast landscape. *Stairway, Chaco Canyon National Historical Park, New Mexico, 1987* (page 57) shows a beautifully incised stairway descending the slick-rock cliff and remnant circular pathway that echoes the rock face above it, revealed only by the massive, dislodged boulder that has broken away. From the Great Gallery area in Utah, *Luke in Horseshoe Canyon, Canyonlands National Park, Utah, 1984* (page 13) portrays the young Luke in a modern mode of transportation a baby stroller—against the ancient pictographs of the canyon wall. It is a jarring juxtaposition made even more amazing given the rigorous hike necessary to get to the site those many years ago!

Sometimes Sutton requires a close observation of his images to understand what is going on in them. *Desert View Point, Grand Canyon National Park, Arizona, 1980* (page 41) shows the dramatic scale of the landscape, void of all inhabitants save the tourists perched behind the railing of the optimal viewpoint on top of the cliff, itself appearing to overhang in space. Far, far below, a trail meanders toward the Colorado River. The image recalls those of the nineteenth century that heralded the accomplishment of a few to reach the highest vantage point from which to view the sublime landscape below. Even subtler is *The Keyhole, Long's Peak Trail, Rocky Mountain National Park, Colorado, 2001* (page 15). Look closely and see a line of hikers climbing up big boulders through the center of the image, trying to accomplish the "keyhole" at the top in order to see the view on the other side. The rock structure to the left is more distinguishable than the climbers.

Sutton, too, is one to climb to the mountaintop and take in the view of what the landscape might have looked like in earlier times. *Painted Desert, Petrified Forest National Park, Arizona, 1987* (page 137) is one view that remains void of human presence, except for the foreground shadows of people and a safety railing. More often the images are from the uppermost regions of the mountains with breathtaking views. *Views from near Stoney Pass, San Juan National Forest, Colorado, 1997 and 1996* (pages 82 and 83) and *View of Tabeguache Peak from Mount Antero, San Isabel National Forest, Colorado, 1995* (page 91) are equally intimate and close, vast and distant. Soft, snow-patched lands undulate to the distance, where sharp mountains rise even higher: alone, with nature, on top of the world—almost touching the sky.

The importance of the moment, the magic and even intimacy of the moment, is evident throughout Sutton's work. He becomes the land—present, respectful, and passionate. But what of the future? If we look back only to 1974, when *The New West* by Robert Adams changed our consciousness about our relationship to the land and about our actions on the land, an intricate dance of photography and the settled West emerges. What will these public lands look like in the next fifty years? How will today's policies on energy and resources transform these places? We don't see (yet) the full impact of recent changes in gas and oil exploration policies in the U.S. that threaten public lands. And, as technology advances, the most obscure energy resource will become even more possible to extract. In ways reminiscent of other pioneer photographers whose work inspired conservation—Ansel Adams in black-and-white and Eliot Porter (1901–1990) in color are among the most notable and influential—Sutton's images are a reminder and a wake-up call to remember and recognize the importance of our public lands as places of refuge, where encounters with nature will forever revive the human spirit.

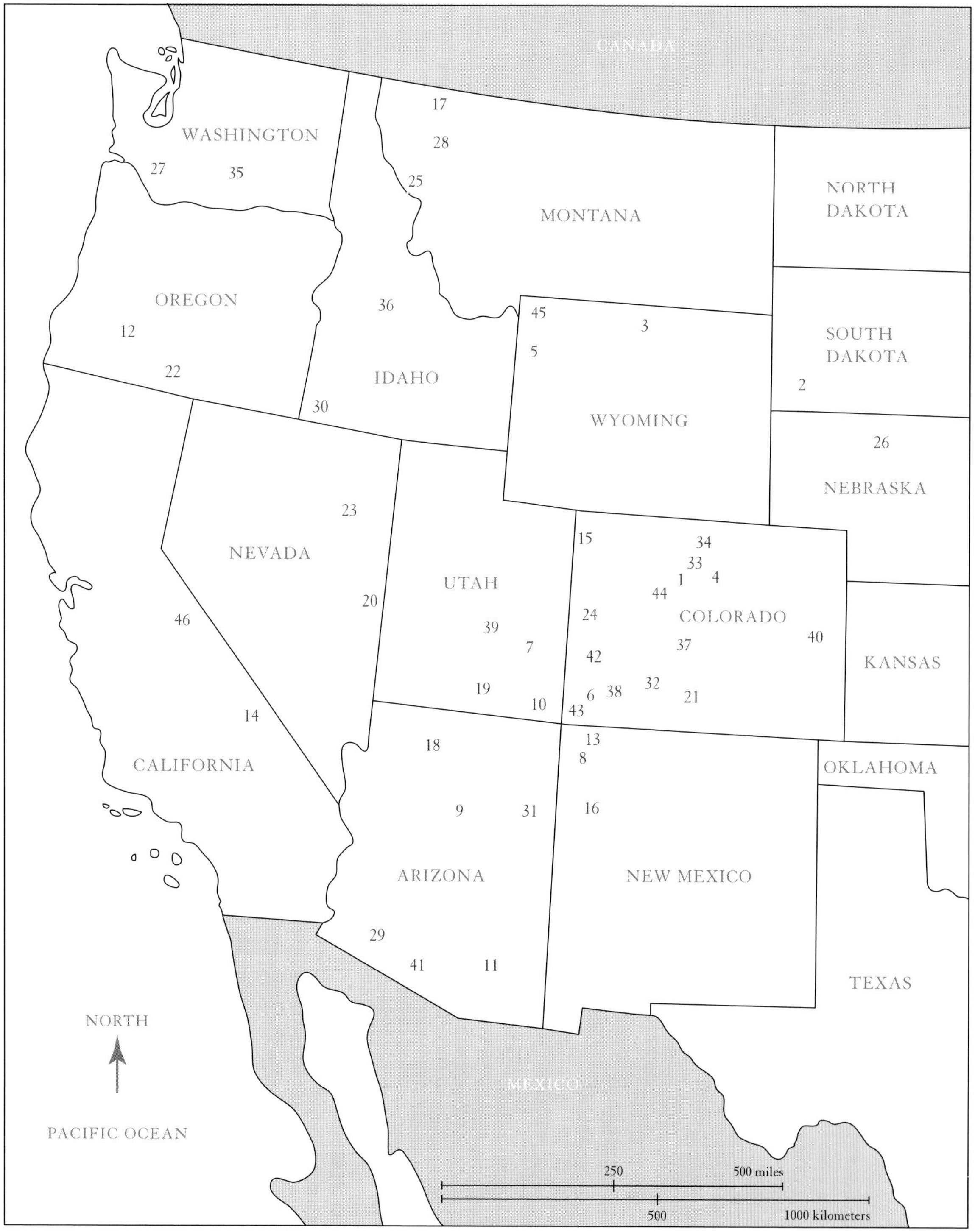

1. Arapaho National Forest (CO)
2. Badlands National Park (SD)
3. Bighorn National Forest (WY)
4. Boulder County Parks and Open Space / City of Boulder Open Space and Mountain Parks (CO)
5. Bridger-Teton National Forest (WY)
6. Canyons of the Ancients National Monument (CO)
7. Canyonlands National Park (UT)
8. Chaco Culture National Historical Park (NM)
9. Coconino National Forest (AZ)
10. Comb Ridge (UT)
11. Coronado National Forest (AZ)
12. Crater Lake National Park (OR)
13. Crow Canyon Archeological District (NM)
14. Death Valley National Park (CA)
15. Dinosaur National Monument (CO)
16. El Morro National Monument (NM)
17. Glacier National Park (MT)
18. Grand Canyon National Park (AZ)
19. Grand Staircase-Escalante National Monument (UT)
20. Great Basin National Park (NV)
21. Great Sand Dunes National Park and Preserve (CO)
22. Hart Mountain National Antelope Range (OR)
23. Humboldt-Toiyabe National Forest (NV/CA)
24. Little Book Cliffs Wild Horse Range (CO)
25. Lolo National Forest (MT)
26. Samuel R. McKelvie National Forest (NE)
27. Mount St. Helens National Volcanic Monument (WA)
28. National Bison Range (MT)
29. Organ Pipe Cactus National Monument (AZ)
30. Owyhee River Wilderness (ID)
31. Petrified Forest National Park (AZ)
32. Rio Grande National Forest (CO)
33. Rocky Mountain National Park (CO)
34. Roosevelt National Forest (CO)
35. Saddle Mountain National Wildlife Refuge / Hanford Reach National Monument (WA)
36. Salmon-Challis National Forest (ID)
37. San Isabel National Forest (CO)
38. San Juan National Forest (CO)
39. San Rafael Swell (UT)
40. Sand Creek Massacre National Historic Site (CO)
41. Tohono O'odham Indian Reservation (AZ)
42. Uncompahgre National Forest (CO)
43. Ute Mountain Ute Indian Reservation (CO)
44. White River National Forest (CO)
45. Yellowstone National Park (WY)
46. Yosemite National Park (CA)

Map by Morgan Pfaelzer.

Copyright © 2013 The American Land Publishing Project and Center for the Study of Place, Inc.

Notes on the Public Lands

The following public lands appear in alphabetical order with page references to Willy Sutton's photographs appearing in parentheses. Information was derived from sources available to the public. All entries were compiled by the author with the assistance of Carmen Rose Shenk and then vetted and verified by the various public agencies that administer the forty-six public lands featured in this book. Some information (such as acreage, elevation, and even land use) over time is subject to change. Each entry concludes with a field observation by Willy Sutton.

Arapaho National Forest (Page 105)

Located in the Rocky Mountains in north-central Colorado, ANF was established on July 1, 1908, by President Theodore Roosevelt, making it one of the oldest national forests. Named for the Indian nation whose people occupied the region, ANF protects 723,744 acres. The topography ranges from the mile-high foothills along the Front Range to snow-covered peaks such as Mount Evans (elevation 14,264 feet) along the Continental Divide west of Denver. There are six Congressionally designated wilderness areas within ANF that are part of the National Wilderness Preservation System. ANF is administered jointly as a field unit with Roosevelt National Forest and Pawnee National Grassland by the U.S. Forest Service, an agency of the U.S. Department of Agriculture.

"Colorado state highway 5 leads virtually to the top of Mount Evans. The idea of driving to the top of a 14,000-foot peak sounded to me like cheating—an unearned and touristy experience—

but all that fell away when I got there. I love being at high altitude and find inspiration in the big views, the sense of space, and thin air."

Badlands National Park (Pages 33 and 35)

Located in southwestern South Dakota, adjacent to the Pine Ridge Indian Reservation and southeast of Rapid City, BNP protects 242,756 acres of sharply eroded canyons, towering spires, flat-topped tables, and currently the largest protected mixed-grass prairie in the United States. Established as a national monument on January 29, 1939, by President Franklin Roosevelt, it was designated a national park by President Jimmy Carter on November 10, 1978. The Badlands contain one of the world's richest fossil beds. Prehistoric mammals such as the oreodonts, three-toed horse, and saber-toothed cat once roamed there. Today, bison, bighorn sheep, and prairie dogs dominate the landscape. Within the BNP is Badlands Wilderness (64,144 acres), which is where the endangered black-footed ferret was re-introduced in 1990. BNP is administered by the National Park Service, an agency of the U.S. Department of the Interior, except for the South Unit, which is managed cooperatively between the NPS and the Tribal Council and Parks and Recreation Authority of the Oglala Lakota Nation.

"When I first explored Badlands National Park in 1985, I was on a journey to begin my first full-time teaching position at the University of Michigan in Ann Arbor. I traveled through the park and came across a herd of bison in the open plains and made this picture. I set up my tripod and camera as close as I dared and made some exposures. When the bison began to march towards me, it was time to go. Back then, the park was small and relatively underdeveloped, and I could wander in the animated badlands without permits and confining regulations. It is an especially good place to visit during the spring, when other public places at higher elevations are still under snow."

Bighorn National Forest (Page 21)

Located in north-central Wyoming, west of Sheridan and Buffalo, BNF protects more than 1,100,000 acres. Created as a U.S. Forest Reserve on February 22, 1897, BNF is one of the oldest government-protected forest lands in the U.S. Named after the Big Horn River, it includes the spine of the Big Horn Mountains (often referred to as the "Big Horns"), an outlying mountain range separated from the rest of the Rocky Mountains by Big Horn Basin. Within BNF is Cloud Peak Wilderness (189,000 acres) and the Medicine Wheel National Historic Landmark. Bighorn sheep, black bear, elk, moose, mule deer, and pronghorn are among the resident large mammals. BNF is administered by the U.S. Forest Service.

"In 2012, I spent fifteen days in Wyoming photographing Nature Conservancy lands with Michael Berman, whom I first met in 1981. He was one of several photographers with whom I traveled and made photographs back before I got married and had kids. We shared our ideas and concerns about photography and the West and through that dialogue developed a lifestyle of picture-making in the great outdoors. After rambling around in the dry, scorching heat of mid-June among the fantastic badlands of the Big Horn Basin, it was refreshing to drive east, up Shell Canyon to the beautiful, higher grounds of Bighorn National Forest. There, the temperature can drop into the lower 40s in the middle of a summer day."

Boulder County Parks and Open Space (Page 146)

The Boulder County (Colorado) Commissioners established a Parks and Open Space Department in 1975. The 1978 Boulder County Comprehensive Plan set out the goals and policies for preserving open space. The county prioritizes the conservation of open space lands for the protection of critical wildlife habitats, protecting farms and ranches, and creating quality recreational experiences. The county currently owns or protects more than 97,000 acres of open space, conserving natural, cultural, and agricultural resources and providing public uses that reflect sound resource management and community values. The Parks and Open Space Department is administered by Boulder County, Colorado.

"The combination of Boulder County and City of Boulder open space and park lands makes living in Boulder so exceptional. Here, people care about preserving the natural environment and are willing to pay for it through taxes. Amusing and serious conflicts are played out in the community's dialogues about such things as accessibility to open space for dogs and mountain bikes and the protection of prairie dogs, mountain lions, and deer. These are good issues around which to clarify a community's thoughts about living in the margins between the domestic and the wild."

Bridger-Teton National Forest (Page 65)

Located in west-central Wyoming, extending from Grand Teton and Yellowstone national parks in the north to Jackson and then the Salt River Range and Commissary Ridge in the south, BTNF protects 3,400,000 acres of forest, making it one of the largest national forests outside Alaska. It includes three designated wilderness areas (Bridger, Gros Ventre, and Teton), the tallest mountain in Wyoming (Gannett Peak at 13,809 feet elevation), and one of the largest, readily visible landslides on Earth (Gros Ventre landslide). Officially established by President Theodore Roosevelt on July 1, 1908, the current forest formed from a 1973 administrative combination of Bridger and Teton national forests, absorbing the Wyoming National Forest (established in 1923) that was previously known as Yellowstone Forest Reserve (1904). John Muir (1838–1914), the famous Scottish-born American naturalist, author, and conservationist, said of this land (*Our National Parks,* Riverside Press, 1901, page

56): "Walk away quietly in any direction and taste the freedom of the mountaineer. Camp out among the grasses and gentians of glacial meadows, in craggy garden nooks full of Nature's darlings. Climb the mountains and get their good tidings, Nature's peace will flow into you as sunshine flows into trees. The winds will blow their own freshness into you and the storms their energy, while cares will drop off like autumn leaves. As age comes on, one source of enjoyment after another is closed, but nature's sources never fail." BTNF is administered by the U.S. Forest Service.

"In 1987, I was in the area exploring Grand Teton and Yellowstone national parks. I was first attracted to make this picture of a Western buck fence because of the way the vegetation created a pattern through it. It was also a good view of Mount Leidy (elevation 10,233 feet) in the Bridger-Teton National Forest. Later, I followed a forest road and trail that led to the peak. In 1871, the Hayden Geological Survey, which included the famous photographer William Henry Jackson (1843–1942), named Mount Leidy in honor of Joseph Leidy (1823–1891), an esteemed scientist at the University of Pennsylvania who made landmark contributions to botany, parasitology, and vertebrate paleontology."

Canyonlands National Park (Pages 13, 37, 62, 63, and 195)

Located in southeastern Utah, southwest of Moab and Arches National Park, CNP protects 337,598 acres of vibrantly colored landscapes shaped by the Green and Colorado rivers and gravity into countless buttes, canyons, and mesas. The first new national park to be approved since 1956, CNP was established on September 12, 1964, by President Lyndon B. Johnson and expanded in 1971 by President Richard Nixon. Official attendance figures have increased from 19,000 to 71,700 by 1975, to 116,672 by 1985, to a record 473,773 in 2011. The Colorado and

Green rivers combine within the park, creating three very different regions: to the north, the Island in the Sky; to the west, the Maze; and, to the east, the Needles. Author-conservationist Edward Abbey (1927–1989) frequented the park and proclaimed Canyonlands as "the most weird, wonderful, magical place on Earth—there is nothing like it anywhere" (*Postcards from Ed: Dispatches and Salvos from an American Iconoclast*, Milkweed Press, 2006, page 175). CNP is administered by the National Park Service.

"One of my first destinations into the Western landscape was to Canyonlands. During the 1970s and 80s, it was considered very remote, and relatively few people visited it. The first time I saw the Great Gallery and the Harvest Panel I was with photographer Steve Fitch, his wife, Lynn, and their six-month-old baby, Luke. Later, on my own, I drove the infamous Elephant Hill to the confluence overlook, Chesler Park, and the Joint Trail. Canyonlands was a place where I could wander in the wondrous red-rock landscapes and explore amazing ancient Pueblo rock art and archeological sites. Today, permits, precise planning, and advance reservations at designated camping sites make it more difficult to experience the freedom and spontaneity of my early visits."

Canyons of the Ancients National Monument (Page 54)

Located in the southwestern corner of Colorado, to the west and northwest of Cortez, Mesa Verde National Park, and Ute Mountain Ute Indian Reservation, CANM was established by President Warren G. Harding on March 2, 1923, to preserve six groups of Pueblo villages that were active for nearly 10,000 years. CANM protects approximately 173,000 acres of incised canyon land, ranging in elevation from 5,000 to 6,700 feet. CANM also surrounds or is adjacent to four units of Hovenweep National Monument in Utah. "Hovenweep" means "deserted valley" in the Ute language, and its ruins were long known to the Ute and Navajo people. CANM was formed when President Bill Clinton signed a presidential proclamation on June 9, 2000, in order to preserve and protect the highest known density of archeological sites in the United States. More than 6,355 distinct structures (c. 750–1350 CE) have been identified among an estimated 20,000 to 30,000 associated with ancestral Pueblo cultures (c. 8000 BCE–1350 CE). CANM is administered by the Bureau of Land Management, an agency of the U.S. Department of the Interior.

"Joe Ben Wheat (1916–1997) started excavating the Yellow Jacket site in 1954, the first of a series of investigations at three Pueblos here that would engage him until 1991. By 1989 I had heard of Joe Ben Wheat and his work, so, when I was traveling through southwestern Colorado on my way to southern Utah, I decided to see if I could find his site. I was only using a Colorado state map, but it had some indication of Yellow Jacket Canyon. It was a brilliantly sunny summer day. Rows of crops receded to a vanishing point, with glorious cumulus clouds in a blue sky. I found the site, and Joe Ben himself was there. He had just excused his graduate students to go to lunch. I asked if I could photograph his site, and he said "yes" with a smile. Before I left, I made his portrait sitting in a recent excavation. The sites reflect all the physical components of past human life: villages, field houses, check dams, reservoirs, great kivas, cliff dwellings, shrines, sacred springs, agricultural fields, petroglyphs, and sweat lodges. Some areas have more than 100 sites per square mile."

Chaco Culture National Historical Park (Pages 19, 51, 52, 53, and 57)

Located on the Colorado Plateau in northwestern New Mexico, to the west of the Continental Divide near Pueblo Pintado and Star Lake, CCNHP protects 33,998 acres in a remote, alluvial canyon bisected by Chaco Wash and surrounded by the dense forests of the Chuska, San Juan, and San Pedro mountains to the west, north, and east. CCNHP hosts one of the most exceptional and densest concentrations of ancestral Pueblo ruins (900–1,150 CE) north of Mexico; thus, it is considered one of the most important pre-Columbian cultural and historical areas in the United States. The site was designated a national monument on March 1, 1907, by President Theodore Roosevelt, was listed on the U.S. Register of Historical Places on October 15, 1966, became a national historical park on December 19, 1980, and, in 1987, became a UNESCO World Heritage Site. CCNHP is administered by the National Park Service.

"Chaco Canyon is one of my favorite places. Although the roads to the park have changed slightly for the better, their condition still limits the type of vehicles that can access the park, including large RVs. Inside the park, facilities are also limited, and the small, primitive campground makes for an intimate experience. Chaco contains some of my favorite hikes, including Pueblo Alto Trail, which provides amazing views of the great houses at Pueblo Bonito and elsewhere and the canyon below."

City of Boulder Open Space and Mountain Parks (Page 4)

In 1967, Boulder, Colorado, became the first city in the nation to pass a sales tax of four-tenths of a cent for the acquisition and management of open-space lands. An additional three-tenths of a cent was approved by voters in 1989 and another fifteen-hundredth of a cent in 2003. As of 2012, approximately $200,000,000 has been raised and spent to acquire, preserve, and protect more than 45,000 acres of open space. City of Boulder OSMP lands form a buffer around the city, help shape the urban mosaic of Boulder Valley, and provide citizens with recreational opportunities. Wildlife habitat, unique geologic features, greenways, and 144 miles of trails are all part of Boulder's OSMP, which receives an average of 4,700,000 visits a year, compared to nearby Rocky Mountain National Park, whose all-time attendance record was 3,380,044 in 2000. City of Boulder OSMP is administered by the City of Boulder, Colorado.

"Within view of this photograph are City of Boulder Open Space and Mountain Park lands. The land before Boulder Reservoir, in the upper left, and the land to the right of the lake are part of the city's greenbelt and contain great hiking and bicycle trails. The Front Range in the upper right-center including the iconic Flatirons, are part of City of Boulder Mountain Parks. The city itself, almost indiscernible, is in a slight valley directly before the four Flatiron formations."

Coconino National Forest (Page 39)

Located on the Mogollon Plateau in north-central Arizona, from Flagstaff in the north to Payson in the south, CNF protects 1,821,495 acres. It was created on July 2, 1908, when President Theodore Roosevelt consolidated all of the San Francisco Mountains National Forest, parts of the Black Mesa and Tonto national forests, and the Grand Canyon National Forest south and east of the Colorado River. It also boasts the orange-red rocks of Sedona that seem to glow in the light of the early morning and late afternoon sun. Given its wide range of elevation (nearly 10,000 feet), CNF is one of the most biologically diverse national forests in the nation, featuring ponderosa pine forests and alpine tundra peaks such as Humphreys Peak, sacred to thirteen Indian nations, which, at an elevation of 12,633 feet is the highest natural point in Arizona. The second-, third-, and forth-highest peaks (Agassiz at 12,356 feet, Fremont at 11,969 feet, and Aubineau at 11,817 feet) are nearby. CNF is administered by the U.S. Forest Service.

"Michael Berman, my long-time photographer buddy, first showed me Strawberry Crater, a red volcanic cider cone with the ancient ring of stones. During another visit with photographer Scott Engel, I made this photograph. I later returned with my family when the children were young. We ran down the cinder slopes, laughing as our feet sank into the cinders, and slid down the hillside. Good memories."

Comb Ridge (Page 45)

Comb Ridge is a distinctive 120-mile-long and one-mile-wide sandstone monocline that trends north to south from southeastern Utah, near Bluff, to northwestern Arizona, near Kayenta, of which sixty-five miles are part of the Navajo Nation. Nearby Monument Valley, sacred to the Diné (the Navajo people), was made famous by Hollywood, from many John Ford films, such as *Stage Coach* (1939), to other classics, among them *2001: A Space Odyssey* (1968), *Easy Rider* (1969)*, and Forrest Gump* (1994). Comb Wash and Butler Wash, tributaries of the San Juan River, include various cliff dwellings built and occupied by the ancestral Pueblo people, among them Butler Wash Ruin, Monarch Cave Ruin, and House on Fire Ruin. Vegetation is typical of the semi-arid Great Basin desert, though at least seven known species of noxious weeds and plants have invaded the watershed. CR is administered by the Bureau of Land Management.

"I have hiked into and on top of Comb Ridge numerous times. There are old Pueblo ruins, cliff dwellings, and rock art sites within the Comb Ridge area, including the complex Procession Panel petroglyph. I enjoy walking up the incline of the sandstone formation from the east to the top and then along the edge, where it drops steeply to the west."

Coronado National Forest (Pages 2*,* 102, and 103)

Located in the southeastern corner of Arizona, northeast of Douglas, and the boot corner of southwestern New Mexico, south of Lordsburg, CNF protects 1,780,000 million acres, ranging in elevation from 3,000 to 10,720 feet. CNF's origins can be traced to 1902, when four forest reserves were proclaimed: Chiricahua, Mount Graham, Santa Catalina, and Santa Rosa. CNF was officially formed on July 1, 1908, and today contains eight designated wilderness areas. The forest was named for Francisco Vásquez de Coronado (1510–1554), the Spanish explorer whose contigent, in 1540, came upon Zuñi and Hopi villages in the search for the mythical Seven Cities of Gold. The twelve widely scattered mountain ranges or "sky islands" of CNF rise dramatically from the desert floor, supporting communities as biologically diverse as those encountered on a trip from Mexico to western Canada. CNF is administered by the U.S. Forest Service.

"The trip to Coronado National Forest marked a change in my life, for I had gotten married the year before and started a family. But I was still photographing the West with Michael Berman, who had recently moved to southern New Mexico and wanted to show me some of the places he was exploring. CNF is one of them. Since then, Michael has created spectacular photographs in the deserts and grasslands along the U.S.-Mexico border from his home in Silver City."

Crater Lake National Park (Page 129)

Located in southwestern Oregon in the Cascade Range, CLNP is America's fifth-oldest national park, protecting 183,225 acres. It is also the only national park in Oregon. Historically, the Klamath, Molala, and Takelma peoples used Crater Lake as a spiritual retreat. When William Gladstone Steel (1854–1934), of Portland, saw Crater Lake for the first time in 1885, the water was so blue it startled him: "All ingenuity of nature seems to have been exerted to the fullest capacity to build a grand, awe-inspiring temple the likes of which the world has never seen before" (*The Mountains of Oregon*, self-published, 1892, page 33). He subsequently devoted his life to establishing the lake as a national park. President Theodore Roosevelt signed the law that created the park on May 22, 1902. The lake's maximum depth is 1,943 feet, the nation's deepest, North America's second-deepest, and the world's ninth-deepest lake. About 7,700 years ago, Mount Mazama (elevation ca. 12,000 feet) violently erupted and collapsed, creating the current caldera whose rim is between 7,000 and 8,000 feet elevation. With no streams flowing into it, Crater Lake is considered to be the world's cleanest and clearest large body of water. The lake had no fish until they were introduced by humans in 1888. CLNP is administered by the National Park Service.

"The light was glorious when I visited Crater Lake National Park in August 2011. My mode of seeing a place is often to hike to the highest terrain around—in this case to Mount Scott (elevation 8,934 feet), the highest point in the park—and then to have a look at the landscape. From this vantage I can see the shape of the earth, the uplifts and drainage patterns and the associated vegetation; from there I can gain an enhanced perception of time."

Crow Canyon Archeological District (Page 61)

CCAD is a historic site located in the heart of Dinétah, the traditional homeland of the Diné (the Navajo people) in northwestern New Mexico, about twenty-three miles southeast of Bloomfield. The site was added to the U.S. Register of Historic Places on July 15, 1974. The site contains extensive and well-known pueblitos (small above-ground structures used for shelter and cooking and for defense against raiding bands of Utes), rock art, and petroglyphs from the sixteenth to eighteenth centuries, including several large panels. CCAD is administered by the Bureau of Land Management.

"Photographer Michael Berman and I explored this area after we heard that Rick Dingus, our friend and fellow photographer, was working there. Crow Canyon is about twenty miles northeast of Chaco Canyon and is said to be the place of origin for the Diné (the Navajo people). There are impressive rock art sites and pueblito ruins on top of giant boulders at this special place."

Death Valley National Park (Page 123)

Located in southeastern California west of the Sierra Nevada, part of the Mojave Desert in California, and bordering the Amargosa Desert (also part of the Mojave) in Nevada, DVNP protects 3,396,192 acres of desert biodiversity, of which all but nine percent is a designed wilderness area. President Herbert Hoover established Death Valley National Monument on February 11, 1933; the area was closed to mining in 1976 and then expanded and designated a national park on October 31, 1994, under the leadership of President Bill Clinton. Death Valley is the the hottest and driest place in North America, due to its low relief (elevation -286 feet) and lack of surface water and other climactic conditions. A record 134° Fahrenheit was measured here on July 10, 1913, the highest official temperature ever recorded in the world. Daily summer temperatures of 120° Fahrenheit or greater are common, as are near-freezing nightly temperatures during winter. DVNP is administered by the National Park Service.

"I stopped in Death Valley National Park on my way to my sister's home in Santa Cruz, for Thanksgiving with a new girlfriend who is now my wife of almost twenty years. We explored some of the remote and desolate landscapes that Edward Weston (1886–1958) had photographed in 1938 and 1939. Death Valley is unlike any other place, but, like any other place, one can invest a lifetime exploring its landscapes and making meaningful photographs."

Dinosaur National Monument (Pages 46, 47, and 49)

Located in the northwestern corner of Colorado and extending into northeastern Utah, this is the place where the Green and Yampa rivers converge. The site was declared by President Woodrow Wilson an eighty-acre national monument on October 4, 1915, to preserve its outstanding fossils of dinosaurs. The boundaries were expanded in 1938 to include the scenic canyon areas of the Green and Yampa rivers. Today, DNM protects 210,844 acres and holds a special place in U.S. environmental history, because of the intense opposition (led by David Brower, of the Sierra Club, and Howard Zahniser, of the Wilderness Society) during the early 1950s to a proposed dam (by the U.S. Bureau of Reclamation) at Echo Park in the middle of the monument. Although dams were built elsewhere in the West, Echo Park Dam was eliminated when President Dwight D. Eisenhower signed the Colorado River Storage Project Act on April 11, 1956, which states, "that no dam or reservoir constructed under the authorization of the Act shall be within any National Park or Monument." Several sites within DNM are listed on the U.S. Register of Historic Places. DNM is administered by the National Park Service.

"Dinosaur National Monument is a good place to go when the weather is still too cold and snowy in other public locations. There are amazing petroglyphs on the north side of the park, but my favorite place is Bobby's Hole in Echo Park, down by the confluence of the Green and Yampa rivers. I love to hike along the cliffs and look down to the river valleys below."

El Morro National Monument (Page 194)

Located on an historic east-west trail between Pinehill and El Morro on the Ramah Navajo Indian Reservation in west-central New Mexico, EMNM protects 1,278 acres, featuring a prominent sandstone cuesta (mesa) with a pool of water at its base. As many as 1,000 people lived in two large pueblos on top of the mesa (c. 1275–1350 CE), and the ruins are accessible by the Headland Trail. This site has seen many centuries of travelers, some who carved their inscriptions into the rock. The Zuñi people to the west call it *A'ts'ina* (Where pictures are on the rock), the Spanish explorers called it *El Morro* (The Headland), and, after the Spanish Colonial period, Europeans and Americans called it *Inscription Rock*. To preserve the historical importance of the area and to initiate preservation of the old inscriptions, El Morro was established as a national monument by President Theodore Roosevelt on December 8, 1906, and further carving was prevented. EMNM is administered by the National Park Service.

"About fifty miles east of El Morro is Acoma Pueblo on top of a prominent mesa—Sky City—and in between the two places is the El Malpais National Monument volcanic area. By the time I visited El Morro, I had seen a lot of petroglyphs and pictographs and read a bit of the history of the Southwest. Looking at the inscriptions on the rock, I imagined a long trail of travelers—prehistoric, native, and European—who had stopped here at the spring in the desert."

Glacier National Park (Pages 74 and 75)

Located in northwestern Montana, northwest of Kalispell and bordering Canada on the north and the Blackfeet Indian Reservation on the east, GNP protects 1,013,322 million acres. The Great Northern Railway, in a concerted effort to stimulate use of its railway by extolling the natural wonders of the region, lobbied the U.S. Congress for preservation status, and, in 1897, the area was designated a forest preserve. On May 11, 1910, President William Howard Taft re-designated the preserve a national park. GNP shares a border with Waterton Lakes National Park in neighboring Alberta and British Columbia, and together they were designated as the world's first International Peace Park in 1932. The Waterton-Glacier, as it is known, was then designated by the United Nations as a Biosphere Reserve in 1976 and in 1995 as a World Heritage site. This vast, pristine ecosystem is a key component of the Crown of the Continent Ecosystem that encompasses approximately 28,000 acres. Unfortunately, due to a warming Earth, only twenty-five of GNP's original 150 glaciers remain active. The Going-to-the-Sun Road to a high glacier, completed in 1932, is a National Historic Civic Engineering Landmark. GNP is administered by the National Park Service.

"I recall the intense, turquoise-blue water in the streams, the big sky views, and the wonder of grizzly bears in Glacier National Park. The presence of bears, especially grizzly bears, changes my experience of the landscape. One can carry bear spray, but my using it successfully as a viable defense against a humongous wild animal that perceives me as either food or as a threat to their livelihood seems doubtful. There are other ways to die in the back country—falling or becoming stranded due to a sudden storm, for example—but the violence of a bear attack is different. Bears were the top predators of the environment before we humans showed up, and who can blame them for a fight against their loss of dominance?"

Grand Canyon National Park (Page 41)

Located in northwestern Arizona, GCNP protects 1,217,262 acres of one of the most spectacular natural wonders of the world: the Grand Canyon, which was formed by the rushing waters of the Colorado River. First established as a forest reserve in 1893 and later proclaimed a national monument by President Theodore Roosevelt in 1908, President Woodrow Wilson designated the Grand Canyon as the nation's fifteenth national park on February 16, 1919. In 1979, UNESCO declared GCNP a World Heritage Site. In addition to its beauty, the Grand Canyon is one of the most studied geological landscapes on Earth, for it reveals the geological history of the past 2,000,000,000 years. Its scale and moods make it a truly amazing place. When President Theodore Roosevelt visited the site, he declared ("At Grand Canyon, Arizona," May 6, 1903, Presidential Addresses and State Papers 1, page 370): "In the Grand Canyon, Arizona has a natural wonder which, so far as I know, is in kind absolutely unparalleled throughout the rest of the world. I want to ask you to do one thing in connection with it in your own interest and in the interest of the country—to keep this great wonder of nature as it now is. I hope you will not have a building of any kind to mar the wonderful grandeur, the sublimity, the great loneliness and beauty of the canyon. Leave it as it is. You can not improve on it. The ages have been at work on it, and man can only mar it. What you can do is to keep it for your children, your children's children, and for all who come after you, as one of the great sights which every American if (he can travel at all) should see. We have gotten past the stage, my fellow-citizens, when we are to be pardoned if we treat any part of our country as something to be skinned for two or three years for the use of the present generation, whether it is the forest, the water, the scenery. Whatever it is, handle it so that your children's children will get the benefit of it." GCNP was the second most visited national park in 2011 (4,298,178 visitors) and is administered by the National Park Service.

"I made this picture of a viewpoint during an extended motorcycle trip through the West in 1979, which took me to Yellowstone, Washington state, and then down the Pacific coast and east to Arizona. It is well worth the effort to visit the North Rim to lose most of the crowds. At the North Rim there is a classic log lodge and cabins from which a primitive road follows the North Rim to many remote viewpoints with no guard rails, although a herd of four-wheelers may show up at exactly sunset, only to be gone in a rumble of dust after toasting the beauty of the colors of the sky."

Grand Staircase-Escalante National Monument (Page 135)

Located in one of the least-populated areas of the United States in south-central Utah, bordered by Bryce Canyon National Park to the west, Capital Reef National Park to the north, and Glen Canyon National Recreation Area to the east and south, GSENM protects 1,820,800 acres. It was established on September 18, 1996, by President Bill Clinton and encompasses the largest land area of all U.S. national monuments, including the Wolverine Petrified Forest, one of North America's largest and oldest fossil forests. Broad terraces, various pinnacles, and dramatic Technicolor cliffs—white, vermilion, gray, and pink—together create one of the most revered natural areas in the West, where escarpments expose 200,000,000 years of Earth's geologic history. Buckskin Gulch, considered the longest slot canyon in the world, is located here. GSENM is the first national monument to be administered by the Bureau of Land Management.

"The Grand Staircase-Escalante National Monument is almost six times the size of Canyonlands National Park and contains much to explore from various access points. I have only scratched the surface with hikes down to the Escalante River and in Wolverine Petrified Forest."

Great Basin National Park (Page 131)

Located in east-central Nevada, adjacent to the Humboldt-Toiyabe National Forest near the Utah border, GBNP protects 77,180 acres of desert mountain land and numerous limestone caverns, including Lehman Caves (elevation 6,825 feet) at the base of Wheeler Peak (elevation 13,063 feet). President Warren G. Harding proclaimed Lehman Caves a national monument on January 24, 1922, which became part of Great Basin National Park on October 27, 1986, when signed into law by President Ronald Reagan, in order to preserve a representative sample of the physiographic (basin and range) Great Basin. Shoshone and Painte peoples have lived in the area since c. 1300 CE. The park's name comes from the uncommon reality that the streams and rivers of this region do not drain into the sea. Although the park's rainfall and snowpack are dependent on elevation, eleven species of trees (including old groves of bristlecone pines), more than 800 species of plants, 238 species of birds, sixty-one species of mammals, eighteen species of reptiles, two species of amphibians, and eight species of fish can be found here. GBNP is administered by the National Park Service.

"Great Basin National Park is one of a series of long, island-like mountain ranges where the ecology shifts dramatically as altitude increases from the basins below at an elevation of 5,000 feet to the deep forests and glacial lakes of the high country of the South Snake Range, where thirteen peaks exceed 11,000 feet in elevation. Thus, the park supports an impressive diversity of species, from those adapted to the desert to the forest and alpine environments."

Great Sand Dunes National Park and Preserve (Pages 85 and 87)

Located in the San Luis Valley of south-central Colorado, one of the largest high-desert valleys of the world on the western base of the Sangre de Cristo Range, GSDNPP protects 84,997 acres and contains six peaks more than 13,000 feet in elevation. The valley contains archeological sites that are 11,000 years old. More recently, it was home to the Ute people and later was a province of Nuevo Mexico before it was ceded to the United States in 1848. President Herbert Hoover proclaimed the dune-field a national monument on March 17, 1932, and it was expanded when the U.S. Congress made it a national park on September 13, 2004. The 750-foot-high dunes evolved over time, as westerly winds picked up sand particles from the nearby Rio Grande and its floodplain and deposited them at the base of the mountains. The dunes continue to grow, albeit slowly, according to geological time. GSDNPR is administered by the National Park Service.

"The first time I visited the dunes there was nothing but a small campground on the side of the road. Now it is difficult to get a camping site without a reservation. Still, it is an incredible place. When our children were young, we would go to the park every spring to play in the dunes and Medano Creek ("Medana" is Spanish for "sand dune"), which surges out of the Sange de Cristo Mountains along the edge of the dunes and pulses like the waves of the ocean. It is a beach scene with all kinds of colorfully dressed people, young and old, lined up and along the river in folding chairs with coolers, sun tents, barbecues, volley ball nets, flying Frisbees and kites, making sand castles, and running dogs chasing their sticks. Higher up in the dunes, visitors attempt to ride sled-saucers down the sandy slopes."

Hart Mountain National Antelope Refuge (Pages 69 and 117)

Located in sparsely populated south-central Oregon, northeast of Adel and east of Warner Valley and its beautiful lakes and wetlands, NMNAR protects 270,966 acres. Bighorn sheep (reintroduced in 1954 from British Columbia stock), mule deer, and pronghorn are among the 300 species of wildlife and 239 species of birds in this sprawling refuge. Franklin D. Roosevelt established the refuge on December 21, 1936, to conserve range for remnant herds of pronghorn. The refuge was named for Hart Mountain, a massive fault-block ridge that rises to an elevation of 8,065 feet. HMNAR is administered by the U.S. Fish and Wildlife Service, an agency of the U.S. Department of the Interior.

"After a wonderful day of hiking in the refuge, I soaked in a beautiful hot spring adjacent to the campground area. The roadway at the eastern entrance to the refuge switchbacks up a high cliff, providing sweeping views of Hart Lake reservoir below. Within the refuge, I hiked up Warner Peak (elevation 8,017 feet). Somewhat nearby and to the northeast is Steens Mountain National Conservation Area, also worth exploring."

Humboldt-Toiyabe National Forest (Pages 125, 126, 127, and 139)

Located in non-contiguous segments throughout northern Nevada and along the Nevada-California border, HTNF protects more than 6,300,000 acres, making it the largest national forest outside of Alaska. An estimated 80,000 to 100,000 prehistoric and historic sites and twenty-three designated wilderness areas exist within the various forest boundaries that range in elevation from 4,600 to 12,067 feet. Toiyabe was established in March 2, 1907, and Humboldt on July 1, 1908. Explorer John C. Frémont (1813–1890) named the East Humboldt Mountain Range and Humboldt River after German naturalist Baron Alexander von Humboldt (1769–1859). "Toiyabe" is a Shoshone word meaning "mountain." The area is home to one of the largest mule deer herds in Nevada and healthy populations of bighorn sheep, Himalayan snowcock, and mountain goats. Streams and lakes support brook, rainbow, and the threatened Lahontan cutthroat trout. The Mount Moriah Wilderness (89,790 acres), designated on December 5, 1989, is part of HTNF, which is administered by the U.S. Forest Service.

"In early August 2011, I walked in snow every day I climbed the peaks of the Humboldt-Toiyabe National Forest. Northern Nevada is a land of basin and range. There are dramatic views from one mountain ridge across basins to other ranges. The basins can be hot and infested with insects, and the ranges are rugged and remote."

Little Book Cliffs Wild Horse Range (Page 99)

One of only three ranges in the United States set aside specifically to protect wild and free-roaming horses, LBCWHR encompasses 36,113 acres of rugged canyons and plateaus in the Book Cliffs, about eight miles northeast of Grand Junction, Colorado. LBCWHR was established by the Wild and Free-Roaming Horse and Burro Act of 1971, signed by President Richard Nixon, which provided for the protection of wild horses on BLM land. Here, wild horses roam the sagebrush and piñon-juniper-covered hills, and natural barriers such as cliffs and canyons are supplemented with fencing to define the area and control the horses' movement. Horses graze the higher range during the spring, summer, and fall and return to lower country in winter, where there is less snow and more plentiful food. LBCWHR is administered by the Bureau of Land Management.

"In the West, the experience of driving a major interstate highway can be astounding. The highways wind through the landscape along a river or over a mountain pass. The shape of the earth is revealed in bright, clear light, layers of time and geology are exposed in a road cut, and the creations of human beings—towns, rows of crops, mines, fences roadways—are fitted within the layers and folds of the topography. "

Lolo National Forest (Page 95)

Located in west-central Montana, LNF borders eight other national forests in Montana and Idaho and lies at the doorstep of both large and small Montana communities, including Missoula, Seeley Lake, and Superior. The forest's western boundary is also the crest of the northern portion of the Bitterroot Mountains, while other districts stretch east into the Bob Marshall Wilderness (1,009,356 acres) and Swan Mountains and northwest toward the boundary with Idaho's Panhandle National Forest. The mixture of continental and some maritime climates produces diverse ecosystems here. LNF protects 2,197,966 acres of forested ridges, rolling meadows, and rivers and streams that offer some of the best fishing in the Rocky Mountains. Grizzly and black bear, mountain goats and bighorn sheep, elk and lynx, moose and mule deer, bald and golden eagles, trumpeter swans and more than a dozen varieties of other waterfowl thrive here. LNF was created on September 20, 1906, from four different previous forests and was combined for administrative purposes. It was later expanded in 1931, 1934, and 1954. "Lolo" is believed to be a shortened version of "Lou-Lou" after a French-Canadian fur trapper killed by a grizzly bear and buried at Graves Creek. The Lewis and Clark Expedition and Nez Perce Indians used the historic Lolo Trail, and, today, visitors may walk the same path. LNF is administered by the U.S. Forest Service.

"I made the picture of the sawmill on a long trip in 1987. For twenty-four years I believed the location of the mill was in Idaho. Through the process of attempting to confirm the location of the picture, I contacted every national forest office in Idaho. No one could locate the mill. Then Spencer Paddock, nephew of curator Eric Paddock, recognized the mill from the highway in Montana while returning from a fire-fighting job. He re-photographed it, thereby identifying and determining the precise location of the picture."

Samuel R. McKelvie National Forest (Page 29)

Located in the Sandhills (also spelled Sand Hills) of north-central Nebraska, southwest of Valentine between the scenic Niobrara and Snake rivers, SMNF protects 116,079 acres of prairie grasslands and approximately 2,200 acres of trees, the largest human-made forest in the United States, featuring islands of eastern red cedar, Scottish pine, and ponderosa pine. The Nebraska National Forest began in 1902 as an experiment when Dr. Charles E. Bessey, a professor of botany at the University of Nebraska who believed an Indian legend that the Sandhills were once covered in trees, convinced President Theodore Roosevelt to set aside, on April 16, 1902, two treeless tracts of Nebraska's Sandhills as "forest reserves" (the Dismal River and Niobrara River forest reserves) due to worries of a national timber shortage. After passage, Bessey himself proceeded to plant the seedlings, an unbelievably arduous task. The Sandhills—the world's fourth-largest vegetated dune region at nearly 20,000 square miles whose native grasses are also among the world's highest in protein—never became a timber-producing plantation forest, but the Charles E. Bessey Tree Nursery, the nation's oldest federal tree nursery located about one mile west of Halsey, still produces 2,500,000 to 3,000,000 tree seedlings per year for distribution to other national forests and state and tribal agencies in the western U.S. Officially created on October 15, 1971, the forest is named for Samuel Roy McKelvie (1881–1956), the nineteenth Governor of Nebraska who helped break ground for the Nebraska State Capital in Lincoln. SRMNF is administered by the U.S. Forest Service.

"In 1989, I explored several of Nebraska's national forests, including the Bessie Ranger District and the McKelvie National Forest, both of which consist entirely of trees planted in rows, with a few picnic tables scattered about beneath the welcoming shade. When I reached McKelvie National Forest, the sun was setting. Being accustomed to Colorado's national forests, I drove out into the grasslands and camped as it got dark. The next day, the sun rose, and I made this picture."

Mount St. Helens National Volcanic Monument (Page 121)

Located in southwestern Washington state, MSHNVM protects 110,000 acres of land, much of it left to respond naturally to the dramatic volcanic eruption and collapse of Mount St. Helens on May 18, 1980. MSHNVM was established by President Ronald Reagan within the Gifford Pinchot National Forest on August 27, 1982, to provide for scientific research, recreation, and education. The slopes of Mount St. Helens (elevation 8,363 feet after the eruption and 9,677 feet before the eruption) are a unique ash-laden home to a diverse population of plants and animals. Windy Ridge is the closest viewpoint where visitors may see firsthand not only the evidence of a volcano's destruction, but also the remarkable but gradual recovery of the land as re-vegetation proceeds and fish and wildlife return. MSHNVM is one of seven national monuments to be administered by the U.S. Forest Service.

"In 1987, I was following the Columbia River from its origins to the Pacific Ocean. One of the side trips during this journey was to Mount St. Helens to see the volcano. This was seven years after the eruption, and the land was stark, raw, and devastated. The remains of burnt trees appeared as sticks or like matted stubble on the mountainsides. The immense scale and utter otherness of the volcanic landscape expanded my perception of the meaning of nature, which can be violent and destructive."

National Bison Range (Page 67)

Located within the Flathead Indian Reservation in northwestern Montana, north of Missoula between the towns of Dixon, Moiese, and Ravalli, NBR protects approximately 18,700 acres. NVR was established in 1908 by Theodore Roosevelt, making it one of the nation's oldest wildlife refuges. As its name implies, the refuge was created to re-establish and protect a small population of American bison, which, by 1890, were nearly extinct. The bison population today ranges from 350 to 500. Other wildlife found in the refuge include bighorn sheep, black bear, mule and white-tail deer, pronghorn, and more than 200 species of birds. The initial herd of American bison was mainly provided by the American Bison Society, and today the refuge serves as the central point for bison research in the United States. The NBR is administered by the U.S. Fish and Wildlife Service.

"The refuge contains one of my favorite drives with great views and rolling grasslands in the foreground. The day I was there the light was beautiful, and I spent the day driving through rolling hills of grass. I made this picture from the roof of my truck."

Organ Pipe Cactus National Monument (Pages 8, 109, 111, 112, and 113)

Located in southwestern Arizona, bordering the Mexican state of Sonora south of Ajo and Why and sharing its eastern boundary with the Tohono O'odham Indian Reservation, OPCNM protects 330,689 acres. It was established on April 13, 1937, by President Franklin D. Roosevelt as a way to preserve a representative area of the spectacular Sonoran Desert of Mexico and the United States. It is the only place in the U.S. where the *Stenocerus thurberi* (organ pipe cactus) grows wild. The land for OPCNM was donated by the Arizona state legislature to the federal government. In 1976, the United Nations designated OPCNM as an International Biosphere Reserve, and, in 1977, Congress declared that ninety-five percent of the land would become a designated wilderness area. Today, the impacts to the park's resources from drug smuggling from Mexico is a serious issue in the everyday management of the monument. OPCNM is administered by the National Park Service.

"Organ Pipe National Monument is one of my favorite desert landscapes. It is a promising example of how the land and vegetation can blossom and grow once cows are removed. It is also a place where I felt lost and believed I might have to spend the night in the desert in nothing but my t-shirt and pants. Photographer Michael Berman and I had hiked east along a dry riverbed from Bates Well in the remote northwestern section of the park. After a few miles we separated to photograph. I climbed a hill and watched the sunlight retreat across the long Valley of the Ajo. On my way back to the truck, it became totally dark, and I did not know where to cut north out of the riverbed and up to where we had parked. I took a last look back to the west and saw a light that I imagined was the interior dome light in the truck. I bee-lined across the desert toward the light. When I arrived at our camp, I found Michael was perched some twenty-five feet up in the air on top of an old windmill with a lantern to guide me back. I thanked him profusely."

Owyhee River Wilderness (Page 71)

Located in the remote and largely unpopulated southwestern corner of Idaho, ORW stretches from the Oregon-Idaho border in the west and Nevada-Idaho border in the south to the Duck Valley Indian Reservation in the east. Traditionally, the watershed is part of a region inhabited by the Bannock and Shoshone people. The river was named in honor of three Hawaiians, who, as part of Donald MacKenzie's Snake River Expeditions of 1819–1820, were sent to trap the uncharted river but never returned. "Owyhee" was the standard spelling of "Hawaii" at the time. The Owyhee River is classified as a "wild river" and is known for its very challenging whitewater. ORW protects 276,328 acres of the upper Owyhee River, its tributary rivers and creeks, and the surrounding high-desert plateau and deeply eroded canyon landscapes. It is a land with few trails, and direct access is difficult. It is the second-largest U.S. wilderness area that is not a national forest, national park, or national refuge. ORW was established by the Omnibus Public Land Management Act, signed into law on March, 30, 2009, by President Barack Obama. This act protected 2,000,000 acres of land in nine states, added ten new national heritage areas and other provisions for conservation, research, and preservation.

QNW is administered by the Bureau of Land Management.

"I had heard about the Owyhee from reading several articles that described it as a beautiful place worthy of preservation. So, on a family trip north to Montana, we decided to check it out. The West is big and full of beautiful places. Some are wild, and some are cared for; some are being protected, and many are overlooked and degraded. Our nation's way has been largely to protect the sensational and overlook the subtle, but the bottomlands and grasslands are often the biologically most interesting and productive part of the topography."

Petrified Forest National Park (Page 137)

Located in northeastern Arizona, to the east of Holbrook near the edge of the Colorado Plateau, PFNP protects 221,621 acres of intact native grassland, of which 50,260 acres are in a designated wilderness area. The Navajo Indian Reservation borders the park to the north, and the Painted Desert section of the park derives its name from the highly eroded and brightly colored badlands. Named for its large deposits of petrified wood, this site was set aside as a national monument in 1906 by President Theodore Roosevelt to preserve and protect the petrified wood for its scientific and aesthetic value. It was declared a national park in 1962 by President John F. Kennedy. PFNP is rich in petrified logs, fossils of more than 200 different plants, animal fossils from invertebrates to great reptiles, and hundreds of living plants and animals, including ten species of bats. Human settlement commenced here around 8,000 years ago, and more than 600 archeological sites have been identified within the park. PFNP is administered by the National Park Service.

"Since Petrified Forest is located adjacent to Interstate 40 and historic Route 66, I almost always take the time to tour the park when traveling here. The animated landscape of colorful, eroding hills embedded with petrified logs expresses time in a fantastic way."

Rio Grande National Forest (Page 85)

Located in south-central Colorado, with the San Juan Mountains on the western boundary, the Sangre de Christo Mountains on the eastern boundary, and the New Mexico border on the south, RGNF was established on July 1, 1908, by President Theodore Roosevelt. Named for the Rio Grande (Rió Grande del Norte) that courses its way south through the southern San Luis Valley, one of the region's main suppliers of barley for beer, RGNF protects 1,820,000 acres of alpine valley, high deserts, and mountains, of which approximately thirty-one percent is covered in spruce-fir forests. There are four designated wilderness areas within RGNF. Unfortunately, like many areas of the West from here to Montana, RGNF is experiencing a severe infestation of the spruce beetle (*Dendroctonus rufipennis*), which kills all spruce trees larger than five inches in diameter, turning the forest's color from dark green to yellow-orange and rust-reds. RGNF is administered by the U.S. Forest Service.

"Several times I have followed the Rio Grande through Rio Grande National Forest, past reservoirs and recreation areas, and then up four-wheel drive roads to the river's source on the east side of the Continental Divide, near Crede. The "great river of the north," made famous in the writings of Paul Horgan (1903–1995), begins as a snowfield."

Rocky Mountain National Park (Pages 15 and 79)

Located in north-central Colorado, to the northwest of Boulder and Denver, RMNP protects 265,761 acres. Known for its incredible mountain views, RMNP also displays grasslands at lower elevations, ponderosa pine and Douglas-fir at mid-latitude, sub-alpine forests above 9,000 feet, and alpine tundra above the tree line at 11,500 feet. It also includes the Continental Divide and the headwaters of the Colorado River. President Woodrow Wilson signed the Rocky Mountain National Park Act on January 26, 1915, focusing on the park's scenic wonders, including more than sixty mountain peaks higher than 12,000 feet in elevation. The park is surrounded by Roosevelt National Forest on the north and east, Routt National Forest on the northwest, and Arapaho National Forest on the southwest. Due to its proximity to a sprawling mini-megalopolis parallel to the Rocky Mountains, from Fort Collins in the north to Pueblo in the south and Denver in the center, RMNP is among the most visited national parks in the nation, ranking fifth in 2011 (3,176,941 visitors). RMNP is administered by the National Park Service.

"The view of Mount Meeker (elevation 13,911 feet) from Mount Lady Washington (elevation 13,281 feet) is a detour from the trail to Long's Peak (elevation 14,255 feet). After the infamous Boulder Field, hikers pass through the Keyhole to the steep north side of the mountain on the way to the peak. I have climbed to Long's Peak several times, starting up the trail at 3:00 or 4:00 a.m. in the dark and sometimes running down amid thunder and lightning. I love the physical exhilaration of being up a 14,000-foot peak, the thin crisp air, and the thrill of being on the top spine of the continent."

Roosevelt National Forest (Pages 11, 101, and 107)

Located in north-central Colorado, RNF protects 813,799 acres of foothills on the eastern side of the Front Range, the upper valleys of Cache la Poudre and Big Thompson rivers, forested areas, and glacial terrain. Today's RNF, which abuts Arapahoe and Routt national forests as well as Rocky Mountain National Park to the west of Fort Collins and Boulder, began in 1897 as part of Medicine Bow Forest Reserve, was renamed the Colorado National Forest in 1910, and renamed again in 1932 to honor President Theodore Roosevelt. There are six designated wilderness areas within RNF. On July 31, 1976, ten to fourteen inches of rain created an intense flash flood approximately twenty feet high that rushed through the canyon of the Big Thompson River, killing 143 people in Colorado's worst natural disaster. The steep narrows literally collapsed and fell apart under the pressure of a discharge estimated to be 35,000 cubic feet per second. Contiguous with Colorado State Forest and Arapaho National Forest, the area is called "ARP" (Arapaho, Roosevelt, Pawnee) and is administered by the U.S. Forest Service.

"I made this picture of the narrows of the Big Thompson River eleven years after the historic flood. In Boulder, I chose to live within Roosevelt National Forest on an old mining claim along the Colorado Front Range at 7,500 feet elevation with a large, south-facing meadow. North Boulder Creek runs about a third of a mile from my home. I worked for thirteen years to protect North Boulder Creek from a proposed City of Boulder construction project to build a new water pipeline along and through the creek. The eight-mile pipeline would have involved a trench eight feet deep and sixteen feet wide and a construction easement sixty feet wide along the stream in which all vegetation would have been removed. Eventually, through the efforts of many concerned individuals, the city was convinced to build the new pipeline along Sugar Loaf Road."

Saddle Mountain National Wildlife Refuge (Page 119)

Located on the Columbia Plateau in south-central Washington, northwest of Richland, SMNWR was established in 1953 to protect 32,000 acres along nineteen miles of riparian and upland shrub-steppe habitat beside the Columbia River. Bald eagles, coyotes, great blue herons, elk, mule deer, porcupine, and white pelicans are frequently seen here; the refuge is also home to numerous rare, threatened, or endangered animal species (forty-three as of 2012) and several insect species found nowhere else on Earth. On June 9, 2000, President Bill Clinton signed a proclamation that integrated SMNWF into the newly created Hanford Reach National Monument (196,000 acres), in the process reclassifying former security land that buffered the

Hanford Nuclear Reservation (now known as the U.S. Department of Energy Hanford Site). During World War II, nine nuclear reactors were built at Hanford, including Reactor B, the world's first full-scale reactor that fueled the atomic bomb that was dropped on Nagasaki, Japan, on August 9, 1945, killing approximately 60,000 to 80,000 people and leading to Japan's surrender to the United States six days later. Reactor B is among the most recognized historic sites in the nation: it is listed on the U.S. Register of Historic Places, is designated as a National Civil Engineering, National Historical, National Mechanical Engineering, and Nuclear Historical landmark, and is being considered as a National Historical Park. The nuclear reservation has suffered environmental damage from radiation, but contaminated areas are being cleaned up. Interestingly, SMNWR is closed to the public, though access is permitted for ecological research through a permit system with the U.S. Department of Energy, which administers SMNWR/HRNM along with the U.S. Fish and Wildlife Service.

"In the late summer of 1987, I set off on a journey to Montana and then followed the Columbia River west to the Pacific Ocean. One way to approach the landscape is through the lens of a river; other journeys might begin as seeking a particular petroglyph or reaching a particular 14,000-foot mountaintop. These goals get me going, but what motivates me most is the experience of being out in the land."

Salmon-Challis National Forest (Page 73)

A large, diamond-shaped region located in north-central Idaho and paralleling the Bitterroot Range along the Idaho-Montana border, from approximately Nez Perce Pass (elevation 6,589 feet) and Lost Trail Pass (elevation 7,014 feet) in the north near Shoup to Saddle Mountain (elevation 10,810 feet) northwest of Idaho Falls and extending near Sun Valley and Ketchum, SCNF protects approximately 4,300,000 acres. The Frank Church-River of No Return Wilderness (2,365,896 acres) is the largest wilderness area outside of Alaska. Borah Peak (elevation 12,667 feet), the highest mountain in Idaho, and a small portion of the Sawtooth Wilderness are also within SCNF. The Salmon River Forest Reserve was one of 150 established by conservationist-minded President Theodore Roosevelt in 1906. It was renamed Salmon National Forest on July 1, 1908; later that same year, the Challis National Forest was created, and the two merged in February 1998. Salmon-Challis is named for the Salmon River and Challis for the town and county seat that commands a superb view of the Salmon River below. The Main Salmon River was called "The River of No Return" in earlier days when boats could navigate down the river but could not return upriver through the fast water and numerous rapids. Frank Church (1924–1984), a respected U. S. senator from 1957 to 1981, was the Senate floor sponsor of the Wilderness Act of 1964, introduced the Wild and Scenic Rivers Act of 1968, and helped created the Central Idaho Wilderness Act of 1980, which created the River of No Return Wilderness. In March 1984, weeks before his death, Congress honored Senator Church by adding his name to this wilderness area. Rugged and remote, this country offers adventure, solitude, and breathtaking scenery for all present and future generations. SCNF is administered by the U.S. Forest Service.

"These rugged mountains are not easy to access without effort. Much of the experience of the wilderness is consumed in the advance planning, getting there, and taking care of one's basic needs. But, when we make that effort and get out of the truck or car and hike the land, even if only for an afternoon, and hike into the land, we are almost always rewarded by some site or event we long remember."

San Isabel National Forest (Pages 6, 89, 91, and 93)

Located in south-central Colorado and extending in a non-contiguous fashion from Cordova Pass (elevation 11,248 feet) northwest of Trinidad in the south to Royal Gorge near Cañon City in the middle, to the Sawatch Range near Leadville in the north, SINF protects 1,120,233 acres. Within SINF are seven designated wilderness areas and nineteen of Colorado's fifty-four "fourteeners," whose elevations exceed 14,000 feet, including the Collegiate Peaks and Mount Elbert (elevation 14,440 feet), the highest point in Colorado and the high point of the Sawatch Range. Established on April 11, 1902, by President Theodore Roosevelt, Pike and San Isabel national forests and Cimarron and Comanche national grasslands are now administered as a unit ("PSICC") by the U.S. Forest Service.

"Mount Princeton (elevation 14,204 feet) and Mount Antero (elevation 14,269 feet) are two of my favorite hikes. It is said, 'Get off the peak by noon,' but that doesn't always cover. Once, in a gathering thunderstorm on top of Mount Princeton, the eyelets on my boots started buzzing. There I was, fully exposed with a metal view camera mounted on a metal tripod. I frantically ran down the mountain along with everyone else, as lightning flashed above and around us."

San Juan National Forest (Pages 27, 81, 82, and 83)

Located in southwestern Colorado, with the towns of Dolores, Durango, and Pagosa Springs to the south and Telluride, Silverton, and the San Juan Mountains to the north and east, SJNF protects 1,878,846 acres, including three designated wilderness areas and one national monument, Chimney Rock. SJNF is also bordered by the Uncompahgre National Forest to the north, Rio Grande National Forest to the east, and the Southern Ute Indian Nation to the south. President Theodore Roosevelt created the national forest by proclamation on June 3, 1905. Known by different names during the past century, including the Montezuma National Forest and Durango National Forest, this federal land is now named for the San Juan Mountains. The diverse terrain includes alpine lakes, canyons, meadows, and waterfalls, and opportunities abound for strenuous hiking and climbing on several of the "fourteeners" in the Needle Mountains, a sub-range of the San Juans, with thousands of miles of back roads and hundreds of miles of trails on which to explore. SJNF is administered by the U.S. Forest Service.

"Rick Bass, in *The Lost Grizzlies* (1995), explores the San Juans as the final location of the last grizzly bear in Colorado. The San Juan National Forest is huge and has some true wild places and some over-recreated places. It is my favorite forest in Colorado. I spent one memorable and frightful night in a tiny tent in the high alpine country of the Weminuche Wilderness, bombarded by thunder and lightning."

San Rafael Swell (Page 43)

Located in south-central Utah, on the western Colorado Plateau west of Green River, SRS is a seventy-five-by-forty-mile dome-shaped anticline of sandstone, shale, and limestone that trends southwest to northeast. Periodic flash floods have eroded the rocks over time into the impressive buttes, canyons, goblins, gorges, mesas, and valleys that we see today. Evidence of the Ute, Painter, and Fremont peoples is commonly found in the form of petroglyph and pictograph panels. Because of its extraterrestrial, alien-looking landscapes, SRS has been used as a Hollywood location for such films as *Star Trek* (2009) and *Galaxy Quest* (1999), and parts of it are protected as wilderness study areas. It is currently under consideration to be designated a national monument. SRS is administered by the Bureau of Land Management.

"The San Rafael Swell, which is bisected by Interstate 90, is a gateway into wonderful red-rock landscapes. I am interested in making photographs that address time through the expression of the geologic structure of Earth, the succession of vegetation, and the interaction with humanity."

Sand Creek Massacre National Historic Site (Page 140)

Located on the plains along Big Sandy Creek near the intersection of county roads 54 and W in Kiowa County, Colorado, SCMNHS protects 2,385 acres that memorialize the massacre of Cheyenne and Arapahoe people on November 29–30, 1864. A 675-man military force, comprised of the First and Third Regiments of the U.S. Calvary and Colorado Volunteers under the command of U.S. Army Colonel John M. Chivington (1821–1894), attacked and destroyed a temporary encampment of about 500 Northern Cheyenne and Arapaho, people who were peacefully camped there. Chivington's soldiers ignored an American flag and a white flag of surrender over the Indian lodges and killed and mutilated nearly 200 Indians, about two-third of whom were women and children. After years of uncertainty about the site's location, the National Park Service was authorized by public law in November 2000 to "recognize the national significance of the massacre in American history, and its ongoing significance to the Cheyenne and Arapaho people and the descendants of the massacre victims." In 1999, archaeological teams from the National Park Service, Colorado Historical Society, descendants of massacre members, and others discovered large numbers of period bullets, camp equipment, and other items, which, combined with other evidence, convinced the participants that they had likely identified the area where the unforgettable massacre took place. SCMNHS was dedicated as a national historic site on April 28, 2007, and is administered by the National Park Service.

"I visited the Sand Creek Massacre site twenty-one years before it was designated a national historic site. I had read about the massacre in various history texts and stopped to see the place where the brutal events took place. A dirt road led to a small grave-like monument atop a rectangular slab of concrete. No one was around, so I camped in the dry stream bed among dead cottonwood trees and spent an eerie night imagining the spirits of the past."

Tohono O'odham Indian Reservation (Page 115)

Located in south-central Arizona between Ajo in the east and Tucson in the west, Casa Grande in the north and the U.S. Mexico border to the south, TOIR is home to the Tohono O'odham people (previously and incorrectly known as the Papago people). The reservation's land area is

4,454 square miles, making it the third-largest Indian reservation in the U.S. (after the Navajo and the Uintah and Ouray). Kitt Peak National Observatory is located on Kitt Peak (elevation 6,880 feet) of the Quinian Mountains. It is one of the twenty-six telescopes on the reservation conducting astronomical observatories for nighttime optical and infrared astronomy and daytime study of the sun. TOIR is administered by the Tohono O'odham Indian Nation, which is governed by its Tribal Council.

"Although I drove through the Tohono O'odham Indian Reservation many times on my way to Organ Pipe Cactus National Monument on its southwestern border, I never stopped there. I feel a little uncomfortable on Indian reservations, although I have attended Pueblo dances in New Mexico and tourist attractions such as Acoma Pueblo and the Hopi Cultural Center, which can connect the general public with the culture of native peoples. I respect these diverse native histories and recognize that the landscapes of the West are vast enough to set aside some places for others to know in their own way."

Uncompahgre National Forest (Page 97)

Located in west-central Colorado, south of Grand Junction and bordering the San Juan National Forest to the south, UNF manages approximately 955,229 acres. President Theodore Roosevelt created the Uncompahgre Forest Reserve on June 5, 1905. Its boundaries have changed over the years to include the Uncompahgre Plateau and portions of the San Juan Mountains, including the Telluride ski area. "Uncompaghre" comes from the Ute language and translates loosely as "dirty water" or "red water spring," likely references to spring water found in the area. UNF offers unparalleled scenic drives, notably the Million Dollar Highway, a twelve-mile stretch between Ouray and Silverton to Red Mountain Pass (elevation 11,075). Three designated wilderness areas lie within the alpine areas of UNF, which is administered jointly with the Grand Mesa and Gunnison national forests by the U.S. Forest Service.

"Several 14,000-foot peaks in the Uncompahgre National Forest are easily accessible, including Mount Sneffels (elevation 14,157 feet), Uncompahgre Peak (14,308 feet), and Wetterhorn Peak (14,016 feet). On a weekday, when climbing a remote fourteener, I might not see a single person all day, but, on a weekend, a sense of camaraderie develops among diverse climbers, who are happy to be out on the trail, enjoying the challenge and exhilaration of the hike."

Ute Mountain Ute Indian Reservation (Page 55)

Located on the Colorado Plateau in the southwestern corner of Colorado and northwestern corner of New Mexico and adjacent to Mesa Verde National Park, Canyons of the Ancients National Monument, and the Southern Ute Indian Reservation, UMUIR consists of 553,008 acres belonging to the Ute Mountain Ute Tribe, one of three tribes of the Ute Nation, but held in trust by the U.S. government. Reservation lands range in elevation from 4,600 feet along the San Jan River to the Peak of Ute Mountain (elevation 9,979 feet), which is held sacred by the Ute people. In the Ute language, "Ute" means "land of the sun." Ute legend suggests that the long profile of the Sleeping Ute Mountains resembles a warrior god asleep while recovering from a great battle with "evil ones." The Ute people historically have roamed Utah, Colorado, Arizona, and New Mexico for 2,000 years, moving on foot to hunting grounds and ceremonial land, based on the season. The tribe moved to the reservation in 1897, and their lands embrace the actual site where the four state corners meet. The official marker noting the "exact spot" where the four corners meet, however, is reported to be a bit off center, as Earth continues its ancestral dance with perpetual orbital motion and axial spinning. UMUIR is administered by the Ute Indian Nation.

"The Four Corners area of Arizona, Colorado, New Mexico, and Utah is mostly comprised of Ute and Navajo Indian reservations. Tourists come to stand at the only intersection of four states in the U.S. (elevation 4,864 feet) and place each foot and hand on all four states. The rectangular borders of the Western states do not consider geographic features and political boundaries and assemble peoples often with little common interests. In a few places, rivers such as the Colorado and the Rio Grande serve as a partial state border, embracing the lay of the land and some sense of ecological continuity. How would our thinking be different today if we followed in the footsteps and world-view of those who lived here for thousands of years prior to Euro-American settlement and paid attention to what the land provides? What would happen if our grandest political entities—the states—were re-defined by topography and we were known as mountain people, forest people, river valley people, or prairie people?"

White River National Forest (Page 77)

Located in northwestern Colorado and nestled between Steamboat Springs to the northeast, Meeker to the northwest, and Glenwood Springs to the south, WRNF protects 2,285,970 acres, including eight designated wilderness areas, twelve ski resorts (among them Aspen, built in 1946, and Vail, Snowmass, and others, built during the 1960s), ten peaks higher than 14,000 feet in elevation, 2,500 miles of trails, and 1,900 miles of U.S. Forest Service roads. Founded in October 1891, when President Benjamin Harrison set aside the White River Plateau Timberland Reserve, President Theodore Roosevelt officially established it as a national forest on June 28, 1902, making it among the oldest and largest national forests in the Rocky Mountains. It is also the nation's fifth most popular, with more than 9,000,000 annual visitors. Of special note is Arthur Carhart's 1919 visit to Trappers Lake in the Flat Tops, which inspired him to become the first U.S. Forest Service official to initiate a plea for wilderness preservation. The WRNF is administered by the U.S. Forest Service.

"I do not like to make myself vulnerable. The day I made the photograph above the town of Gothic I was exploring how far up a Forest Service road I could get to lead me up to Schofield

Pass (elevation 10,705 feet). The road is a shelf road on a mountainside, and in places snow remained, drifted down across the road. I was pushing my truck through these small areas of snow, sometimes with a certain amount of momentum attained through the speed of the truck. And then I came around a bend in the road and hit a big one. The truck bounced back off the snow, and the rear wheel ended up hanging off the edge of the road, suspended over the deep valley below. I felt that, if I shifted my weight the wrong way, the truck would tip over and tumble down the mountainside. I gently pulled a little shovel out of the back of the truck and removed snow from the front and hillside wheels and very carefully maneuvered the truck back onto the road. That was as high as I got up the pass that day. Today, in addition to a first-aid kit, tire chains, tow chain, come-along, full tool kit, and a big roll of toilet paper, I carry a tire patch kit and a small air compressor in my truck at all times."

Yellowstone National Park (Pages 16 and 31)

Located in the northwestern corner of Wyoming and extending into Montana and Idaho, YNP protects 2,219,791 acres of land, featuring more than 10,000 hydrothermal features, including more than 300 geysers such as Old Faithful, incredibly beautiful valleys and lakes, canyons and mountains, and spectacular habitat for wildlife. It was established by the U.S. Congress at the considerable urging of Ferdinand V. Hayden (1829–1887), who explored and documented the area during the Hayden Geological Survey of 1871, and was signed into law by President Ulysses S. Grant on March 1, 1872, making it the first national park in both the nation and the world. The area was used by many Indian peoples for more than 11,000 years as a special place for hunting and fishing, and, today, Yellowstone's Lamar Valley is reported to be one of the best places to see wolves in the northern Rockies. "Yellowstone" comes from the Minnetaree word "Mitsia-dazi" (Rock Yellow River); French trappers during the late

1700s called it "Roche Jaune," which was later translated as "Yellow Stone," possibly for the yellow rocks in the unforgettable grand canyon of the Yellowstone River. It became a UNESCO World Heritage Site in 1978. YNP is also the centerpiece of the Greater Yellowstone Ecosystem, the largest nearly intact ecosystem in a northern temperate zone anywhere on Earth. It is administered by the National Park Service.

"The national parks of the American West are very popular places. The first time I visited Yellowstone was on a motorcycle trip in the fall of 1979. In my idealistic mind at the time, the tourists were overwhelming but so was the landscape. I tried to leave the park each evening in order to avoid the large, crowded campgrounds and to sleep in the solitude of the nearby national forests. It was futile, because the park is so large. Today, I see Yellowstone as a wonderful and amazing expression of American culture, one that protects, values, and genuinely enjoys natural landscapes and being outside but also underfunds the maintenance of the public lands and lacks a depth of understanding of what is at stake and required for their protection."

Yosemite National Park (Page 133)

Located in the central Sierra Nevada of California, YNP protects 761,268 acres of granite cliffs, amazing waterfalls, thousands of glacial lakes, ponds, and clear streams, two federally designated wild and scenic rivers (the Merced and Tuolumne), and unforgettable Yosemite Valley. YNP is also surrounded by national forests: Stanislaus to the northwest, Humboldt-Toiyabe to the northeast, Inyo to the southeast, and Sierra to the southwest and southeast. "Yosemite" is derived from the Miwok word "Yehemite," which translates "some among them are killers." Only in 1851, however, was Yosemite coined a place name when the Mariposa Battalion first entered the valley in search of the Yosemite people. Galen Clark (1814–1910), in 1857, was the first to count and measure the Mariposa Grove of giant sequoia trees, and Senator John Conness (1821–1909) advocated for protection of the Yosemite area. A bill creating the Yosemite Grant passed both houses of the 38th U.S. Congress and was signed by President Abraham Lincoln on June 30, 1864. This is the first time that park land was set aside by the federal government for preservation and public use, and it set the precedent for the creation in 1872 of the nation's first national park at Yellowstone. Writer and naturalist John Muir (1838–1914) then lobbied Congress for further protection, which led to the creation of Yosemite National Park on October 1, 1890. Ansel Adams (1902–1984) made YNP even more famous with his artful portraiture of the park's natural wonders. Ranging in elevation from 2,127 to 13,114 feet, YNP contains five vegetation zones, accounting for twenty percent of California's 7,000 plant species, including more than 160 rare plants. YNP was designated a UNESCO World Heritage Site in 1984 and was the third most visited national park in 2011 (3,951,393 visitors). It is administered by the National Park Service.

"The first time I saw Yosemite National Park was on a motorcycle trip in 1979. As a photographer, it is impossible to visit Yosemite without thinking about Ansel Adams. When I was young, I was critical of Ansel for the way his photographs tended to eliminate humanity and idealize the pristine. I much preferred the work of Robert Adams, who focused on the vernacular and commonplace, and I considered a picture that did not acknowledge the influence of humans on the landscape as a lie. Today, I very much admire Ansel Adams not only for his photographs, but for the way he provided the conservation movement with a landmark visual vocabulary for scenic beauty."

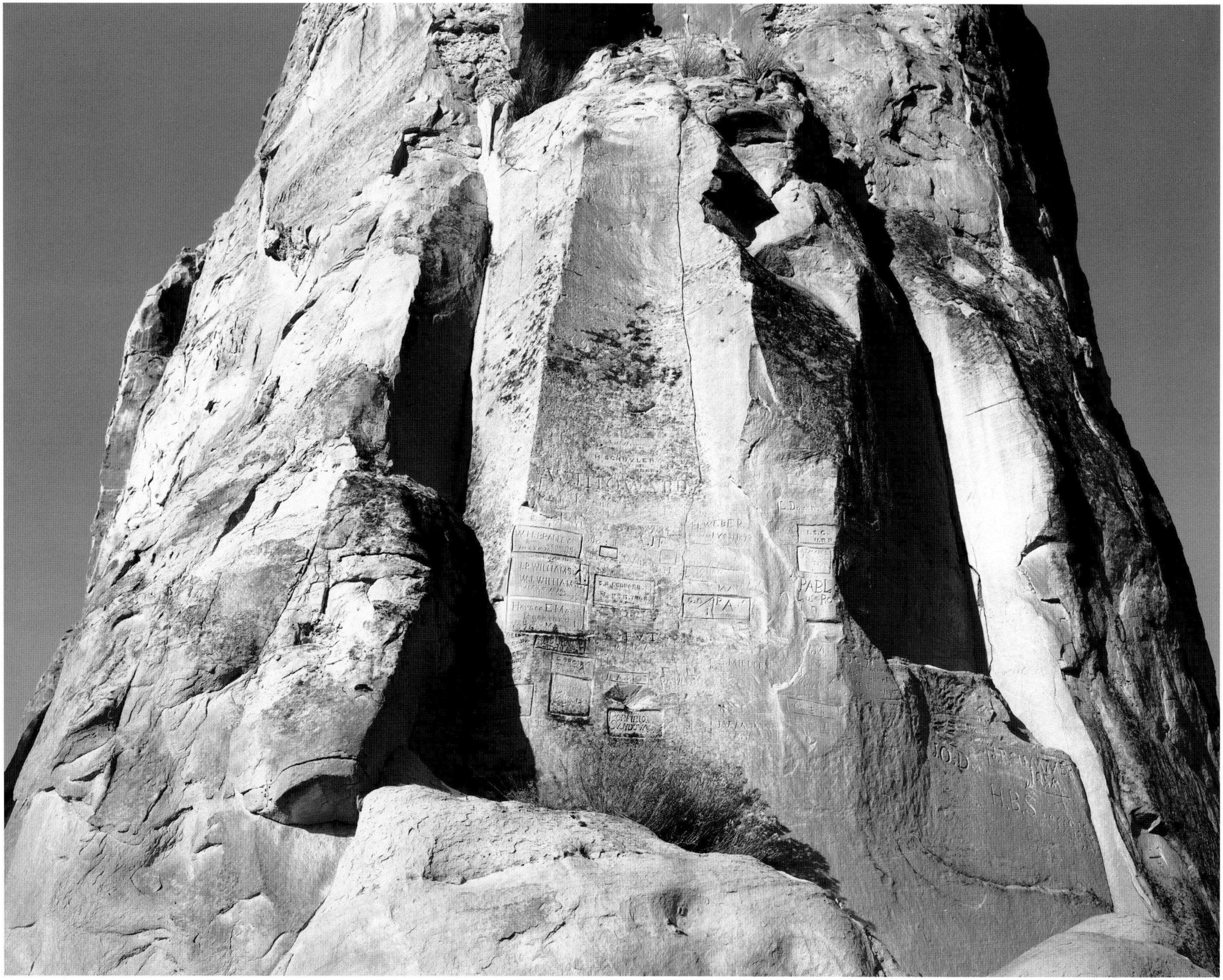
H SCHUYLER
H. WEBER
J.P. WILLIAMS
PABL
H.B.S

Acknowledgments

I express my deep appreciation to George F. Thompson, whose dedication to the wonder and meaning of places and whose patience and commitment to this project created a publication so much better than I ever imagined. I also thank David Skolkin, for designing a book I always dreamed of; Carmen Rose Shenk, for her research assistance; Susan Moldenhauer and Toby Jurovics, for their enthusiasm for my pictures and their insightful essays; Bill Wylie, for helping George and me in the early selection and editing of the pictures; and Jeanne and Richard S. Press and Nancy and Ralph Segall, for their generous support of my work.

My colleagues at Regis College, especially Eugene Stewart-Huidobro, have provided me with an academic home and a wonderful cohort of kindness, spirit, and intellectual discourse. Bill Tydeman, Anthony R. Mayer, Rick Koopman, Deborah Hollis, David Hills, John Grant, Robert Feitler, and Joshua Chuang have also supported my work and this publication, for which I am grateful.

I owe a great debt to my teachers and friends who, over the years, have inspired and guided me with dialogue and pictures through the journey: Michael Berman, Christopher Curtis, Rick Dingus, Scott Engel, Steve Fitch, Eric Paddock, Timmy Pickard, Ted Ringer, Charles Roitz, and Richard Van Pelt. I remember fondly and thank my first teacher of great inspiration, Gary Metz.

My ultimate appreciation and love go to my parents, Bill and Lucia Sutton, who somehow managed always to support and believe in me, and to my wife, Lynn, and our children, Justin and Jaime, for the love of family.

(Left) El Morro National Monument (elevation 7,219–7,419 feet), New Mexico, 1989.

About the Essayists

Toby Jurovics was born in 1965 in Pacoima, California, and was raised in the San Fernando Valley. He completed his B.A. in art history and English at the University of North Carolina, Chapel Hill, and his M.A. in art history at the University of Delaware. He is Chief Curator and Richard and Mary Holland Curator of American Western Art at the Joslyn Art Museum in Omaha, Nebraska. Previously, he was Curator of Photography at the Smithsonian American Art Museum and Associate Curator of Photography at the Princeton University Art Museum. He has organized exhibitions on Robert Adams, Lewis Baltz, Barbara Bosworth, and Emmet Gowin, among many other artists, and he has written seminal essays on Thomas Joshua Cooper, John Gossage, and the New Topographics. He is the author of *Framing the West: The Survey Photographs of Timothy H. O'Sullivan* (Yale University Press, 2010).

Susan B. Moldenhauer was born in 1951 in Chicago, Illinois, and was raised there. She completed her B.F.A. in printmaking and drawing at Northern Illinois University and her M.F.A. in photography at the Pennsylvania State University. A museum curator for more than twenty-five years, she has served since 2002 as Director and Chief Curator at the University of Wyoming Art Museum. She has curated more than 130 exhibitions, overseen more than 200 exhibitions, and produced more than thirty exhibition publications. She is also a practicing photographer whose work, inspired by the landscape and human presence, has been exhibited throughout Canada and the United States, including images from the series "Desert Varnish," "Place/Mind/Spirit," and "Compositions from the Land."

About the Author

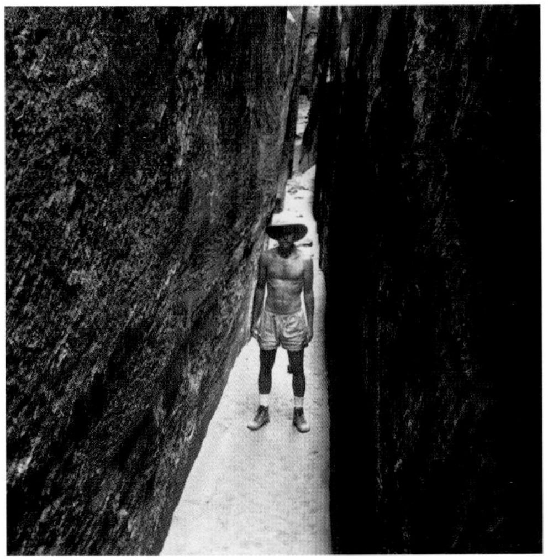

Self-portrait, Joint Trail, Canyonlands National Park, Utah, 1989.

William S. Sutton was born in 1956 in Toledo, Ohio, and was raised in New York State, Scottsdale, Arizona, and the western suburbs of Chicago. He began his academic journey at Arizona State University, completed his B.F.A. and M.F.A. in photography at the University of Colorado in Boulder, and received a National Endowment for the Arts Fellowship in Photography in 1981. His photographs have been exhibited widely and are in the permanent collections of numerous institutions, including the Amoco Collection, Arizona State University, Bellevue Art Museum, Bibliothèque Nationale de France, Center for the Study of Place, Chase Manhattan Bank, Colorado Historical Society, Denver Art Museum, Joslyn Art Museum, Library of Congress, Museum of Modern Art, Phoenix Arts Commission, Princeton University Art Museum, Southwest Collection at Texas Tech University, University of Chicago, University of Colorado Special Collections, University of Wyoming Art Museum, and Yale University Art Gallery, among others. Mr. Sutton is an associate professor of art at Regis College in Denver, and he lives in the mountains west of Boulder, Colorado. His Website is www.academic.regis.edu/wsutton.

About the Craft

Most of the pictures in this book were made with one of two view cameras. In 1982, I purchased a Toyo 45A field camera and a Fujinon 135mm f/5.6 lens. Later, I acquired a Schneider 90mm f/8 lens and a Fujinon 210 mm f/5.6 lens. I used a Gitzo Studex tripod. Around 1992, I acquired a Linhof Technika 5 x 7 inch field camera, with a Rodenstock 150 mm f/5.6 lens and a Linhof tripod. I used the 5 x 7 exclusively from then until 1997.

I used Kodak T-Max 100 primarily in the view cameras, processed with the Photographer's Formulary TFX2, Kodak T-Max, and later D-76 developers. A few pictures were made with medium-format cameras. From 1977 through 1981, I used a Mamiya 645 SLR. In 1997, I purchased a Mamiya 7, a range-finder camera, with 65 mm and 150 mm lenses. I used these cameras on tripods with slow film: Kodak Pan X and Illford Pan F.

On the road I would change the film holders in the back of my pickup truck at night. I had canvas curtains that attached to the windows of the truck bed's shell with Velcro. I had seven different boxes into which I put the exposed film, dependent on the quality of light the film was exposed in, and how I intended to process it according to my version of the zone system.

The original gelatin silver prints were made with a Durst 5 x 7 inch Labrador 138s enlarger, with Rodenstock and Schneider lenses, on Kodak Elite graded photographic paper, and processed with the Beers formula developer to further adjust contrast. Some pictures were printed with a Condit registration masking system. The silver prints were archivally processed and toned with Kodak selenium toner. More recently, I made inkjet prints with an Epson Pro 4000 printer with Cone Piezography K7 monochrome inks on Hahnemuhle Photo Rag 308 paper from digital files scanned from the negatives and directly from digital images made with a Canon 1Ds MIII digital camera.

About the Book

At Home in the West: The Lure of Public Land was brought to publication in an edition of 1,300 hardcover copies. The text was set in Granjon, the paper is Lumisilk, 170 gsm weight, and the book was professionally printed and bound in China.

Editor and Publisher: George F. Thompson
Photographic Adviser: William Wylie
Manuscript Editor: Purna Makaram
Editorial and Research Assistant: Carmen Rose Shenk
Book Design and Production: David Skolkin

Special Acknowledgments: Eric Paddock, for making the initial connection with Willy; Annie Proulx, for making the initial connection with Susan; the many dedicated administrators, employees, researchers, and volunteers at the forty-six featured public lands, for vetting and verifying the information that appears in the *Notes on the Public Lands* section; the assistance of the American Land Publishing Project, an educational program since 2001 of the Center for the Study of Place, a nonprofit organization founded in 1990; and Cotton Mather (1918–1999), the legendary geographer and friend of the Pueblo people, for introducing hundreds upon thousands of dignitaries, scholars, students, writers, artists, and citizens from all walks of life, from all over the globe, to the wonders of the American West. He fully understood the critical connections between art and geography and the comprehension of place.

Copyright © 2013 George F. Thompson Publishing, L.L.C.
Photographs and *Finding My Place* copyright © 2013 William S. Sutton
Four-Wheel Drive copyright © 2013 Toby Jurovics
Willy Sutton's West copyright © 2013 Susan B. Moldenhauer
All rights reserved. Nothing in this book may be used, reprinted, or reproduced
in any form or medium without written permission.
Published in 2013. First Edition.
Printed in China on acid-free paper.

George F. Thompson Publishing, L.L.C.
217 Oak Ridge Circle
Staunton, VA 24401-3511, U.S.A.
www.gftbooks.com

21 20 19 18 17 16 15 14 13   1 2 3 4 5

The Library of Congress Preassigned Control Number is 2012937227.

ISBN: 978–1–938086–08–3

Captions

Page 2. Coronado National Forest (elevation 3,000–10,720 feet), Arizona, 1994.

Page 4. View of the Rocky Mountains and Front Range, including City of Boulder Open Space and Mountain Parks, from Haystack Mountain (elevation 5,545 feet), Colorado, 1989.

Page 6. Salida (elevation 7,080 feet) and the surrounding Methodist and Poncha mountains (elevations 11,690 and 10,135 feet) and San Isabel National Forest, Colorado, 1989.